D0908448

MAY - - 2015

CALGARY PUBLIC LIBRARY

MAY - - 2015

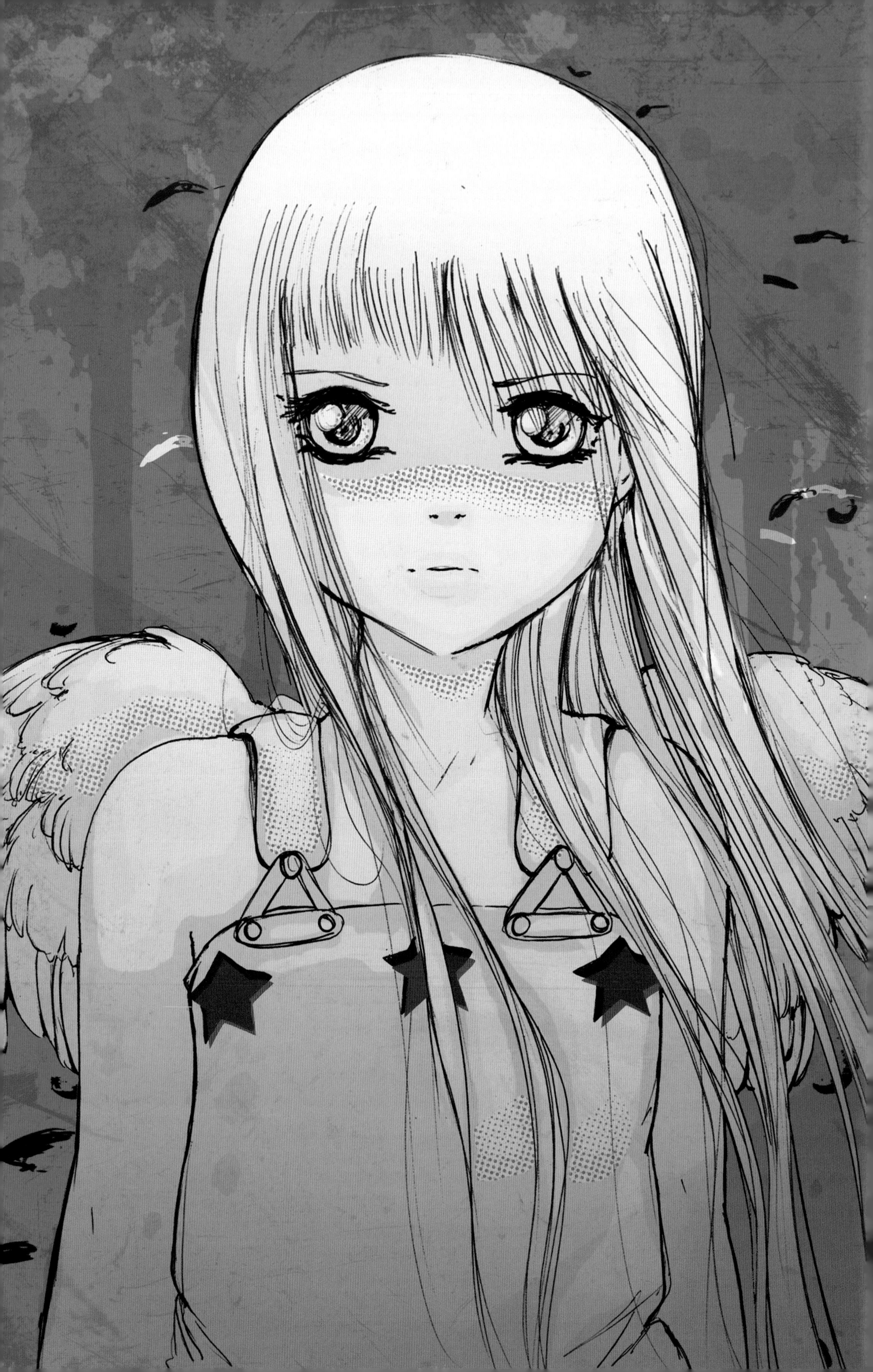

tanpopo™

VOLUME
2

by camilla d'errico

Written and Illustrated by Camilla d'Errico

Co-Author/Producer:
AdaPia d'Errico

Hardcover Edition Asst. Editor:
Jasmine Amiri

Hardcover Edition Editor:
Dafna Pleban

Hardcover Edition Designer:
Kelsey Dieterich

ROSS RICHIE CEO & Founder • JACK CUMMINS COO & President • MARK SMYLIE Chief Creative Officer • MATT GAGNON Editor-in-Chief • FILIP SABLIK VP of Publishing & Marketing • STEPHEN CHRISTY VP of Development
LANCE KREITER VP of Licensing & Merchandising • PHIL BARBARO VP of Finance • BRYCE CARLSON Managing Editor • MEL CAYLO Marketing Manager • SCOTT NEWMAN Production Design Manager • IRENE BRADISH Operations Manager
DAFNA PLEBAN Editor • SHANNON WATTERS Editor • ERIC HARBURN Editor • REBECCA TAYLOR Editor • CHRIS ROSA Assistant Editor • ALEX GALER Assistant Editor • WHITNEY LEOPARD Assistant Editor
JASMINE AMIRI Assistant Editor • CAMERON CHITTOCK Assistant Editor • HANNAH NANCE PARTLOW Production Designer • KELSEY DIETERICH Production Designer • DEVIN FUNCHES E-Commerce & Inventory Coordinator
ANDY LIEGL Event Coordinator • BRIANNA HART Executive Assistant • AARON FERRARA Operations Assistant • JOSÉ MEZA Sales Assistant • ELIZABETH LOUGHRIDGE Accounting Assistant

TANPOPO Volume Two, April 2014. Published by BOOM! Studios, a division of Boom Entertainment, Inc. Tanpopo is ™ & © 2014 d'Errico Studios
Ltd. All rights reserved. BOOM! Studios™ and the BOOM! Studios logo are trademarks of Boom Entertainment, Inc., registered in various countries and
categories. All characters, events, and institutions depicted herein are fictional. Any similarity between any of the names, characters, persons, events,
and/or institutions in this publication to actual names, characters, and persons, whether living or dead, events, and/or institutions is unintended and purely
coincidental. BOOM! Studios does not read or accept unsolicited submissions of ideas, stories, or artwork.

A catalog record of this book is available from OCLC and from the BOOM! Studios website, www.boom-studios.com, on the Librarians Page.

BOOM! Studios, 5670 Wilshire Boulevard, Suite 450, Los Angeles, CA 90036-5679. Printed in China. First Printing.
ISBN: 978-1-60886-337-2, eISBN: 978-1-61398-191-7

TANPOPO

Chapter 1

Inspired by William Shakespeare's
"Richard III"

"Alone" Edgar Allan Poe
"Two Loves I Have of Comfort and Despair"
William Shakespeare

Chapter 2

Inspired by Edgar Allan Poe's Short Stories
"The Pit and the Pendulum" &
"The Masque of the Red Death"

"Sonnet 27" William Shakespeare

Chapter 3

Inspired by *1001 Arabian Nights'* story
"The City of Brass"

"Waste Land" T.S. Eliot
"The Raven" Edgar Allan Poe

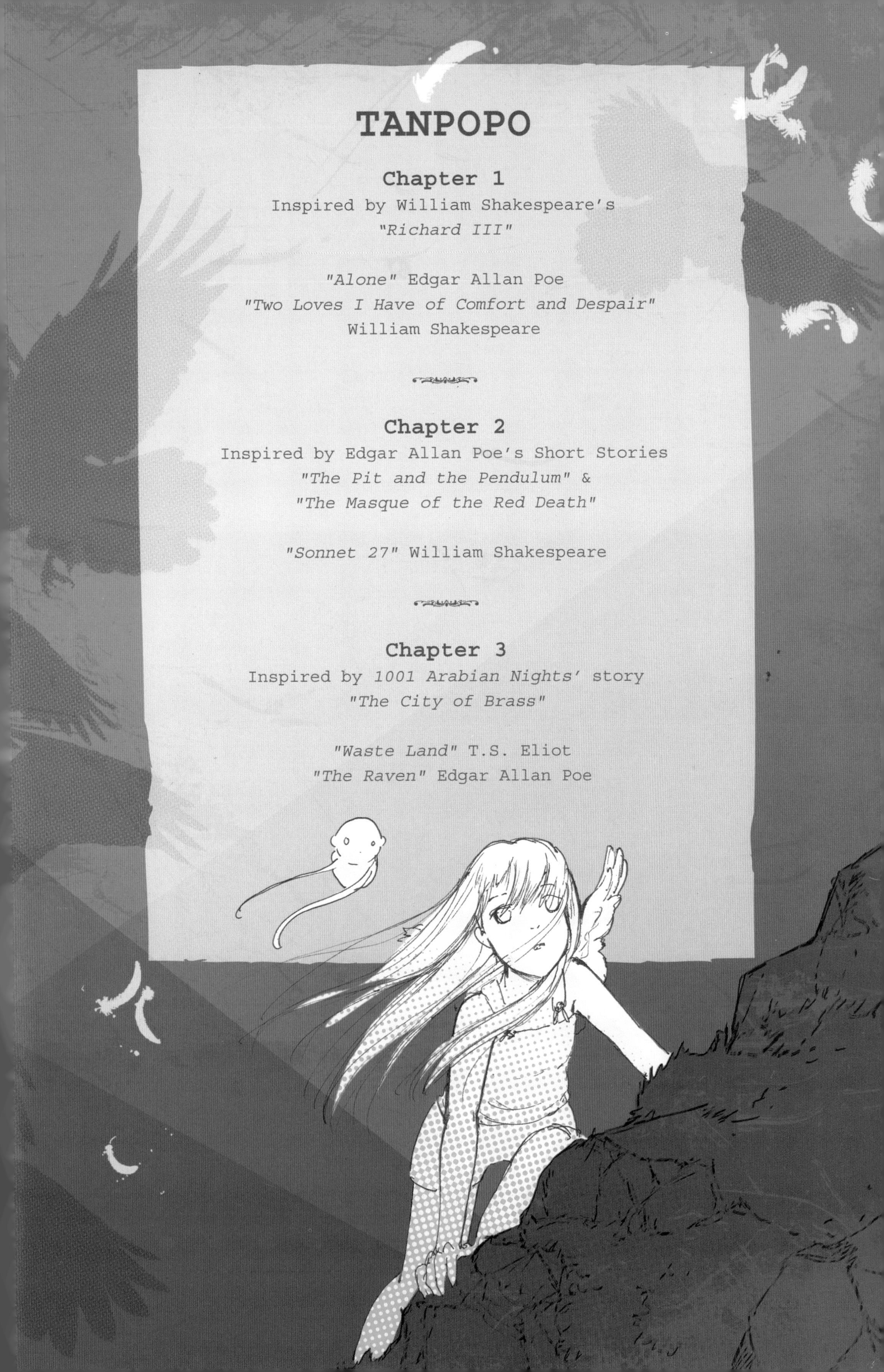

CHAPTER 1

FROM CHILDHOOD'S HOUR I HAVE NOT BEEN
AS OTHERS WERE; I HAVE NOT SEEN
AS OTHERS SAW; I COULD NOT BRING
MY PASSIONS FROM A COMMON SPRING.
FROM THE SAME SOURCE I HAVE NOT TAKEN
MY SORROW; I COULD NOT AWAKEN
MY HEART TO JOY AT THE SAME TONE;
AND ALL I LOVED, I LOVED ALONE.
THEN IN MY CHILDHOOD, IN THE DAWN
OF A MOST STORMY LIFE WAS DRAWN
FROM EVERY DEPTH OF GOOD AND ILL,
THE MYSTERY WHICH BINDS ME STILL:
FROM THE TORRENT, OR THE FOUNTAIN,
FROM THE RED CLIFF OF THE MOUNTAIN,
FROM THE SUN THAT ROUND ME ROLLED
IN ITS AUTUMN TINT OF GOLD,
FROM THE LIGHTNING IN THE SKY
AS IT PASSED ME FLYING BY,
FROM THE THUNDER AND THE STORM,
AND THE CLOUD THAT TOOK THE FORM
(WHEN THE REST OF HEAVEN WAS BLUE)
OF A DEMON IN MY VIEW.

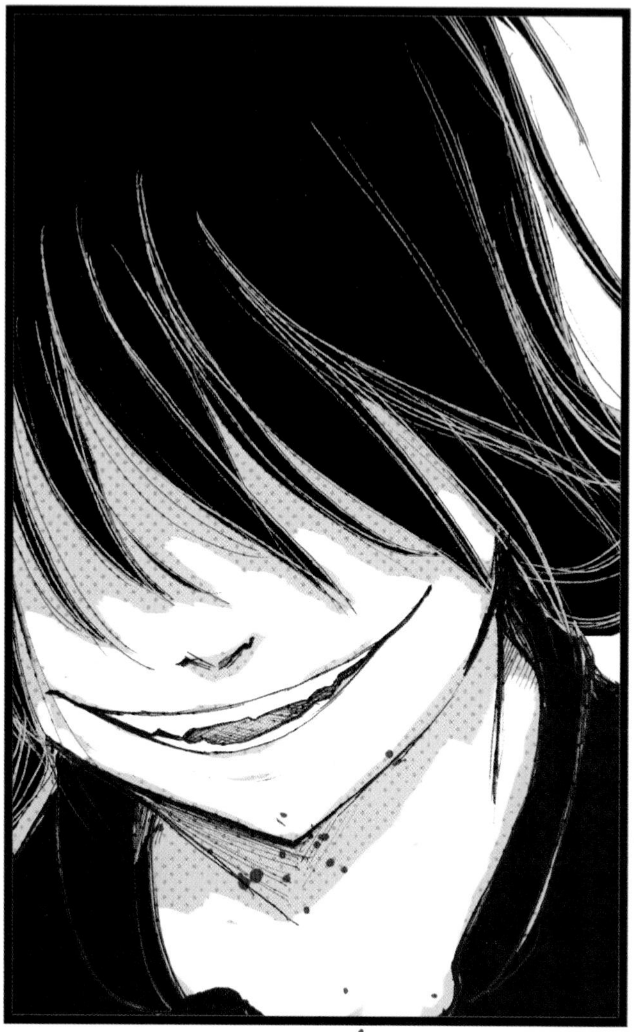

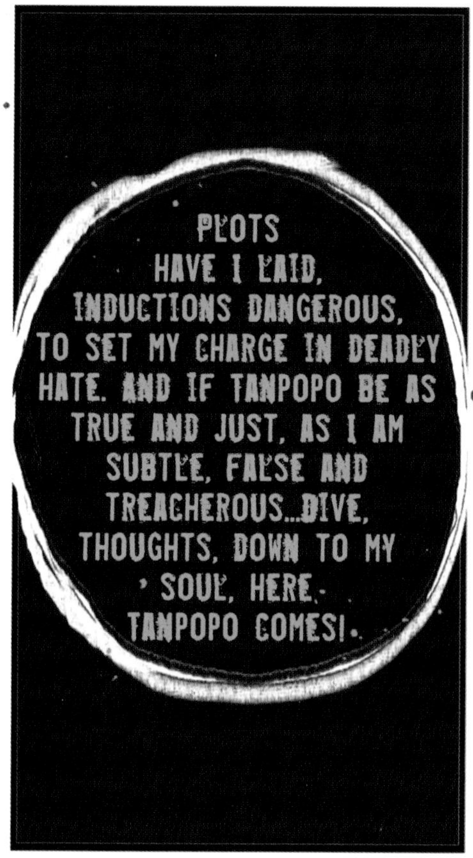
PLOTS HAVE I LAID, INDUCTIONS DANGEROUS, TO SET MY CHARGE IN DEADLY HATE. AND IF TANPOPO BE AS TRUE AND JUST, AS I AM SUBTLE, FALSE AND TREACHEROUS...DIVE, THOUGHTS, DOWN TO MY SOUL, HERE. TANPOPO COMES!

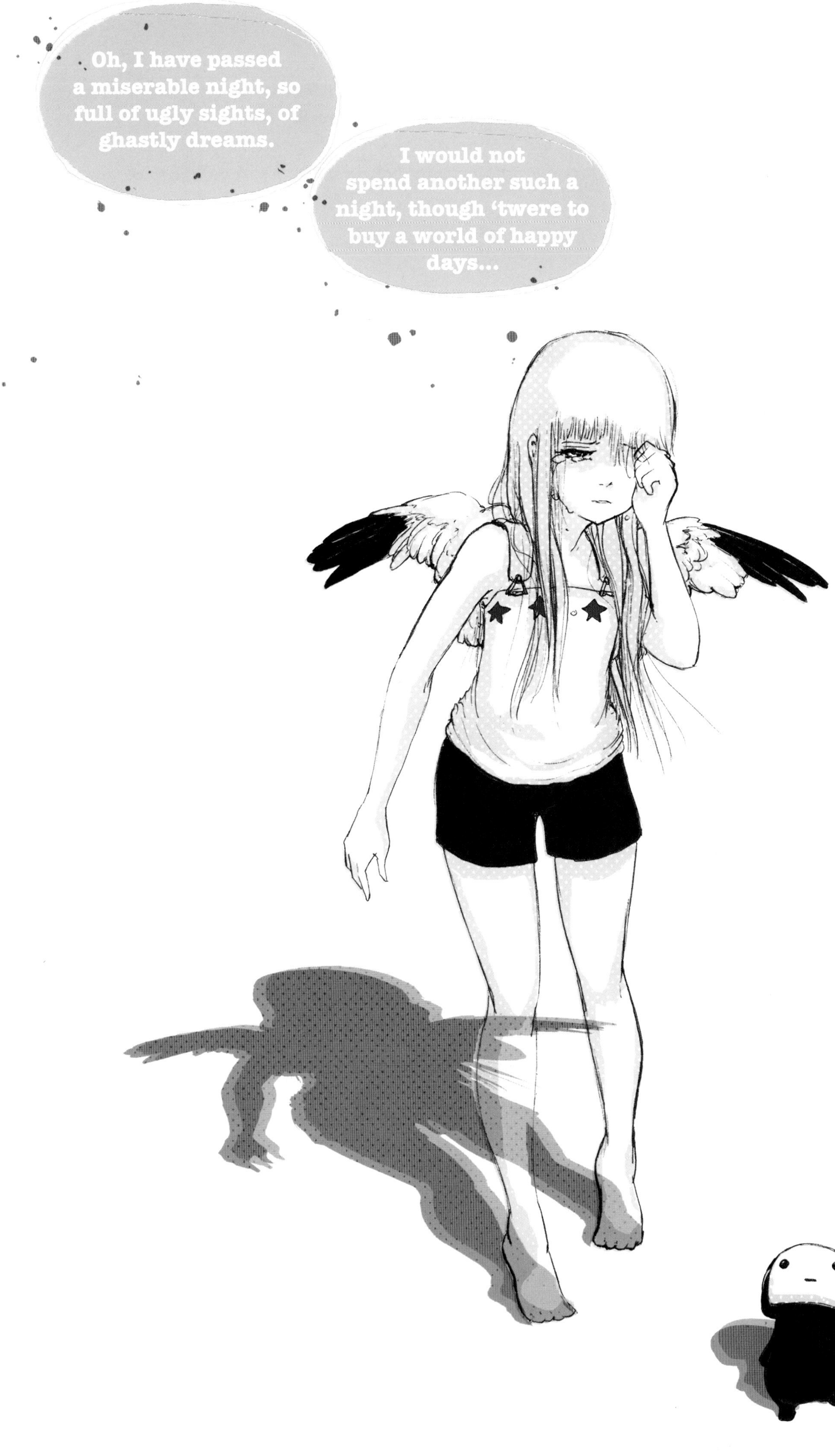
Oh, I have passed a miserable night, so full of ugly sights, of ghastly dreams.
I would not spend another such a night, though 'twere to buy a world of happy days...

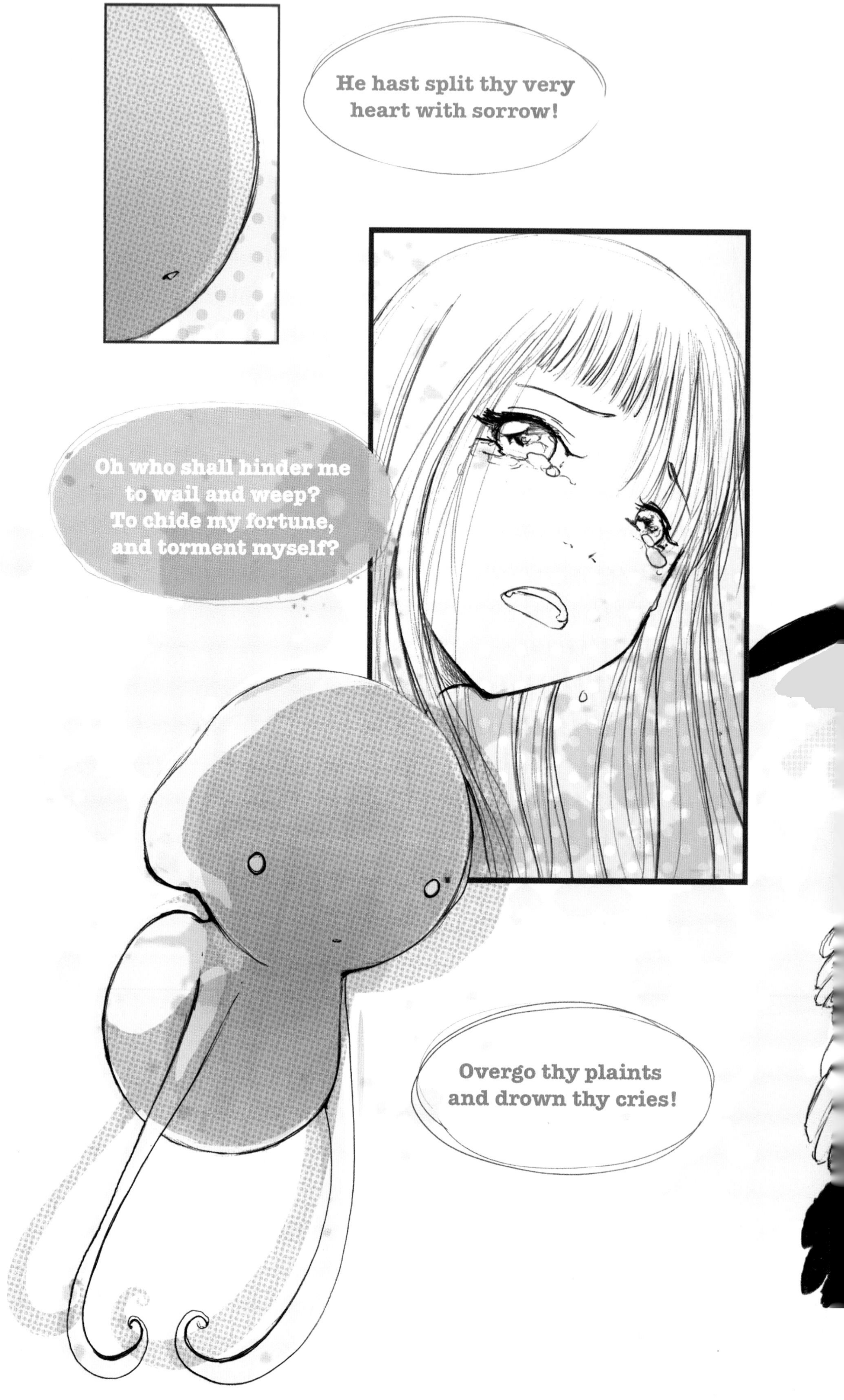
He hast split thy very heart with sorrow!
Oh who shall hinder me to wail and weep? To chide my fortune, and torment myself?
Overgo thy plaints and drown thy cries!

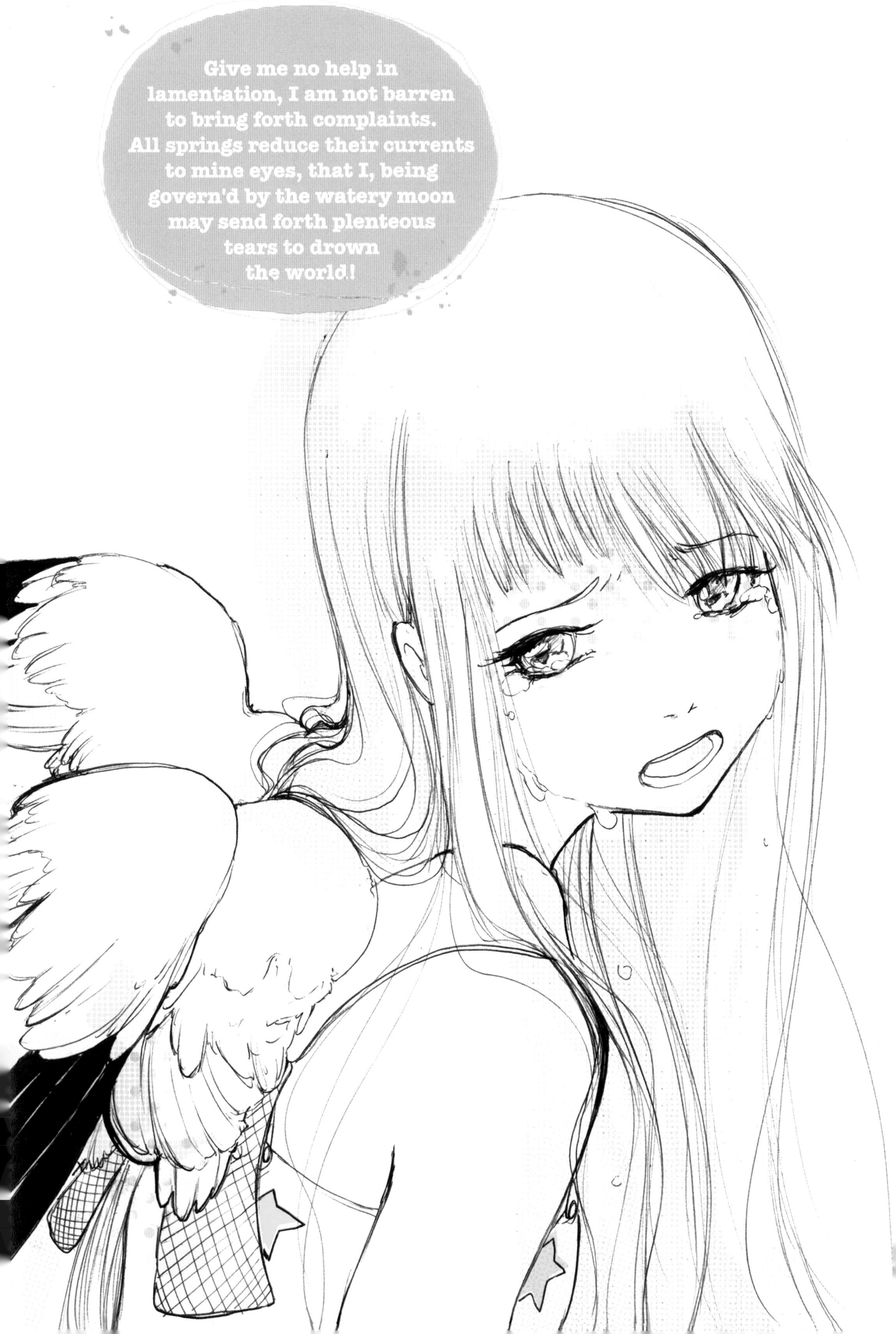
Give me no help in lamentation, I am not barren to bring forth complaints. All springs reduce their currents to mine eyes, that I, being govern'd by the watery moon may send forth plenteous tears to drown the world!

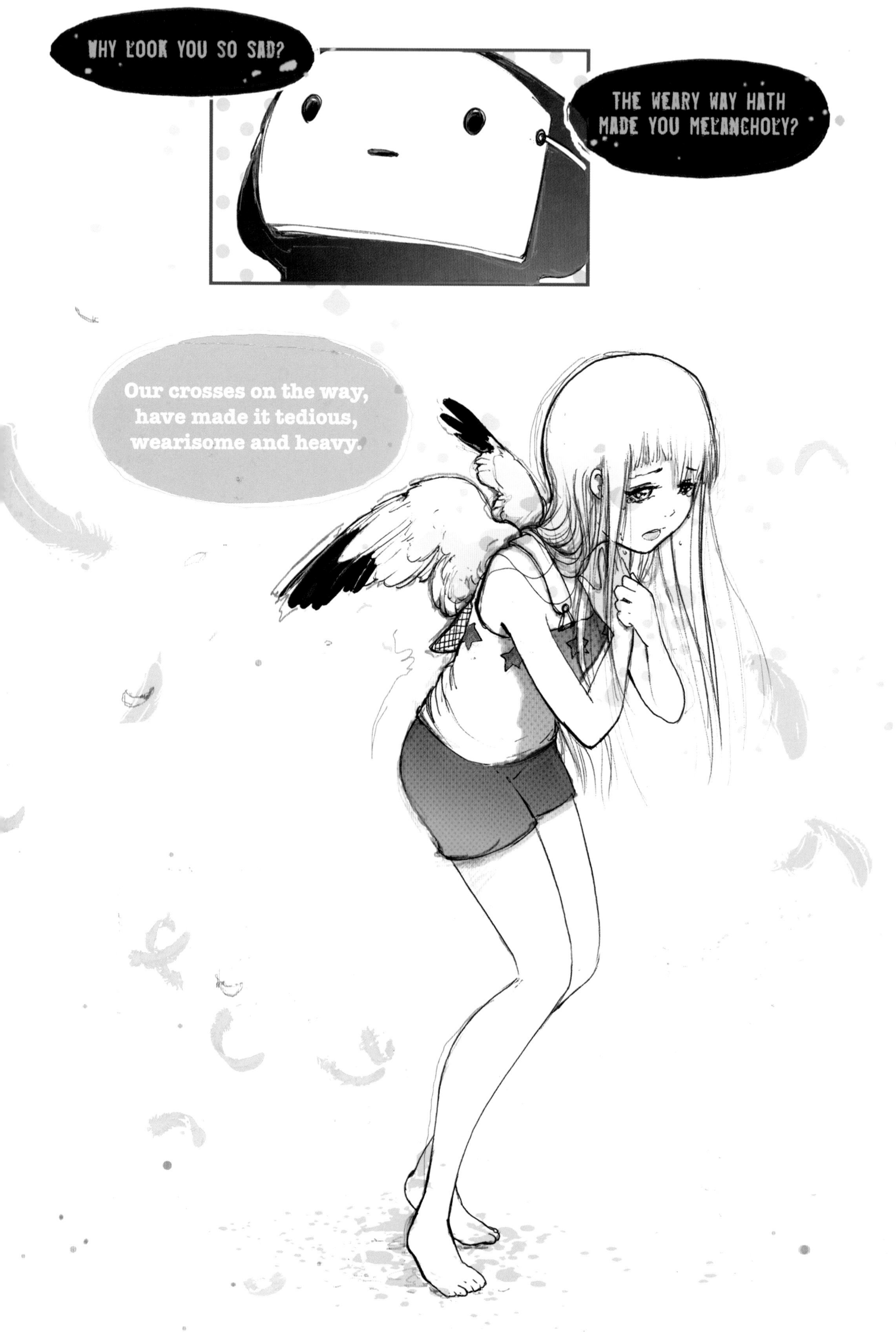
WHY LOOK YOU SO SAD?
THE WEARY WAY HATH MADE YOU MELANCHOLY?
Our crosses on the way, have made it tedious, wearisome and heavy.

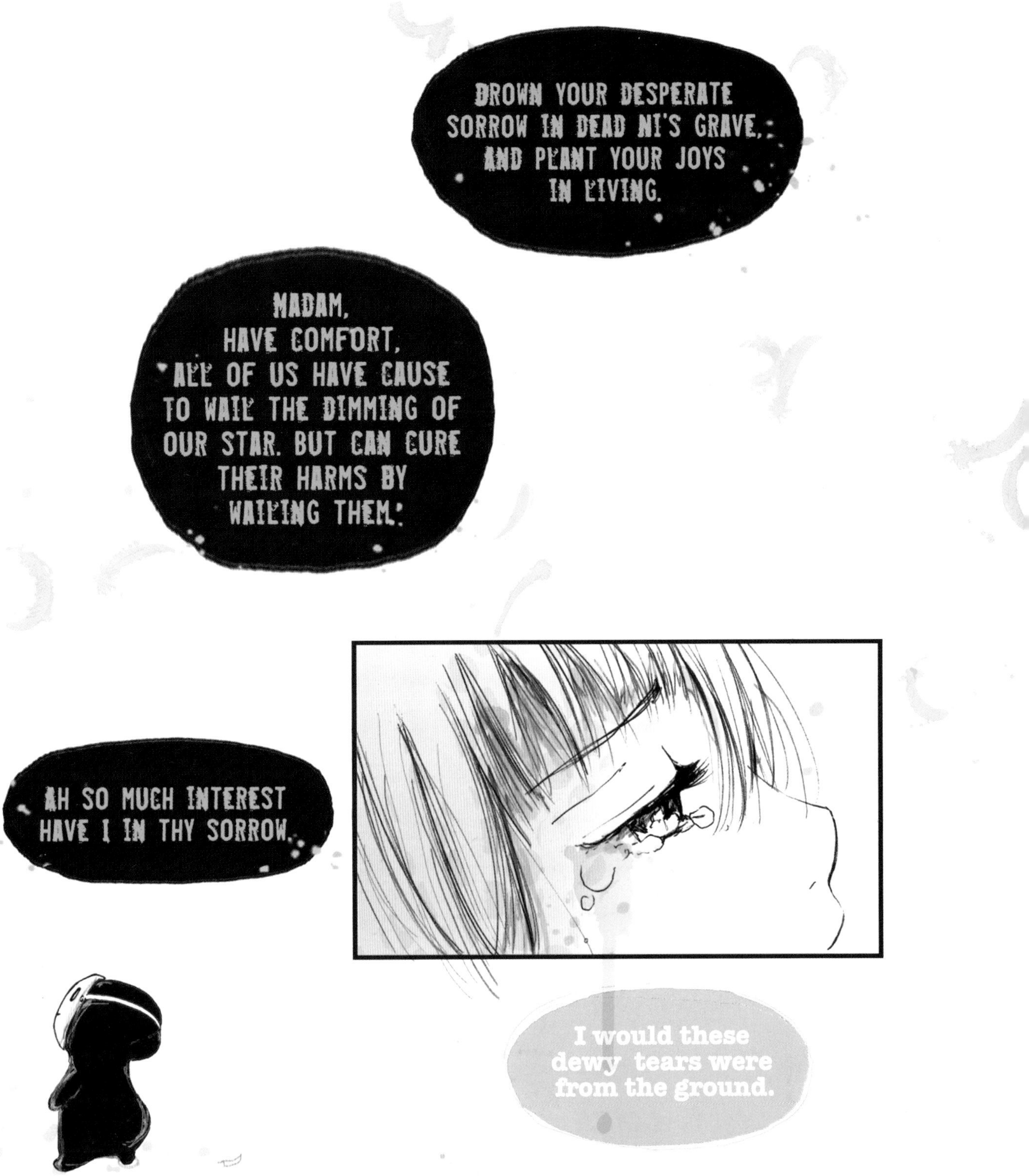
DROWN YOUR DESPERATE SORROW IN DEAD NI'S GRAVE, AND PLANT YOUR JOYS IN LIVING.
MADAM, HAVE COMFORT, ALL OF US HAVE CAUSE TO WAIL THE DIMMING OF OUR STAR. BUT CAN CURE THEIR HARMS BY WAILING THEM.
AH SO MUCH INTEREST HAVE I IN THY SORROW.
I would these dewy tears were from the ground.

Come, come, we fear the worst, all shall be well!
I, like a child, will go by thy direction.

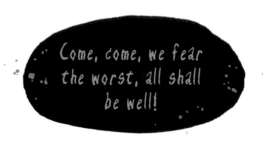

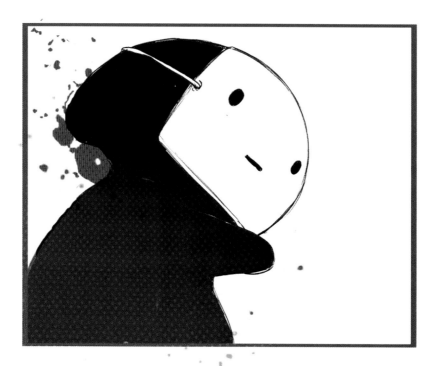

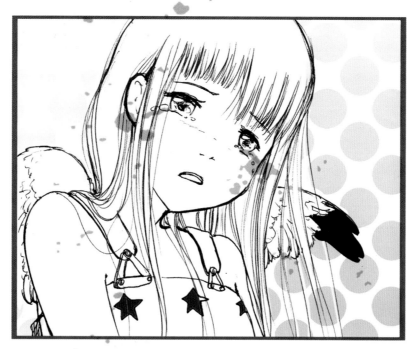

O Tanpopo,
take heed of yonder dog!
He, that is shaped for
sportive tricks, that
is rudely stamp'd,
cheated of feature by
dissembling
nature.

Look, when He fawns,
He bites; and when He bites,
His venom tooth will rankle to
the death. Have not to do with
Him, beware of Him!
Sin, death, and hell have
set their marks on Him.

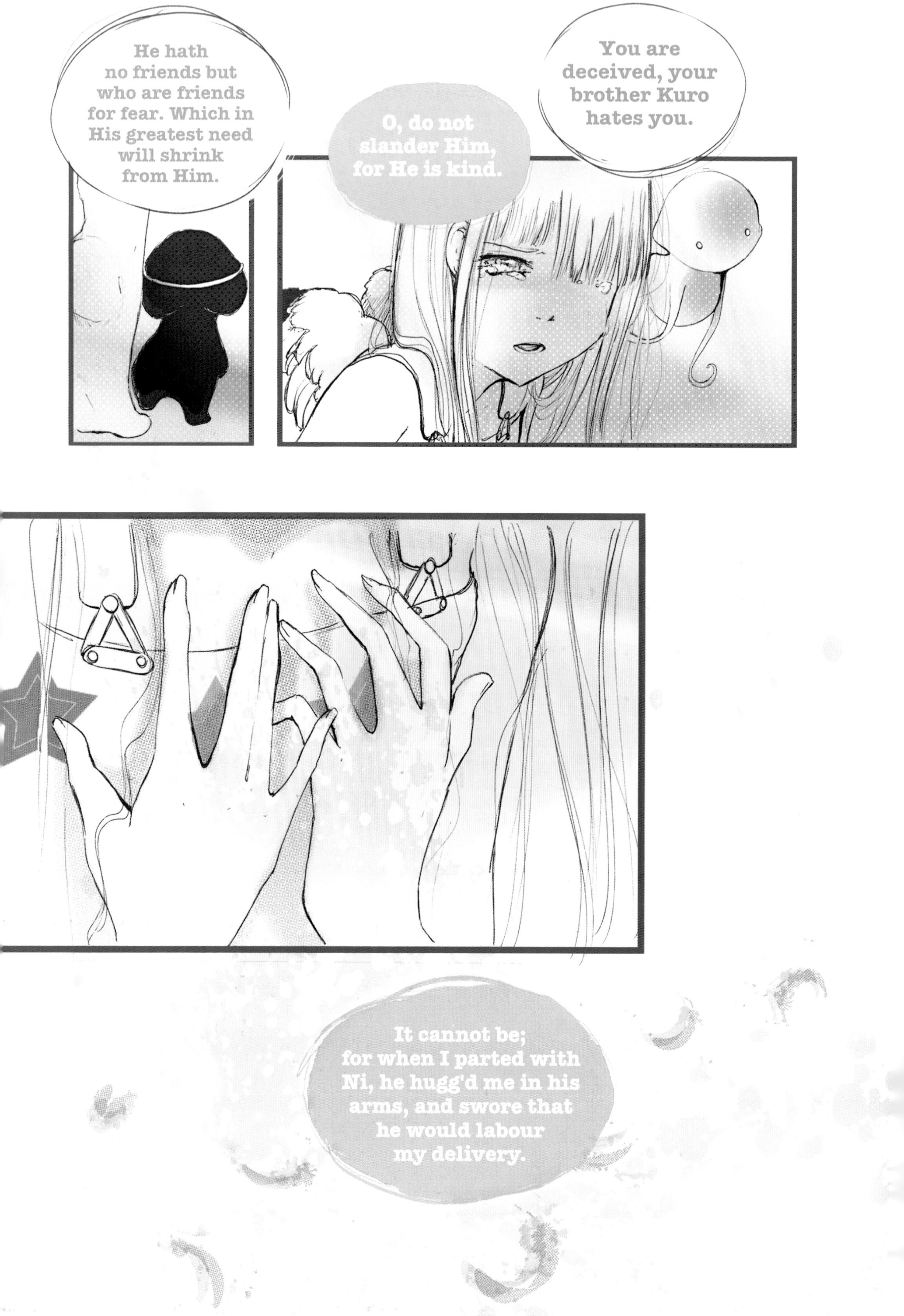
You are deceived, your brother Kuro hates you.
O, do not slander Him, for He is kind.
He hath no friends but who are friends for fear. Which in His greatest need will shrink from Him.
It cannot be; for when I parted with Ni, he hugg'd me in his arms, and swore that he would labour my delivery.

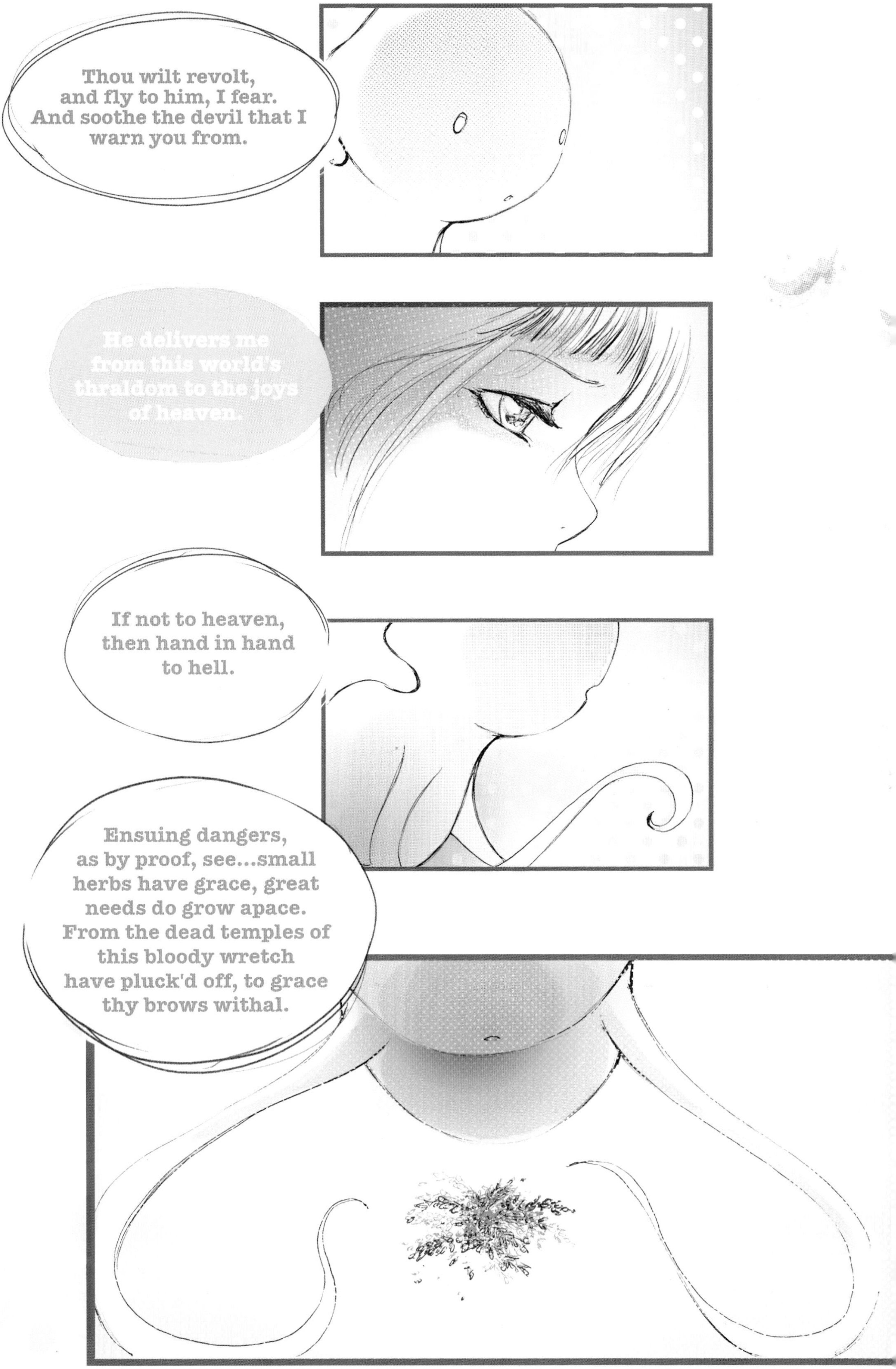
Thou wilt revolt, and fly to him, I fear. And soothe the devil that I warn you from.
He delivers me from this world's thraldom to the joys of heaven.
If not to heaven, then hand in hand to hell.
Ensuing dangers, as by proof, see...small herbs have grace, great needs do grow apace. From the dead temples of this bloody wretch have pluck'd off, to grace thy brows withal.

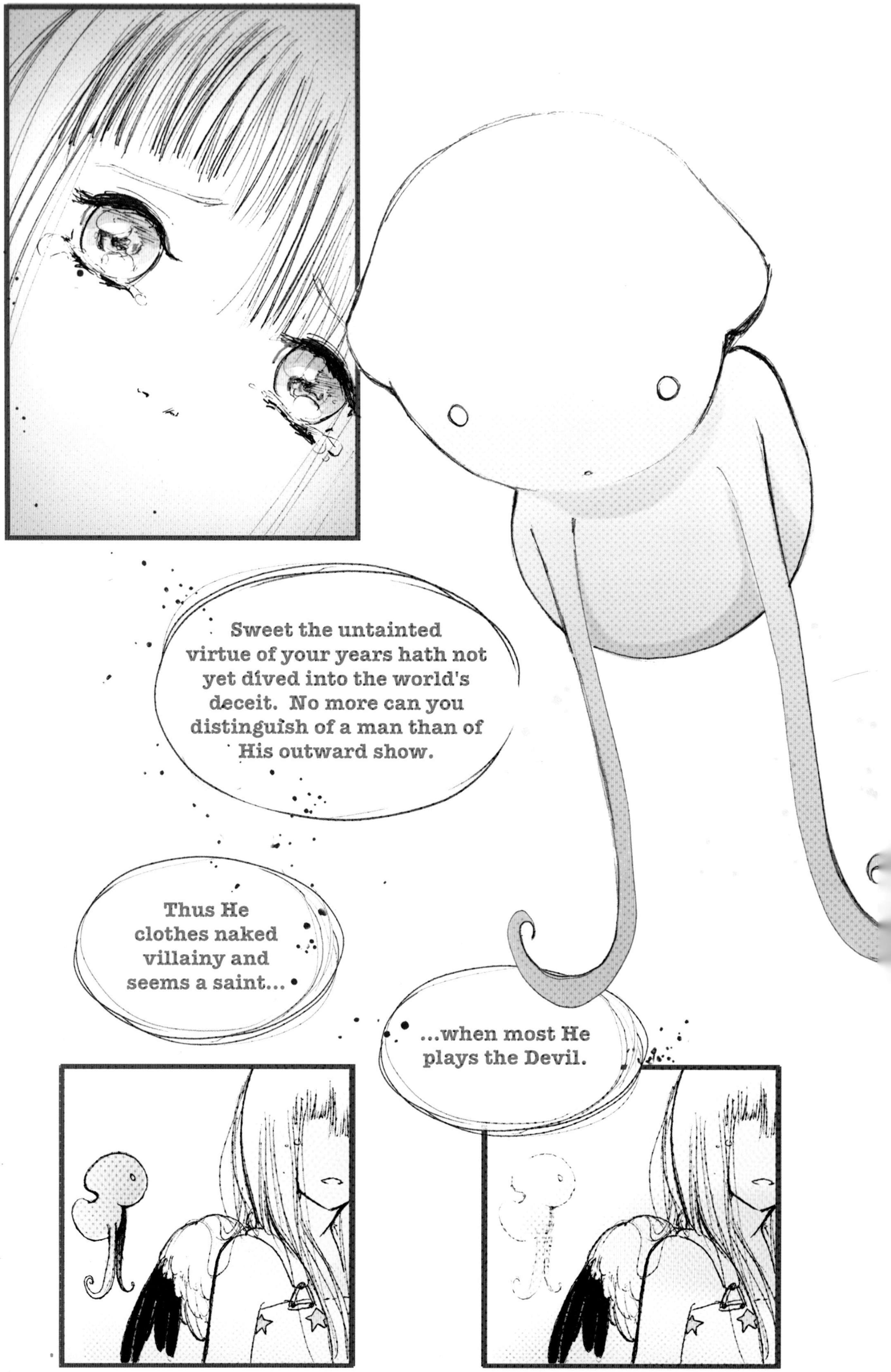
Sweet the untainted virtue of your years hath not yet dived into the world's deceit. No more can you distinguish of a man than of His outward show.
Thus He clothes naked villainy and seems a saint...
...when most He plays the Devil.

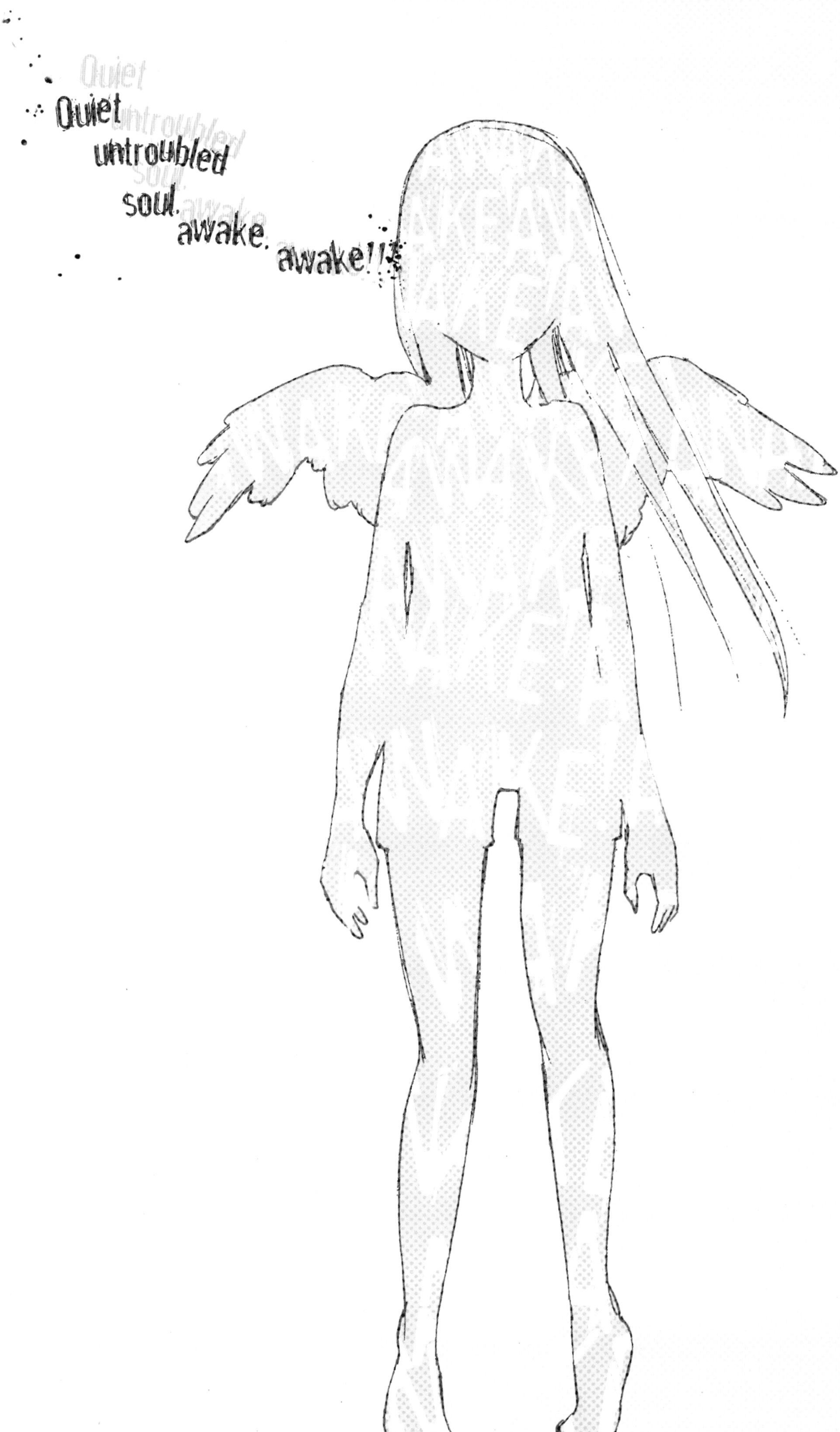
Quiet
untroubled
soul.
awake.
awake!!

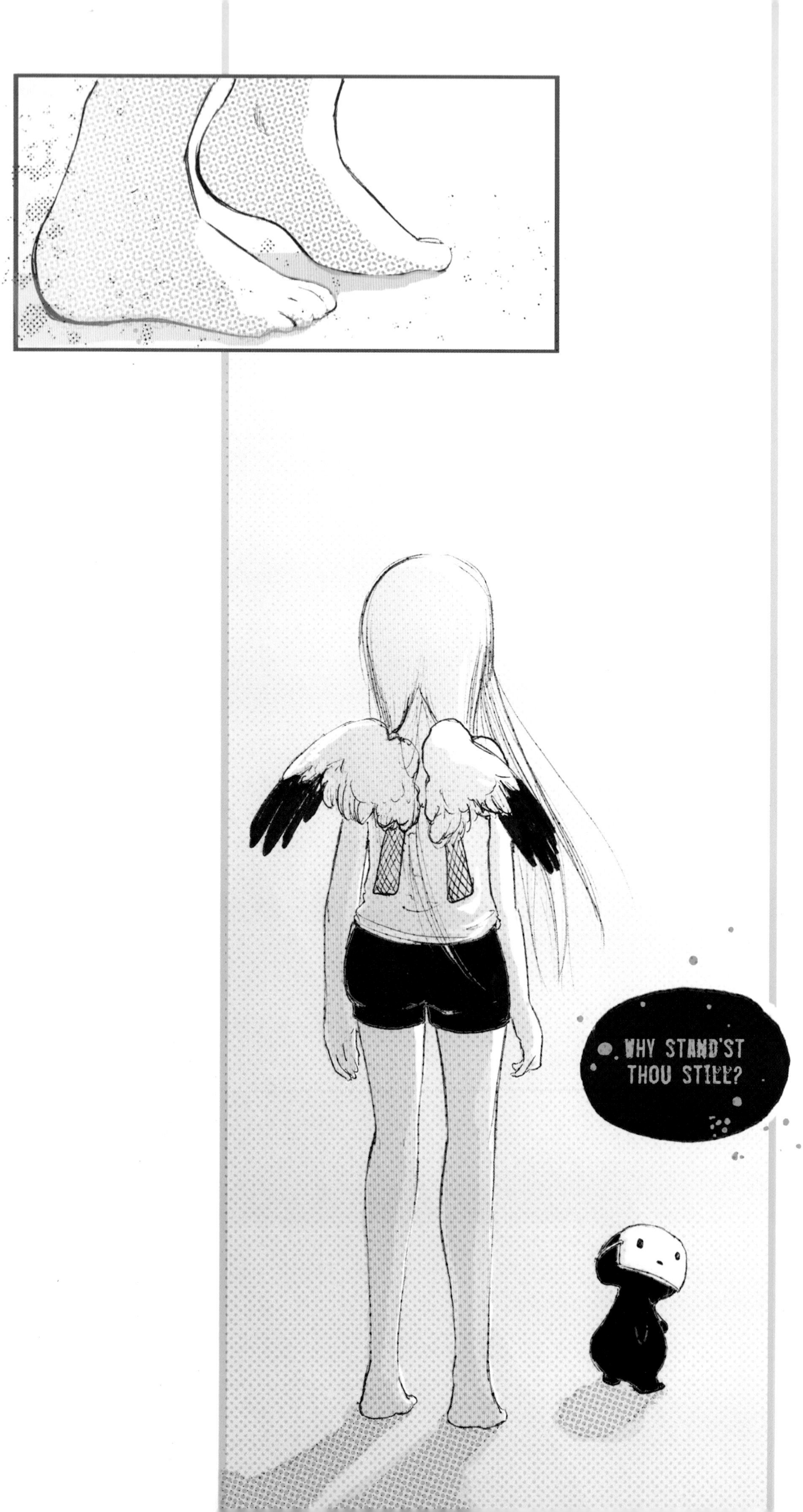
WHY STAND'ST THOU STILL?

First, mighty sovereign, let me know your mind.

Shall I forget myself to be myself?

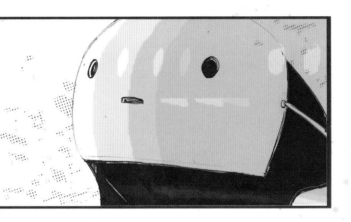

I SIGH, AND TELL THEE THAT GOD BIDS US DO GOOD FOR EVIL.

Shall I be tempted of the devil thus?

AY, IF THE DEVIL TEMPT THEE TO DO GOOD.

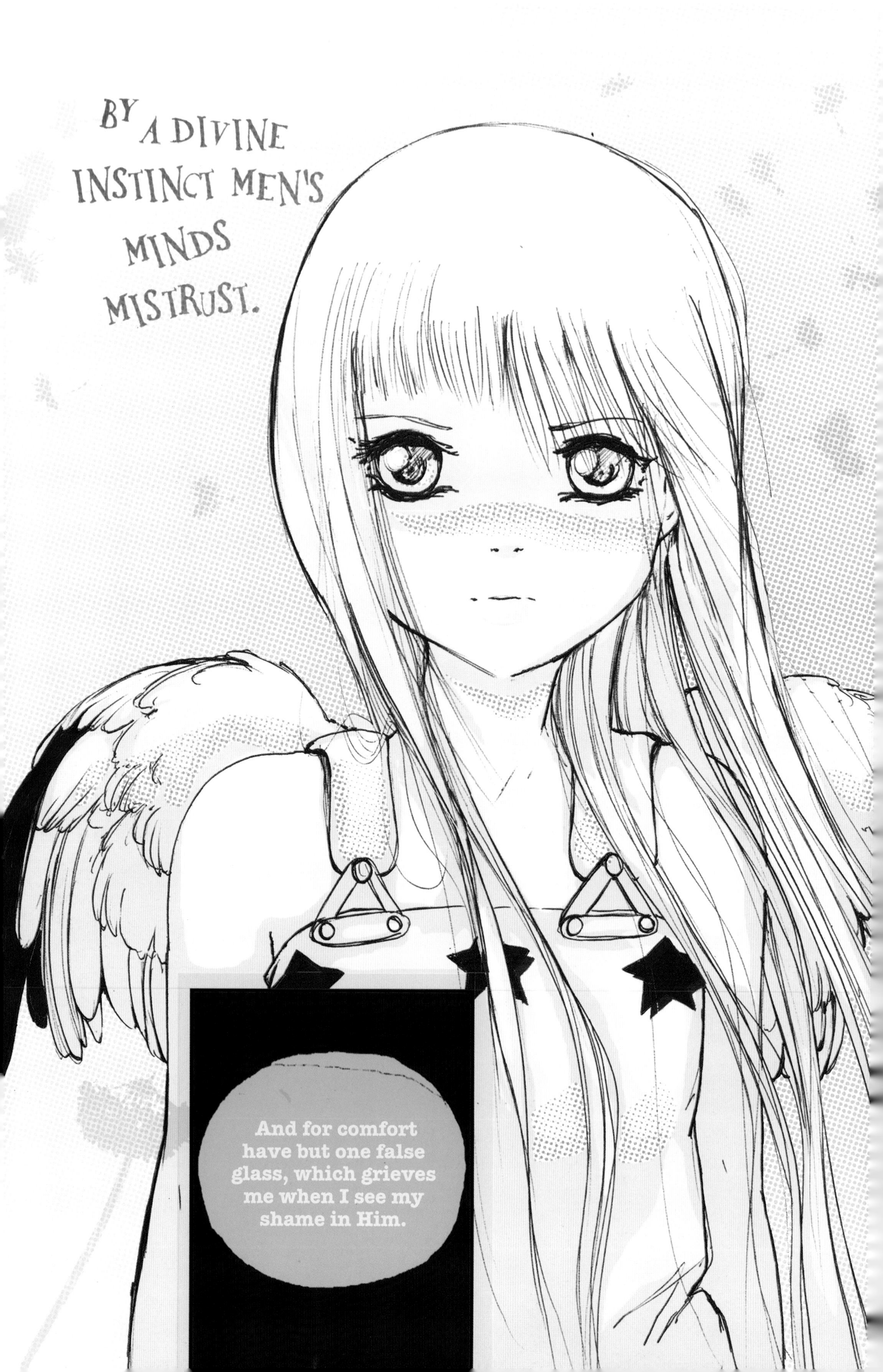
BY A DIVINE INSTINCT MEN'S MINDS MISTRUST.
And for comfort have but one false glass, which grieves me when I see my shame in Him.

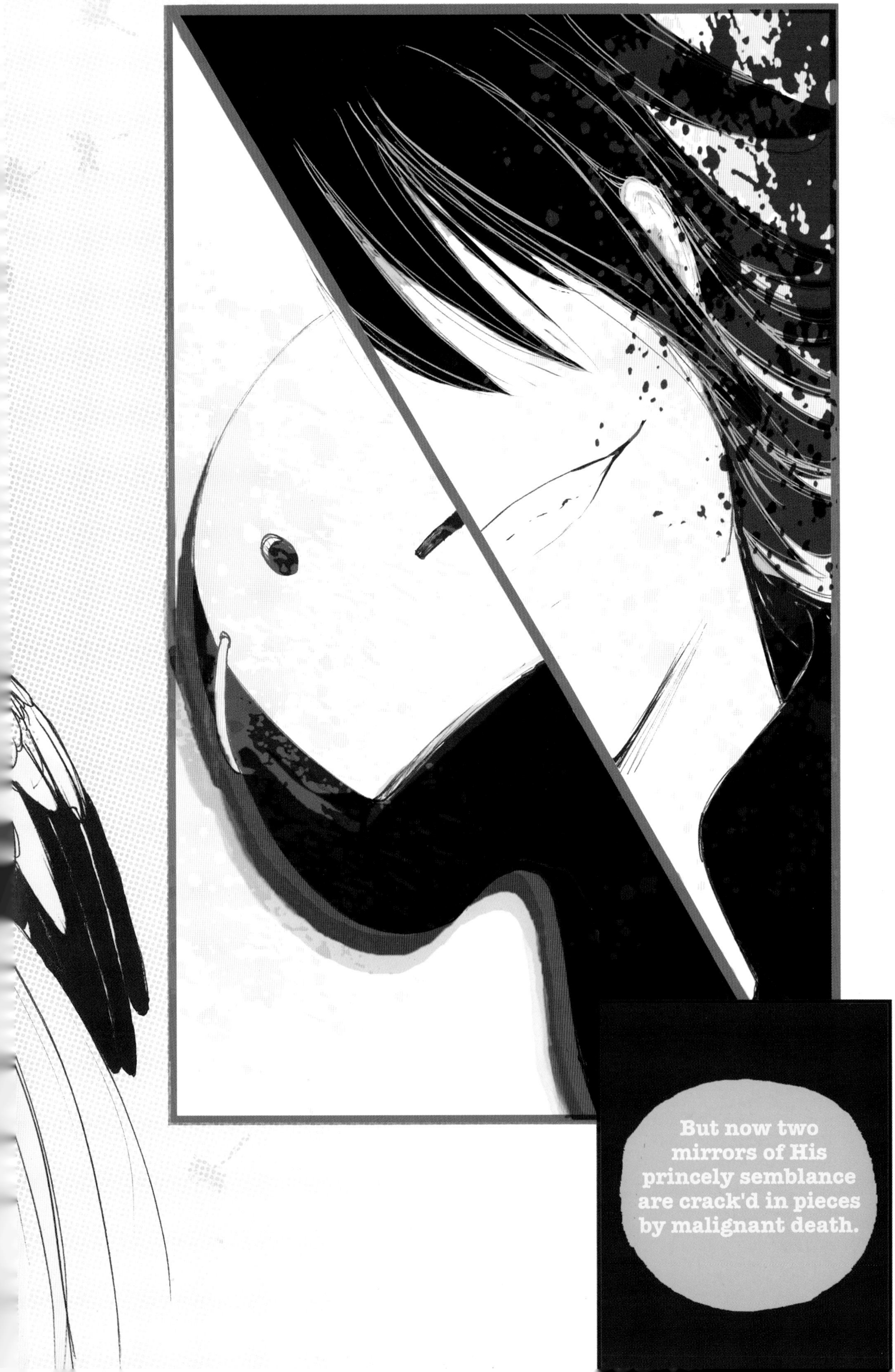
But now two mirrors of His princely semblance are crack'd in pieces by malignant death.

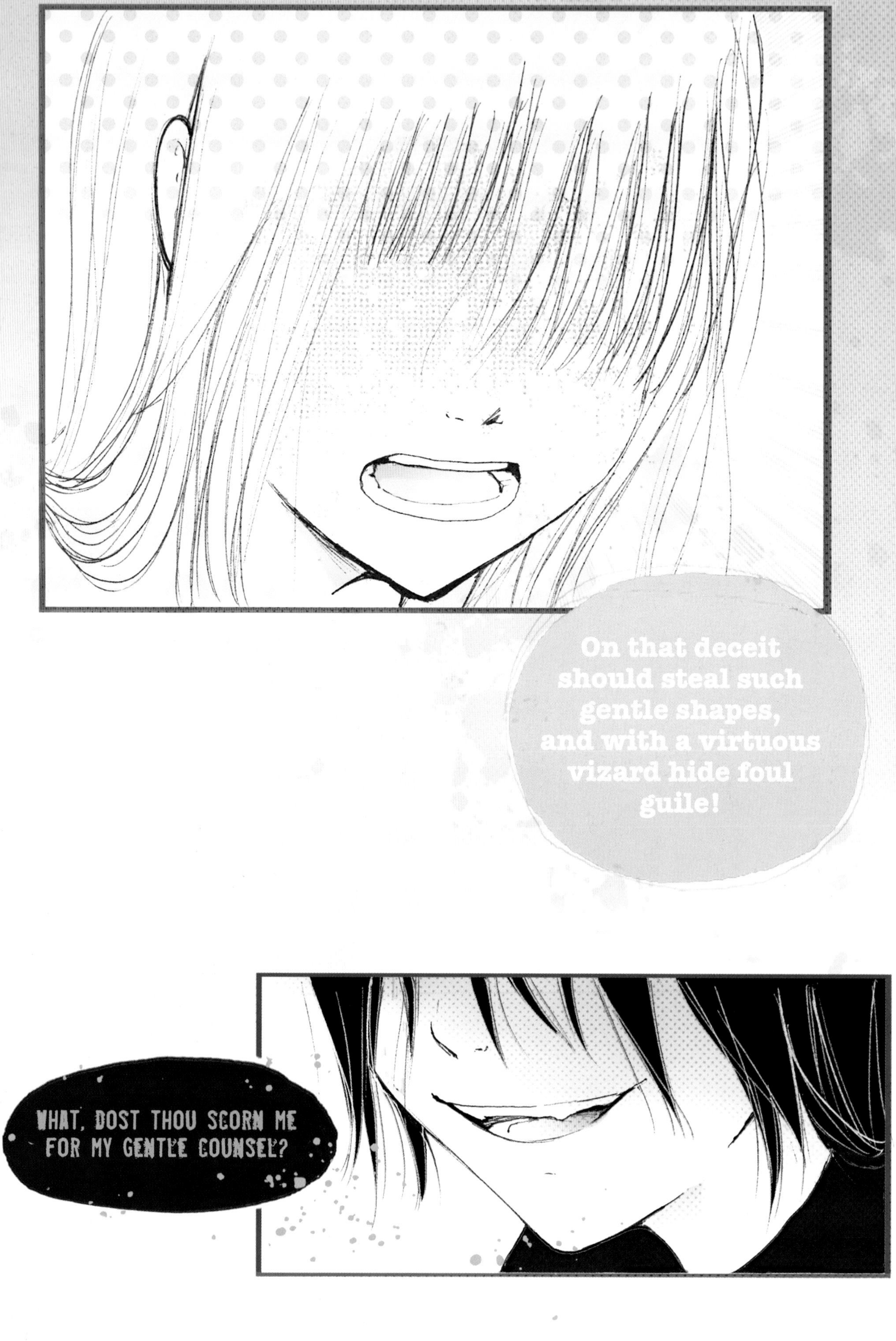
On that deceit should steal such gentle shapes, and with a virtuous vizard hide foul guile!
WHAT, DOST THOU SCORN ME FOR MY GENTLE COUNSEL?

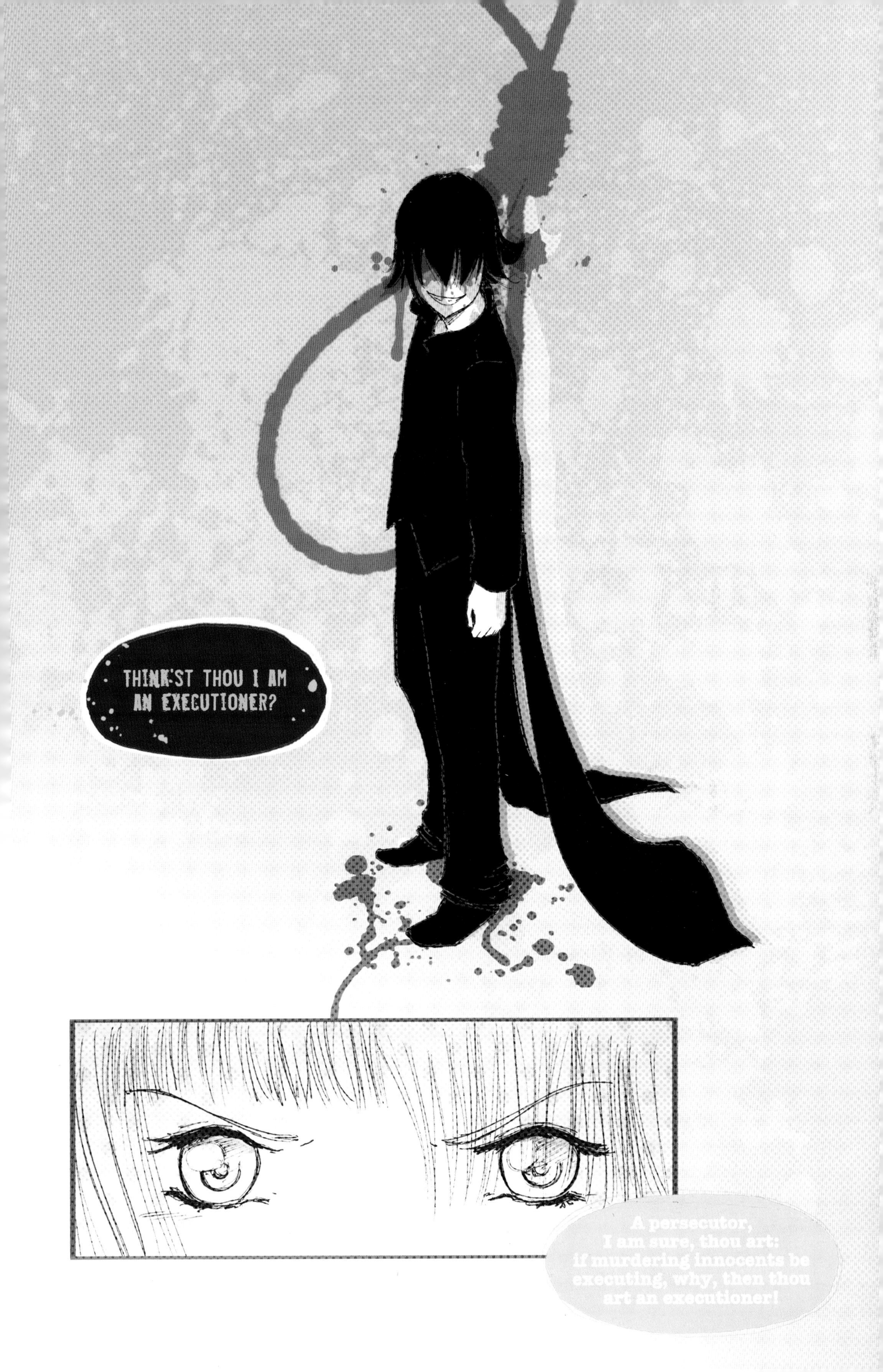
THINK'ST THOU I AM AN EXECUTIONER?
A persecutor, I am sure, thou art: if murdering innocents be executing, why, then thou art an executioner!

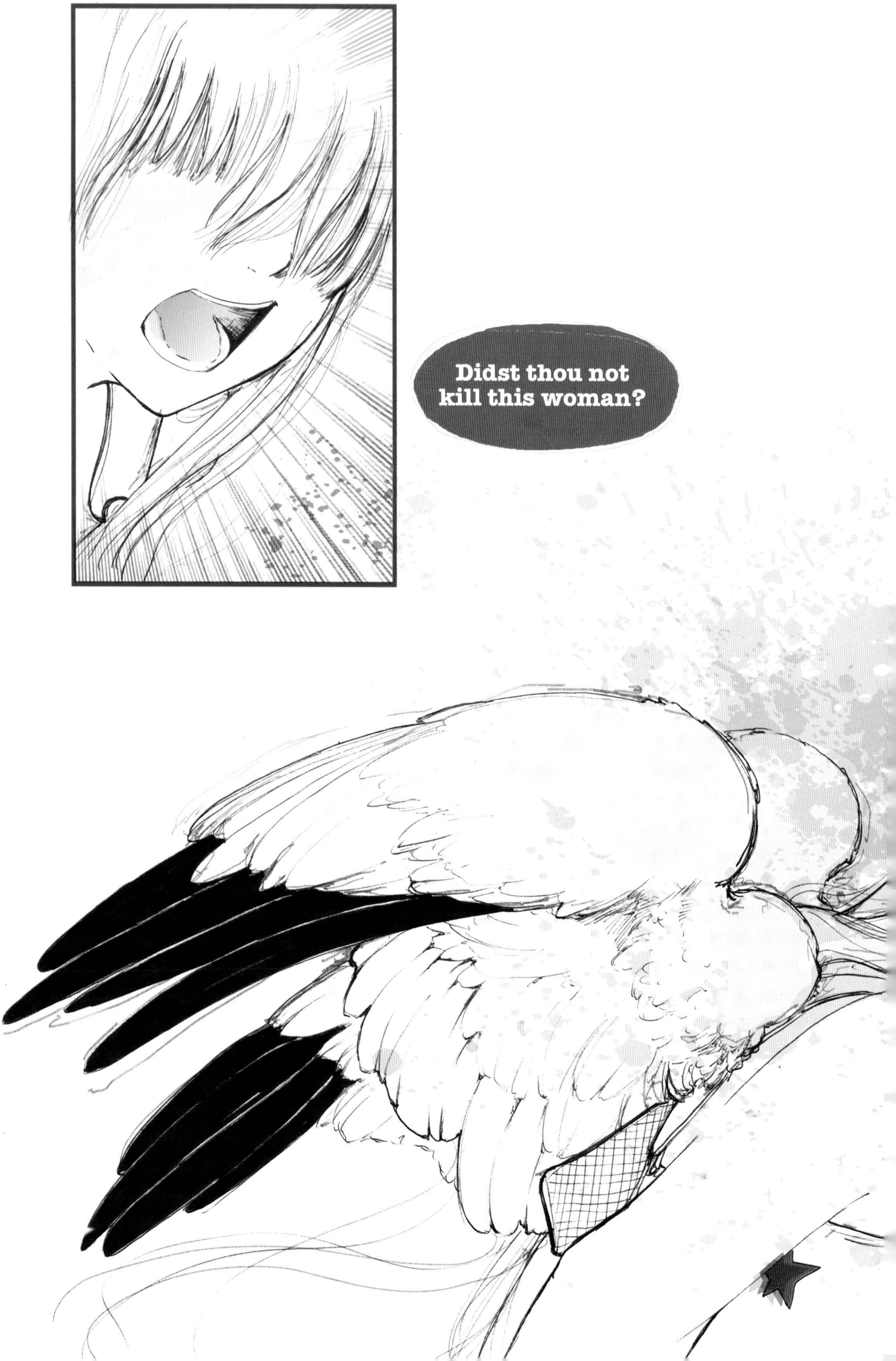
Didst thou not kill this woman?

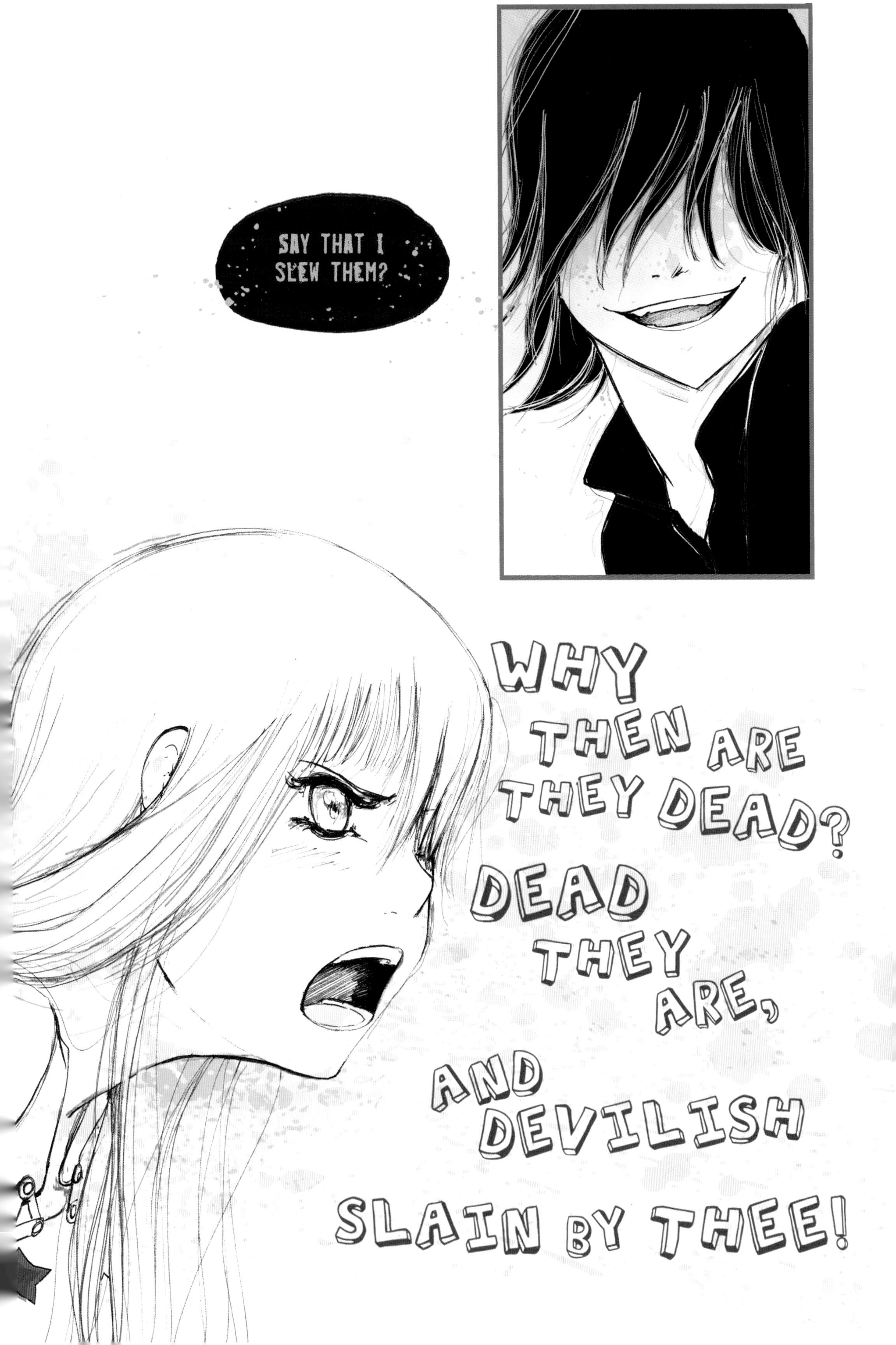
SAY THAT I SLEW THEM?
WHY THEN ARE THEY DEAD? DEAD THEY ARE, AND DEVILISH SLAIN BY THEE!

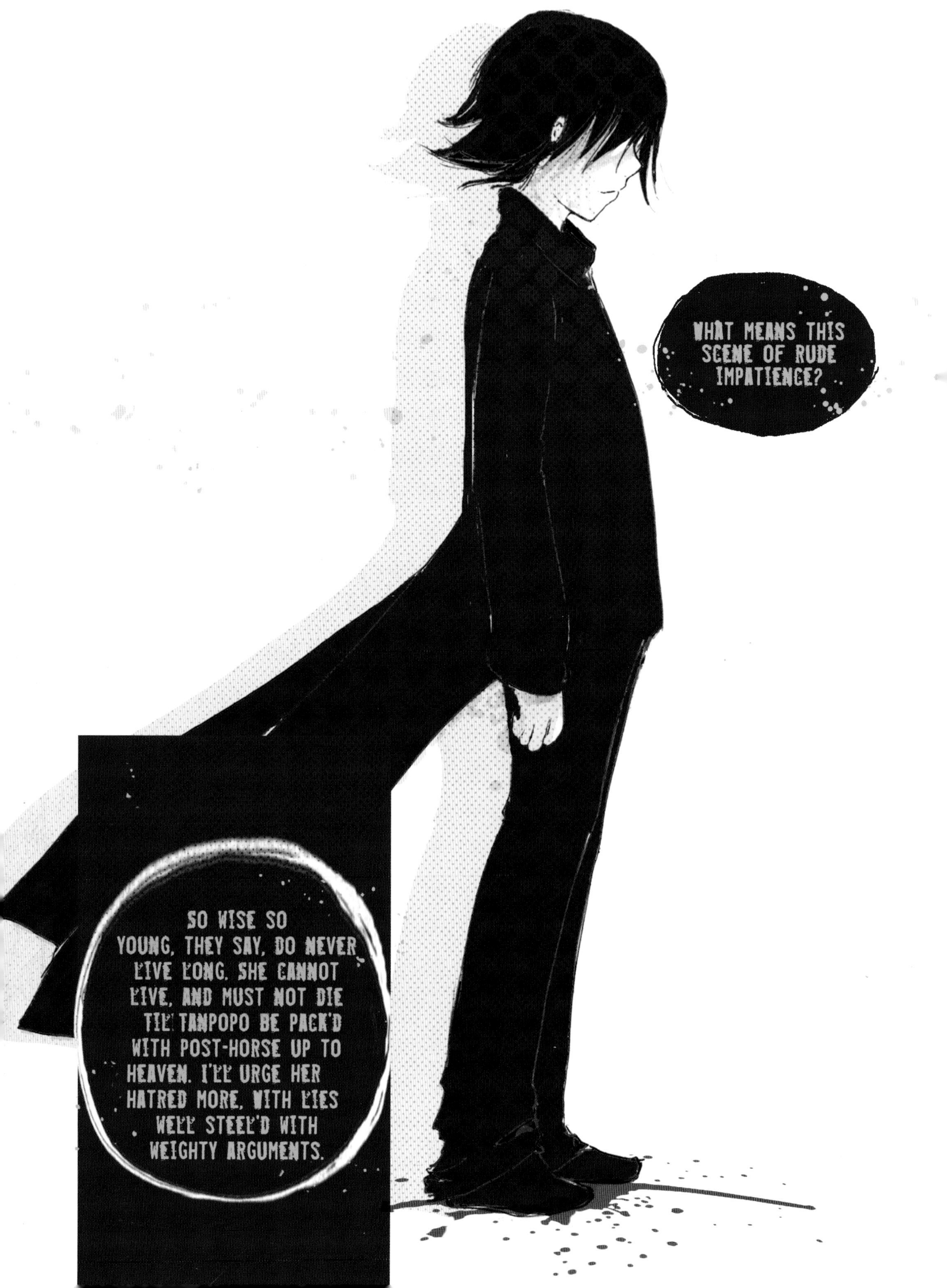
WHAT MEANS THIS SCENE OF RUDE IMPATIENCE?
SO WISE SO YOUNG, THEY SAY, DO NEVER LIVE LONG. SHE CANNOT LIVE, AND MUST NOT DIE TILL TANPOPO BE PACK'D WITH POST-HORSE UP TO HEAVEN. I'LL URGE HER HATRED MORE, WITH LIES WELL STEEL'D WITH WEIGHTY ARGUMENTS.

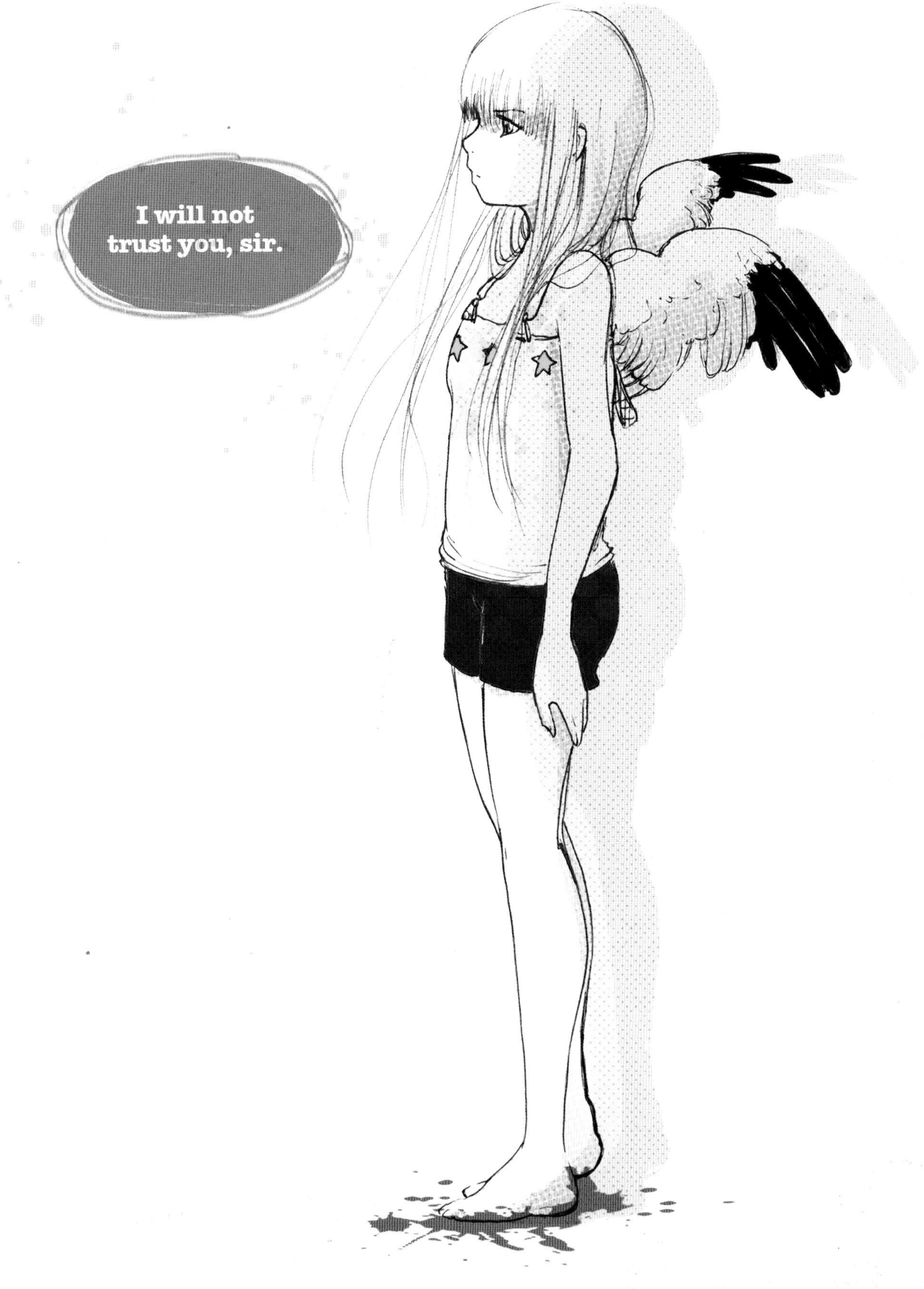
I will not trust you, sir.

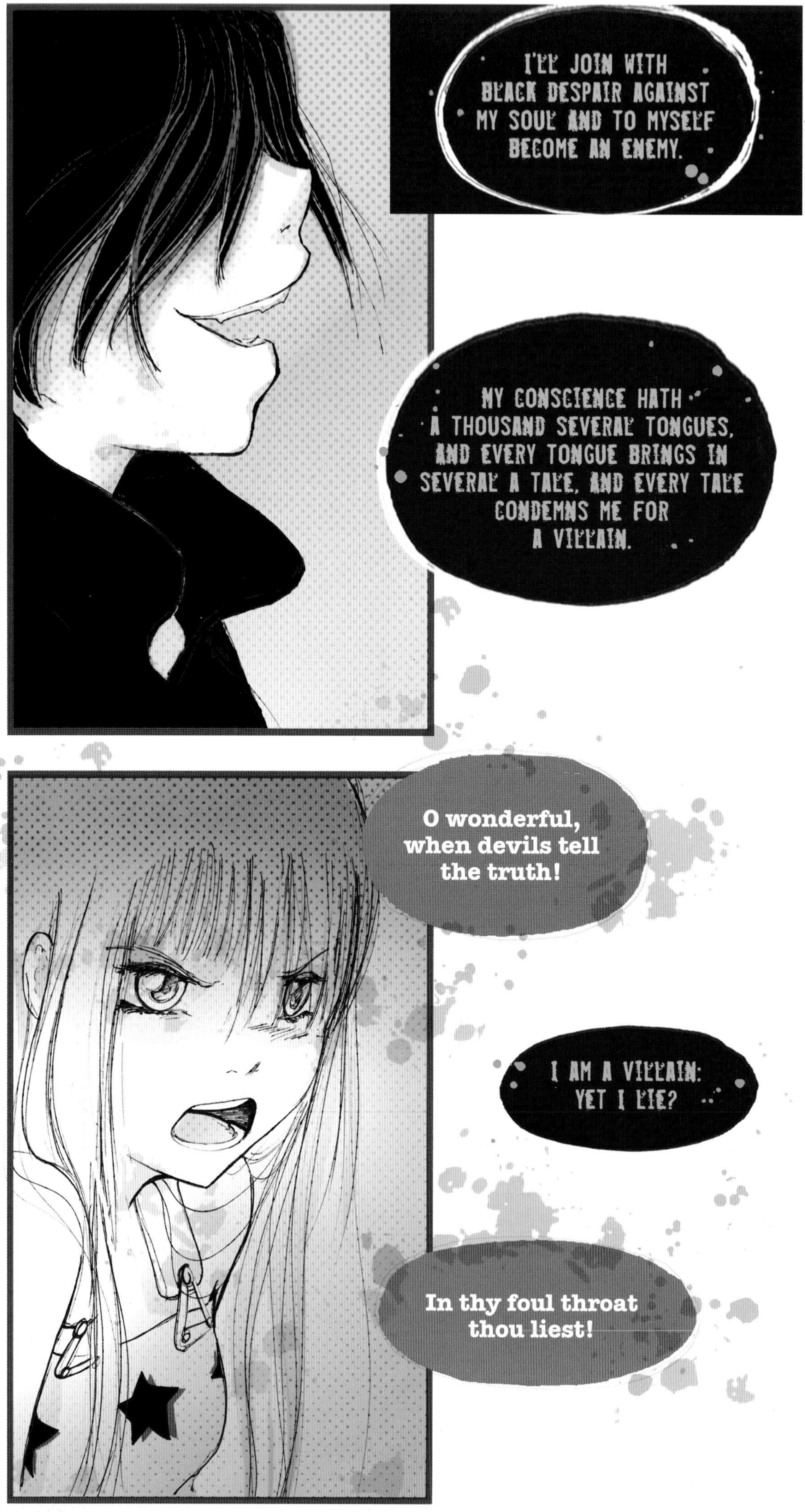
I'LL JOIN WITH BLACK DESPAIR AGAINST MY SOUL AND TO MYSELF BECOME AN ENEMY.
MY CONSCIENCE HATH A THOUSAND SEVERAL TONGUES, AND EVERY TONGUE BRINGS IN SEVERAL A TALE, AND EVERY TALE CONDEMNS ME FOR A VILLAIN.
O wonderful, when devils tell the truth!
I AM A VILLAIN: YET I LIE?
In thy foul throat thou liest!

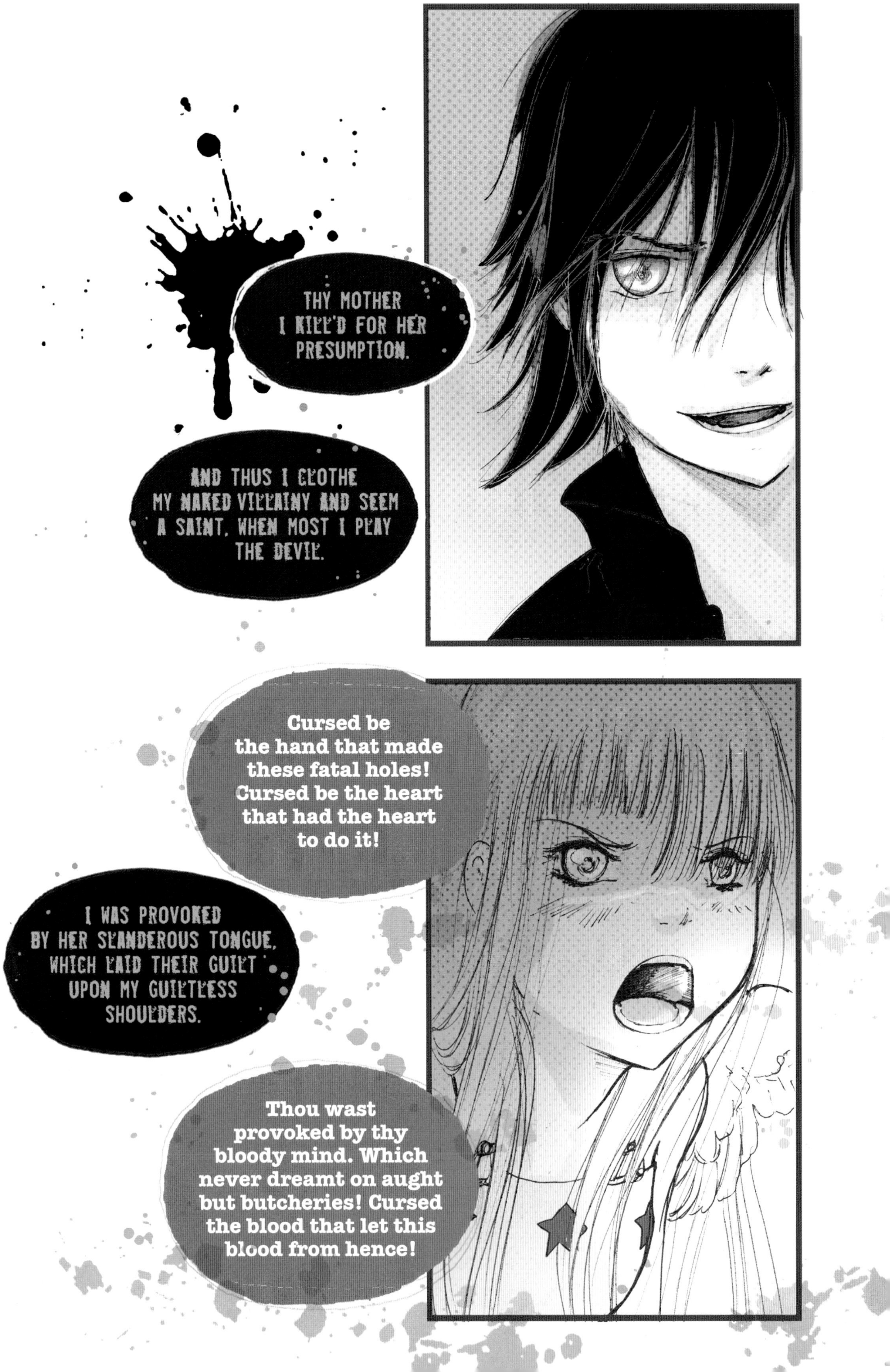
THY MOTHER I KILL'D FOR HER PRESUMPTION.
AND THUS I CLOTHE MY NAKED VILLAINY AND SEEM A SAINT, WHEN MOST I PLAY THE DEVIL.
Cursed be the hand that made these fatal holes! Cursed be the heart that had the heart to do it!
I WAS PROVOKED BY HER SLANDEROUS TONGUE, WHICH LAID THEIR GUILT UPON MY GUILTLESS SHOULDERS.
Thou wast provoked by thy bloody mind. Which never dreamt on aught but butcheries! Cursed the blood that let this blood from hence!

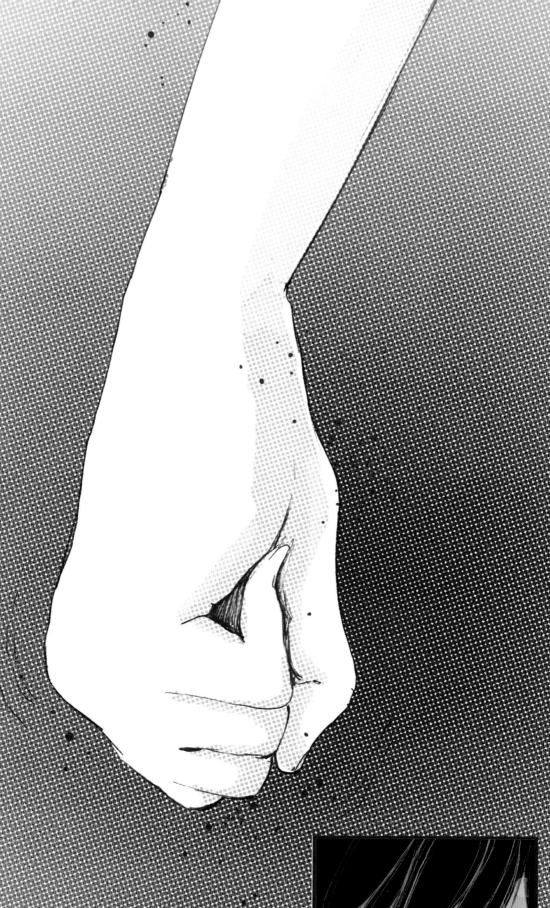

WHAT, DO YOU TREMBLE?

Thou didst kill my mother!

THE FITTER FOR THE KING OF HEAVEN, THAT HATH HER.

She is in heaven, where thou shalt never come.

LET HER THANK ME, THAT HELP TO SEND HER THITHER; FOR SHE WAS FITTER FOR THAT PLACE THAN EARTH.

And thou unfit for any place but hell!

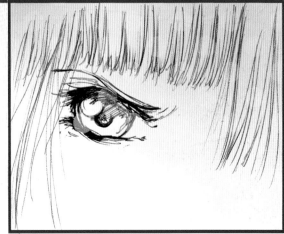

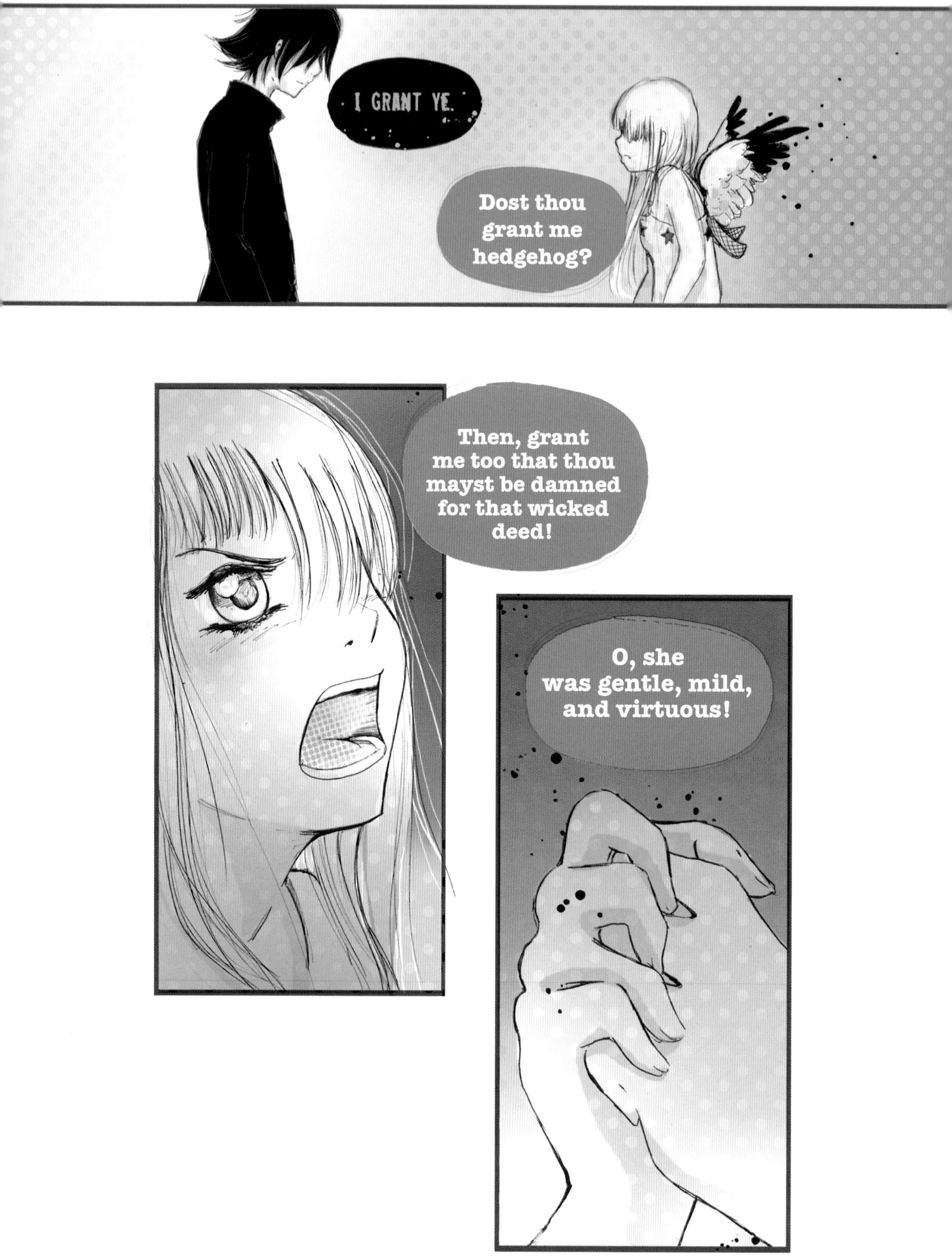
Dost thou grant me hedgehog?
I GRANT YE.
Then, grant me too that thou mayst be damned for that wicked deed!
O, she was gentle, mild, and virtuous!

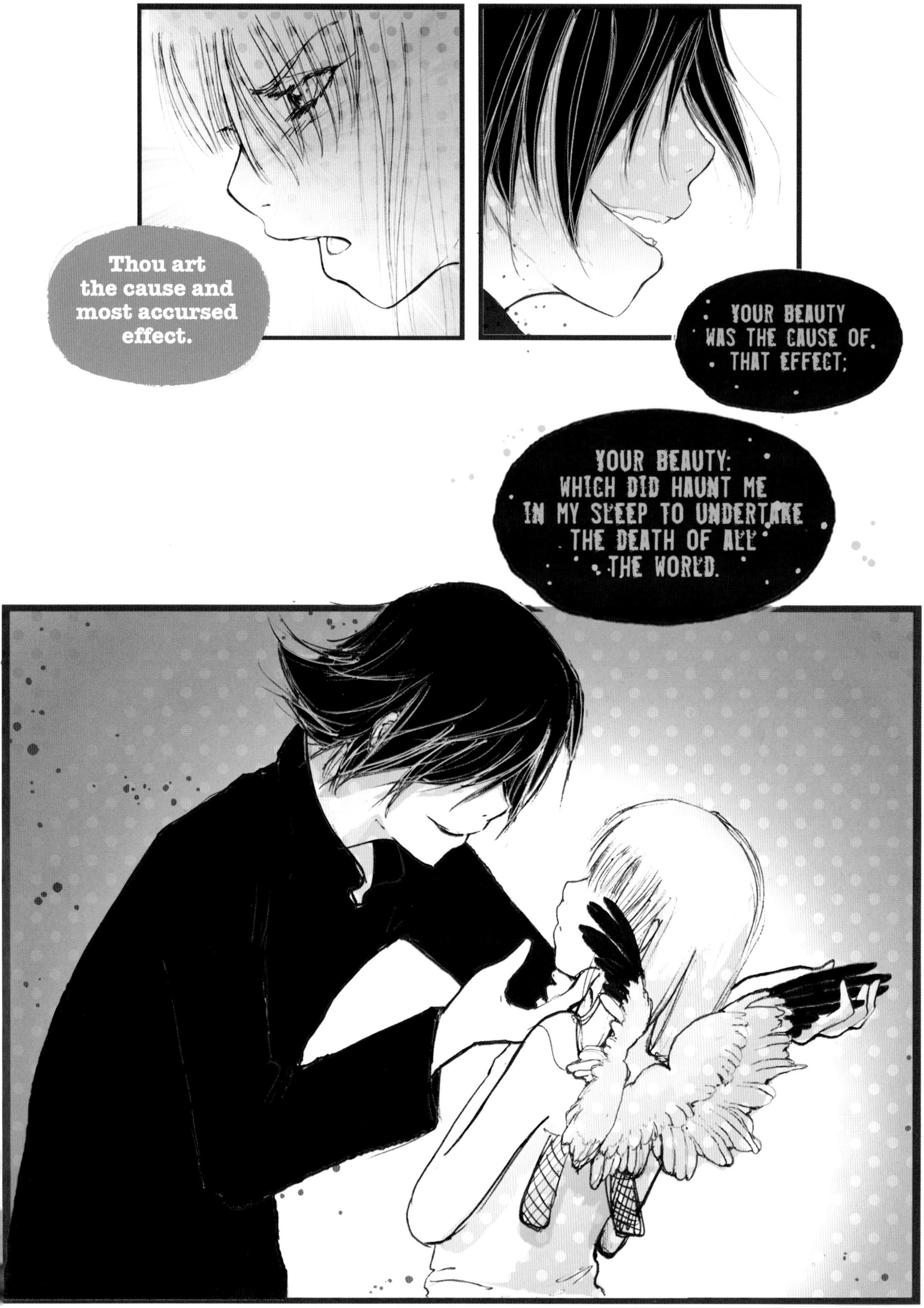
Thou art the cause and most accursed effect.
YOUR BEAUTY WAS THE CAUSE OF THAT EFFECT:
YOUR BEAUTY: WHICH DID HAUNT ME IN MY SLEEP TO UNDERTAKE THE DEATH OF ALL THE WORLD.

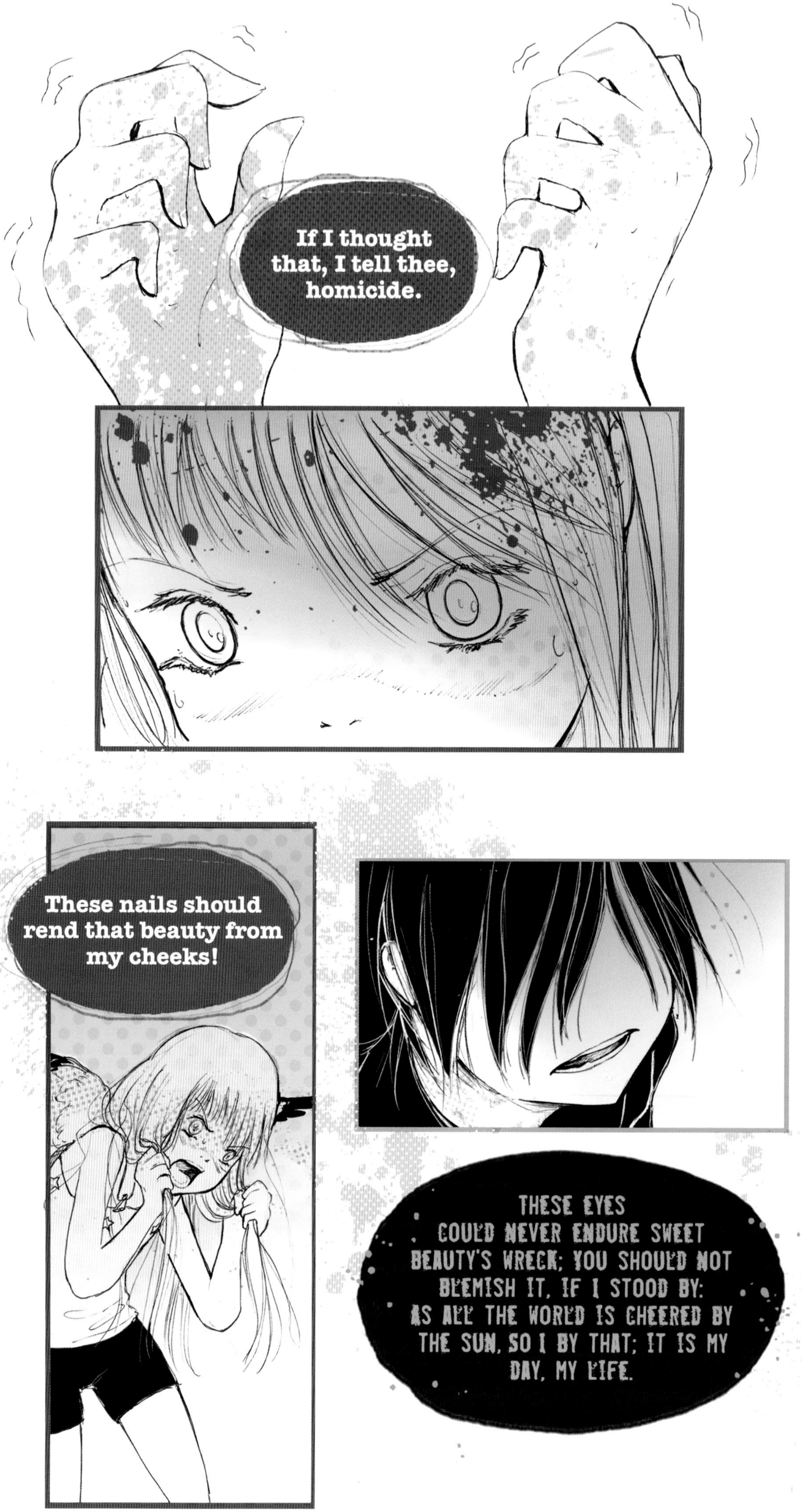
If I thought that, I tell thee, homicide.
These nails should rend that beauty from my cheeks!
THESE EYES COULD NEVER ENDURE SWEET BEAUTY'S WRECK; YOU SHOULD NOT BLEMISH IT, IF I STOOD BY: AS ALL THE WORLD IS CHEERED BY THE SUN, SO I BY THAT; IT IS MY DAY, MY LIFE.

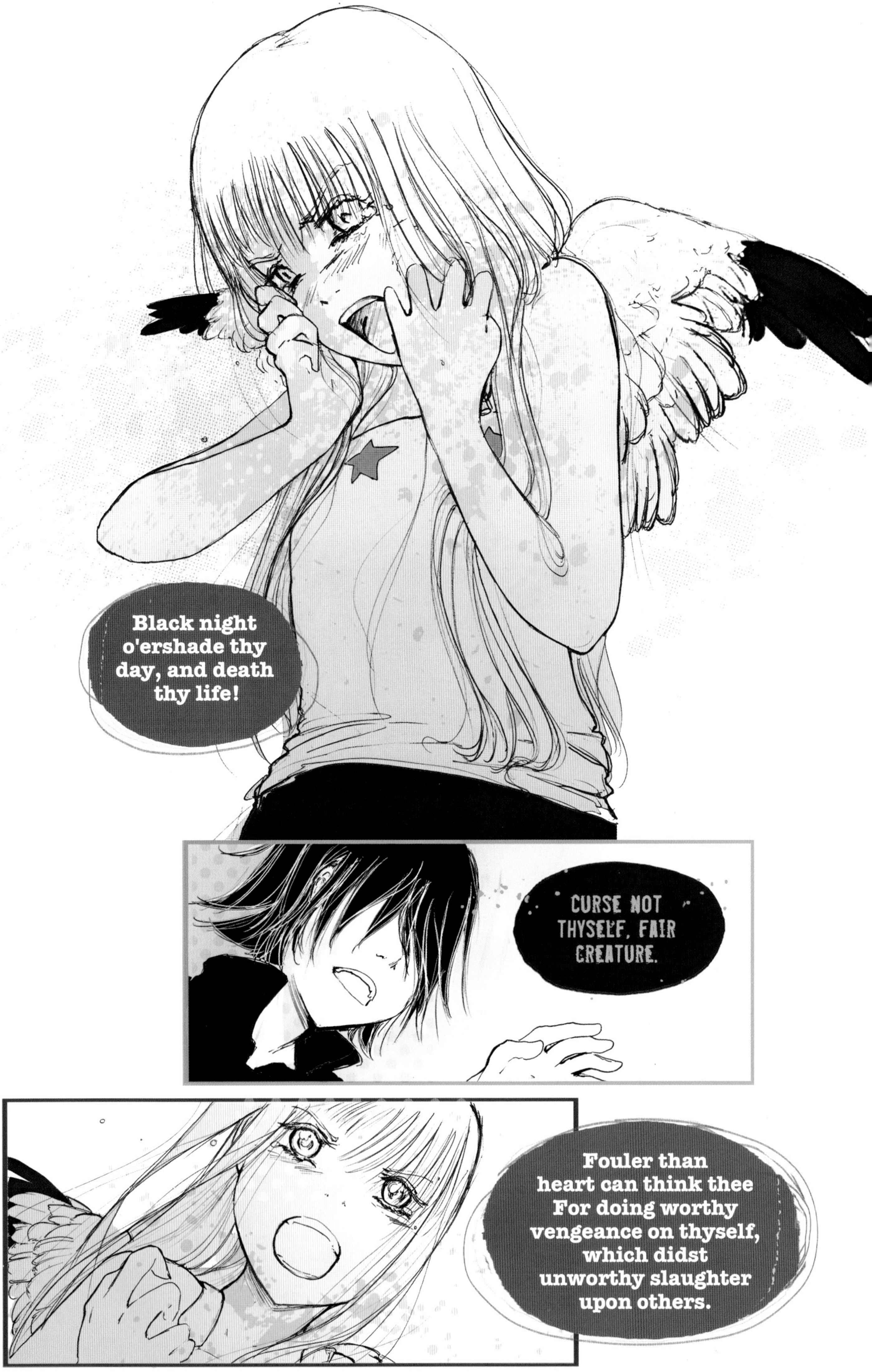
Black night o'ershade thy day, and death thy life!
CURSE NOT THYSELF, FAIR CREATURE.
Fouler than heart can think thee For doing worthy vengeance on thyself, which didst unworthy slaughter upon others.

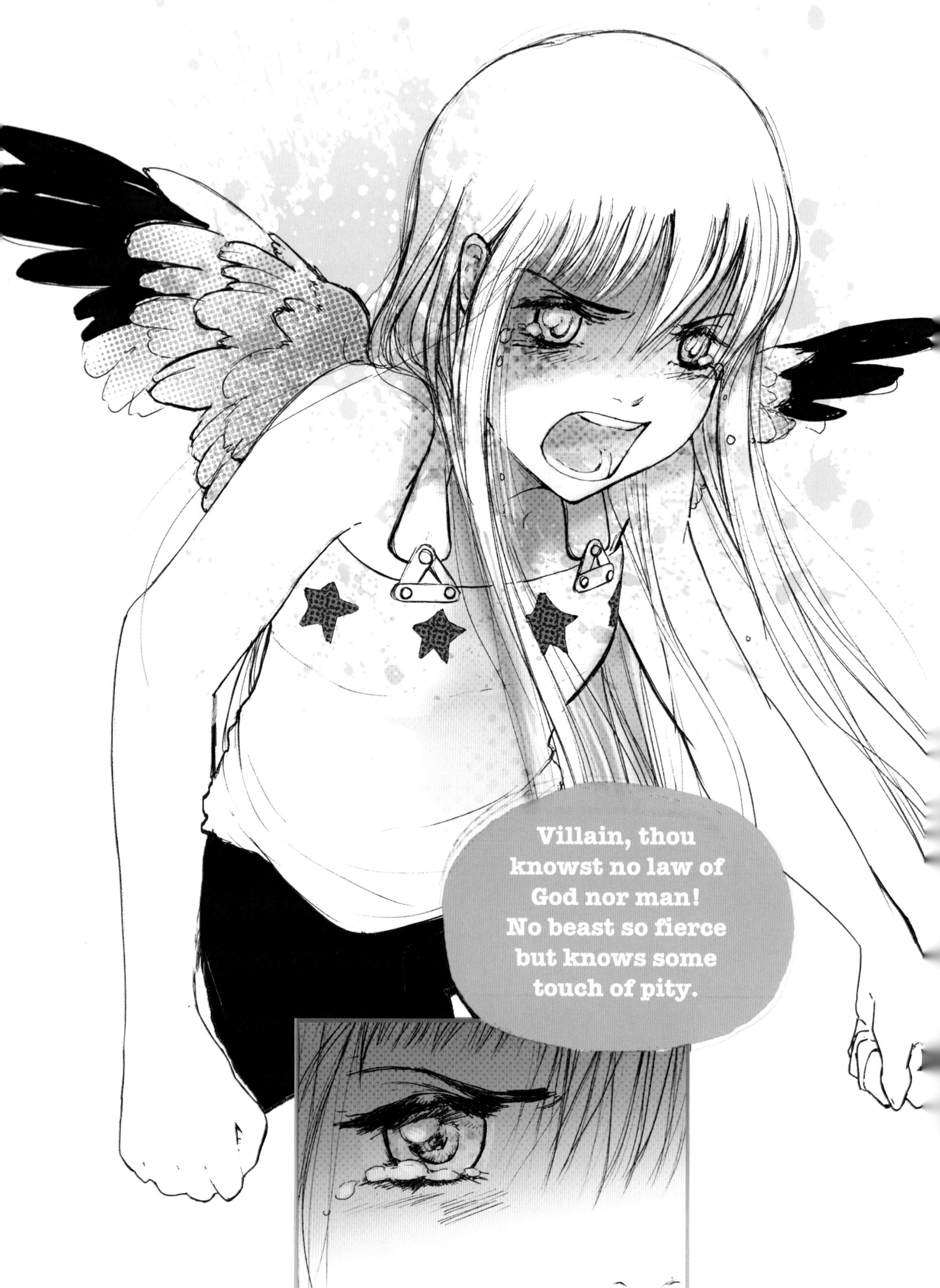
Villain, thou knowst no law of God nor man! No beast so fierce but knows some touch of pity.

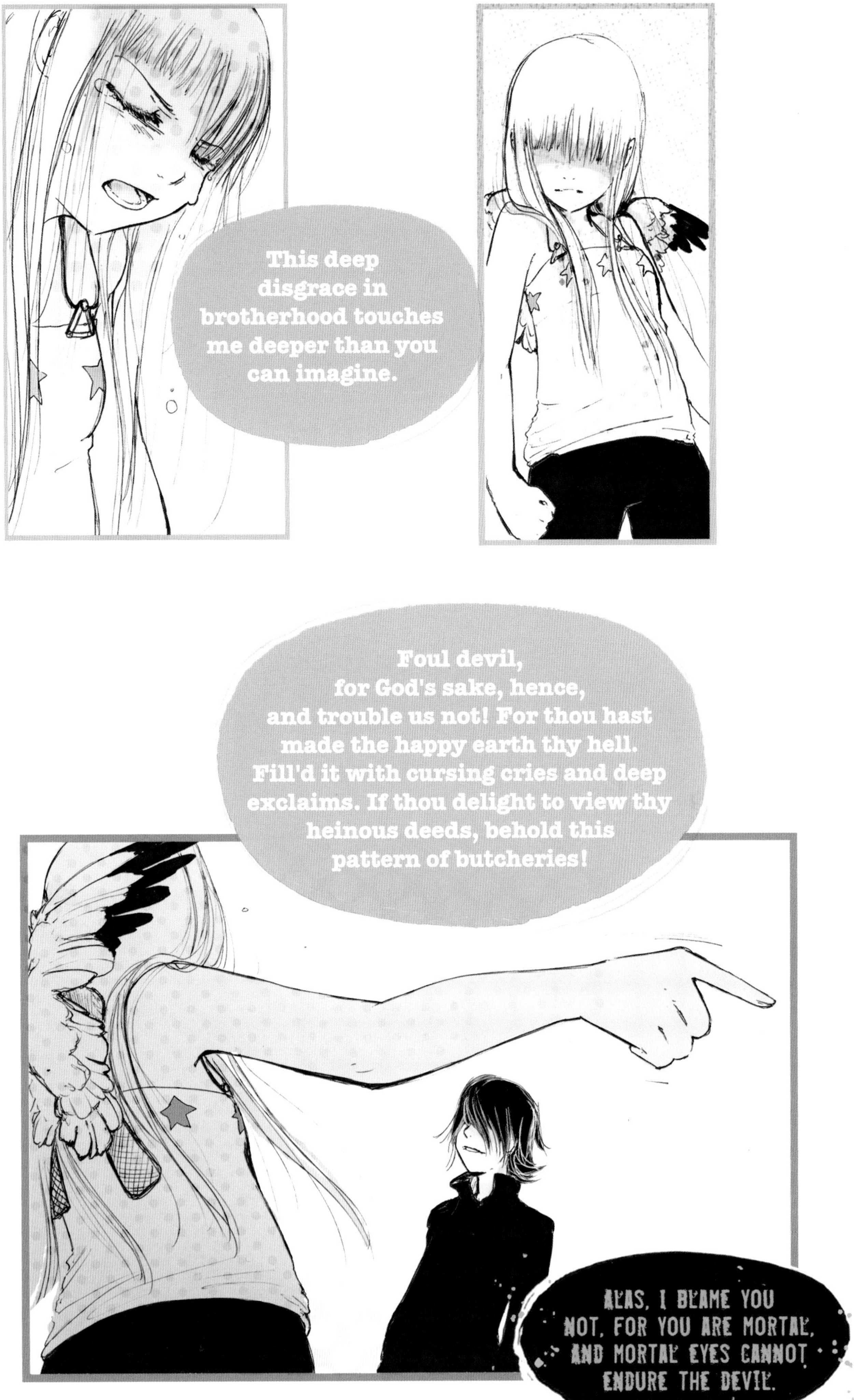
This deep disgrace in brotherhood touches me deeper than you can imagine.
Foul devil, for God's sake, hence, and trouble us not! For thou hast made the happy earth thy hell. Fill'd it with cursing cries and deep exclaims. If thou delight to view thy heinous deeds, behold this pattern of butcheries!
ALAS, I BLAME YOU NOT, FOR YOU ARE MORTAL, AND MORTAL EYES CANNOT ENDURE THE DEVIL.

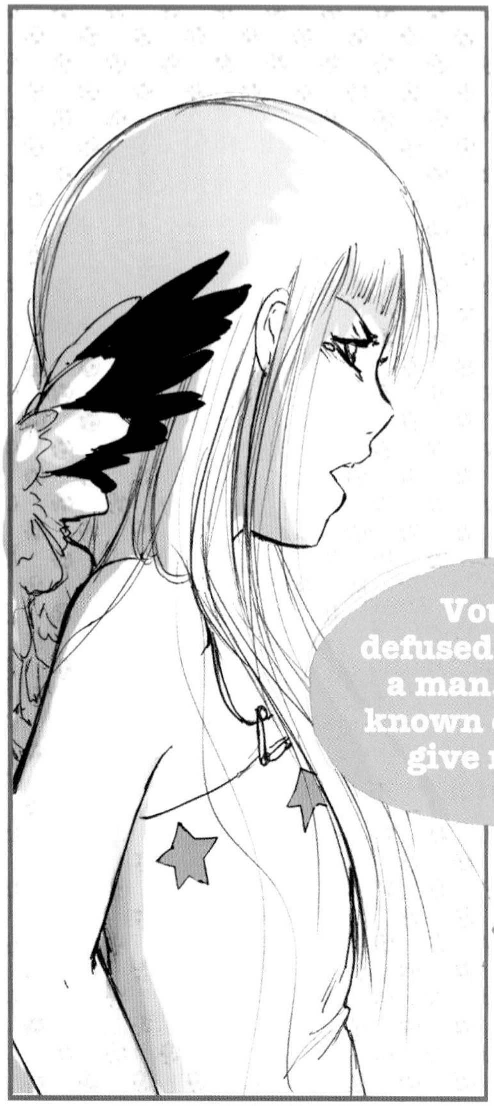
Vouchsafe defused infection of a man. For these known evils, but to give me leave.

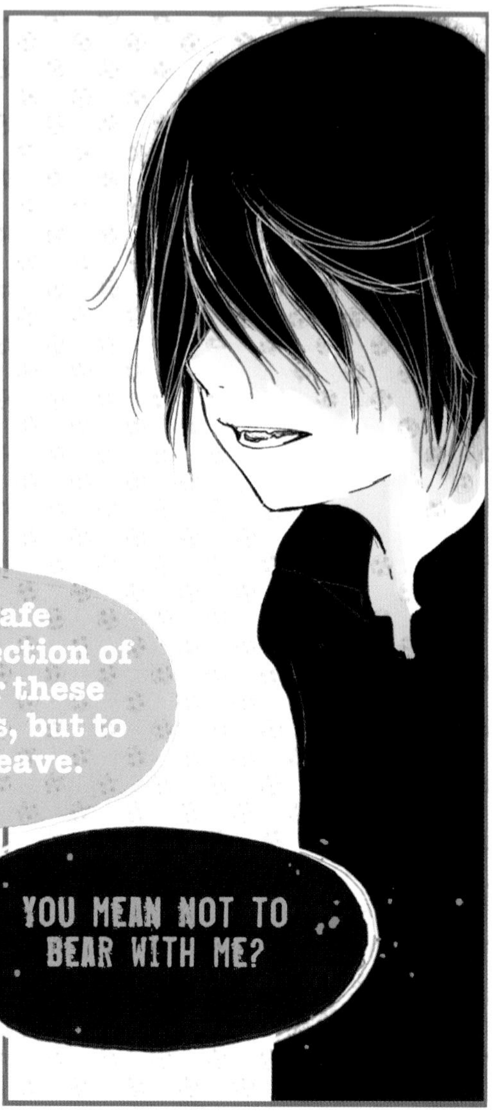
YOU MEAN NOT TO BEAR WITH ME?

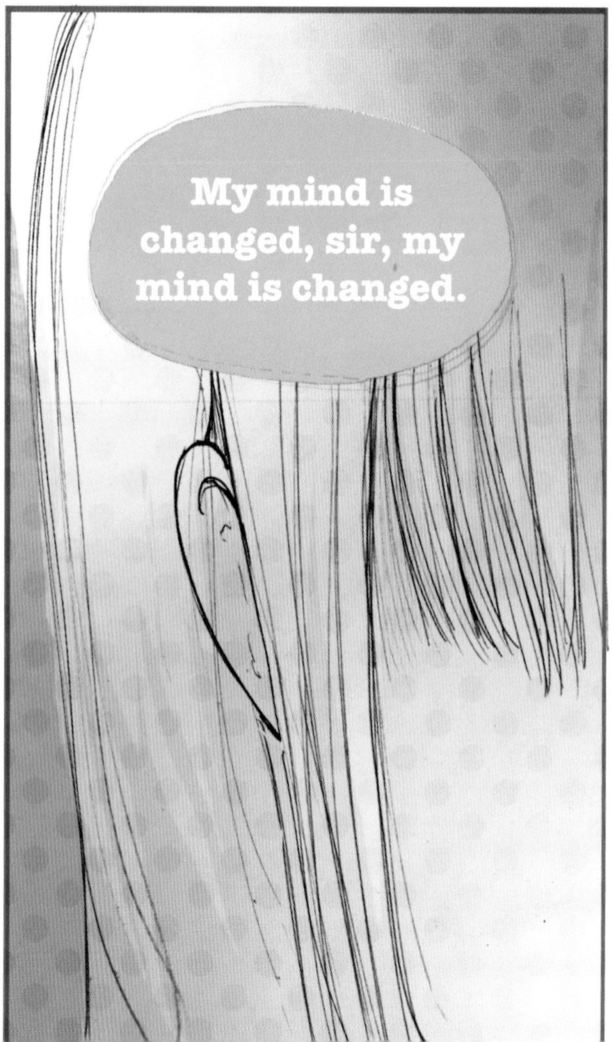
My mind is changed, sir, my mind is changed.

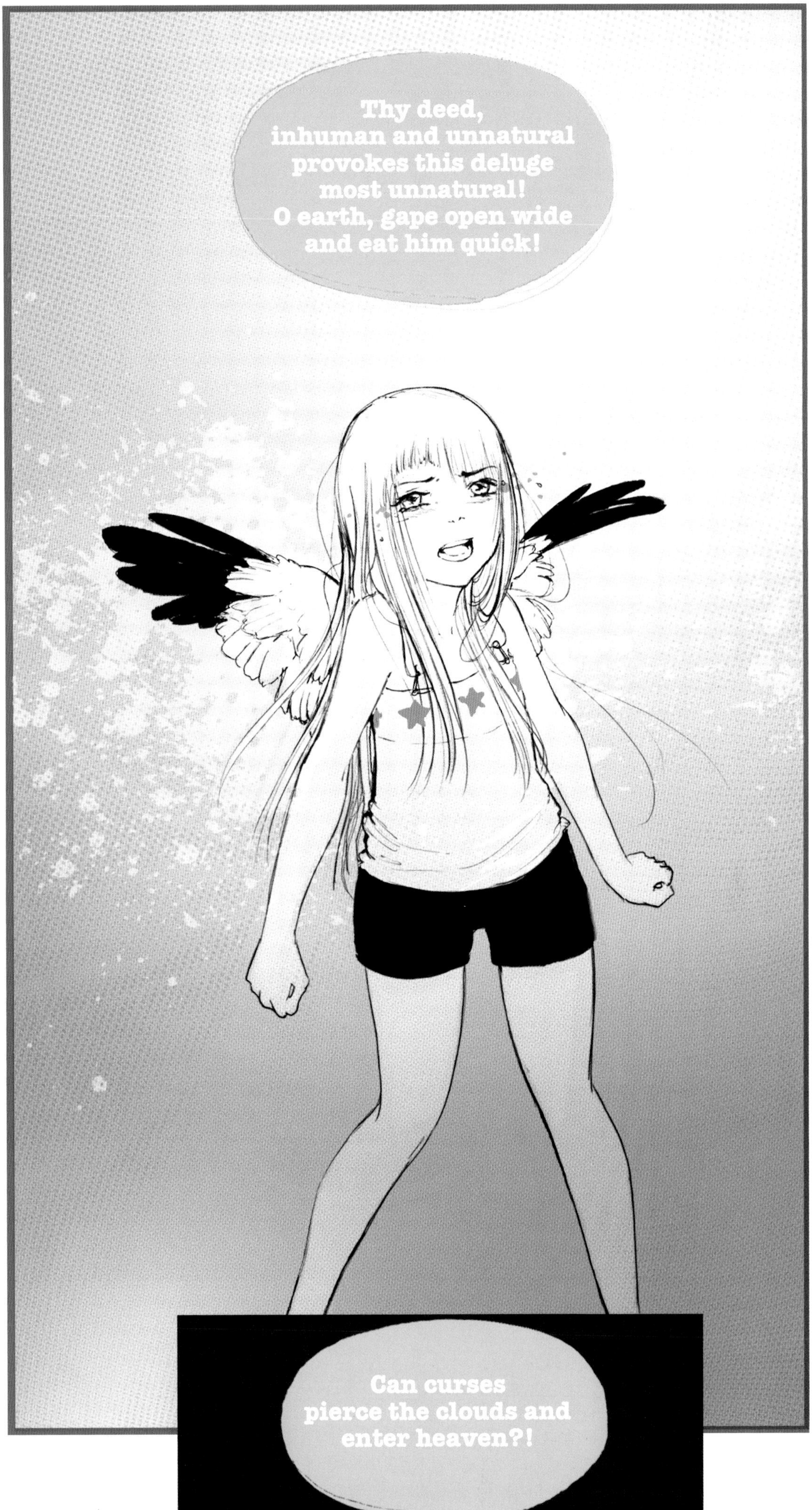
Thy deed, inhuman and unnatural provokes this deluge most unnatural! O earth, gape open wide and eat him quick!
Can curses pierce the clouds and enter heaven?!

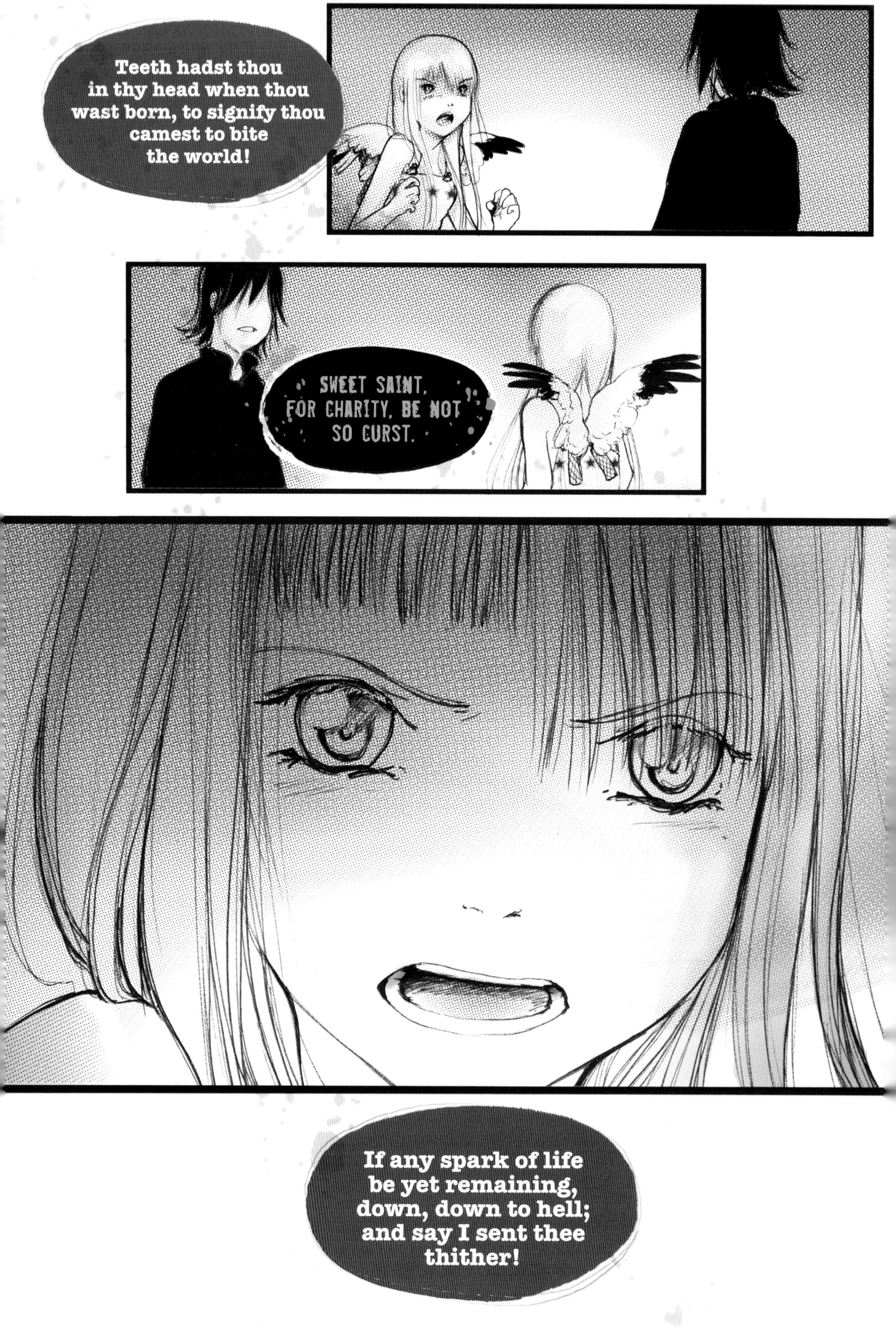
Teeth hadst thou in thy head when thou wast born, to signify thou camest to bite the world!
SWEET SAINT, FOR CHARITY, BE NOT SO CURST.
If any spark of life be yet remaining, down, down to hell; and say I sent thee thither!

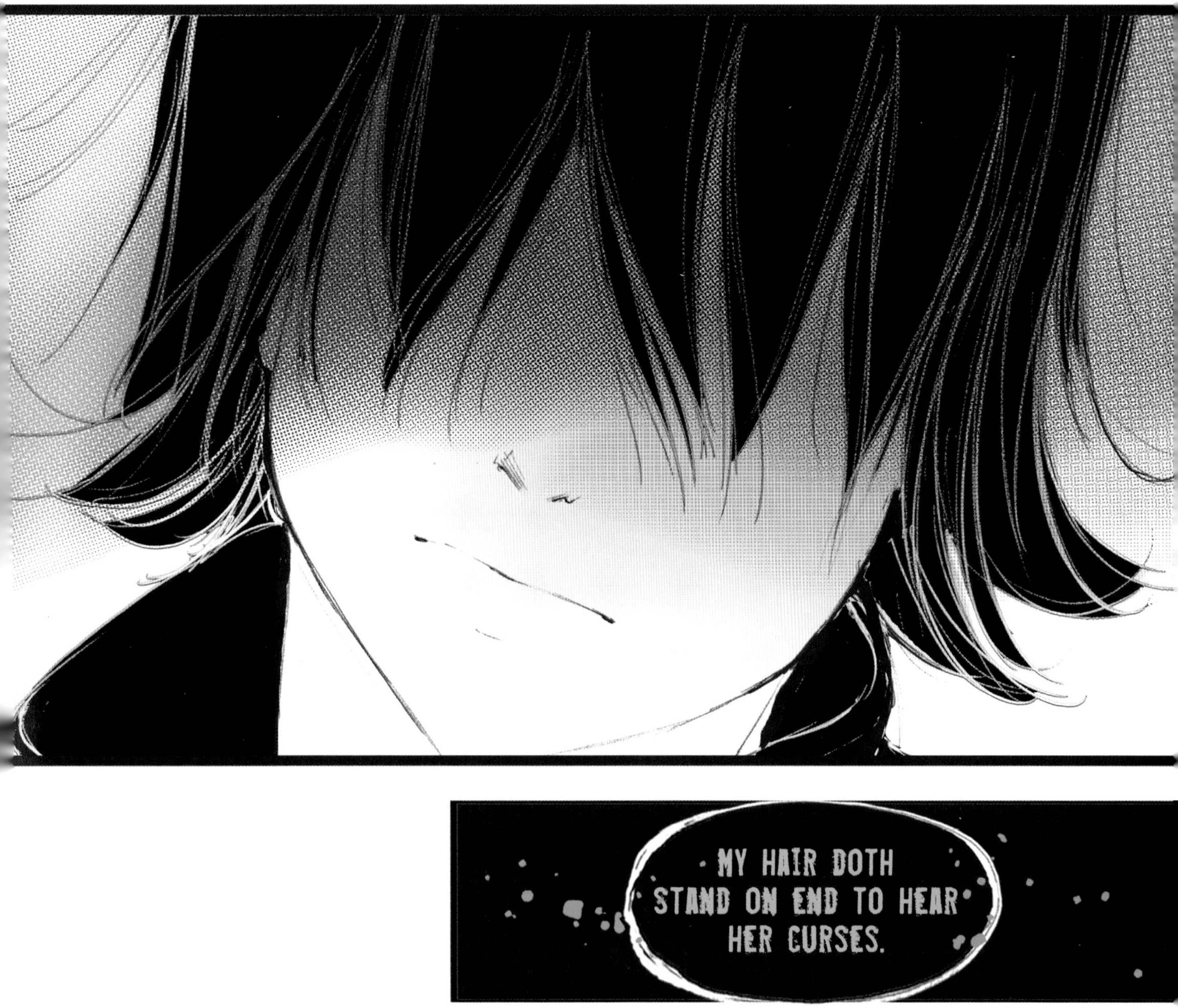
MY HAIR DOTH STAND ON END TO HEAR HER CURSES.

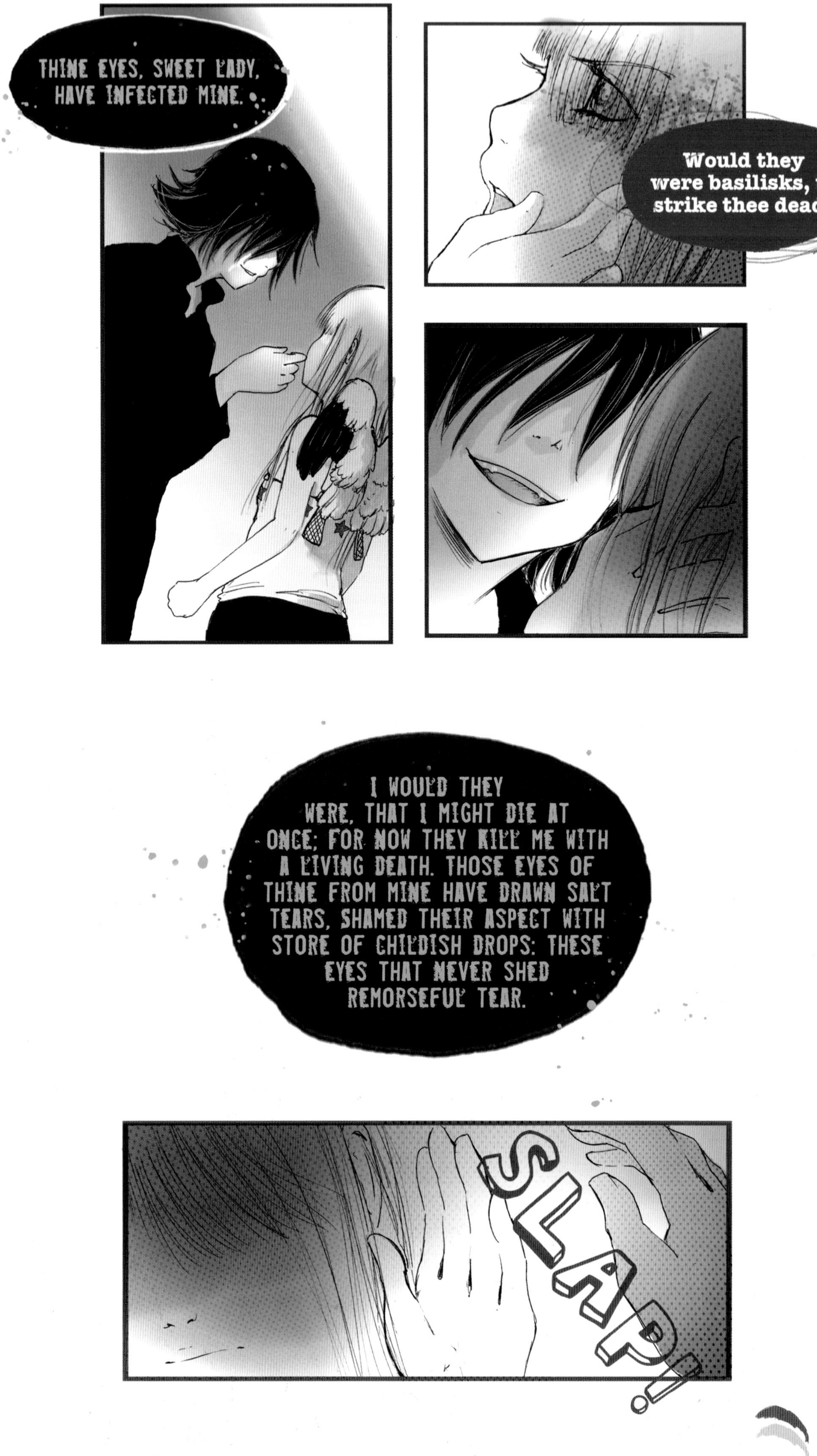
THINE EYES, SWEET LADY, HAVE INFECTED MINE.
Would they were basilisks, to strike thee dead!
I WOULD THEY WERE, THAT I MIGHT DIE AT ONCE; FOR NOW THEY KILL ME WITH A LIVING DEATH. THOSE EYES OF THINE FROM MINE HAVE DRAWN SALT TEARS, SHAMED THEIR ASPECT WITH STORE OF CHILDISH DROPS: THESE EYES THAT NEVER SHED REMORSEFUL TEAR.
SLAP!

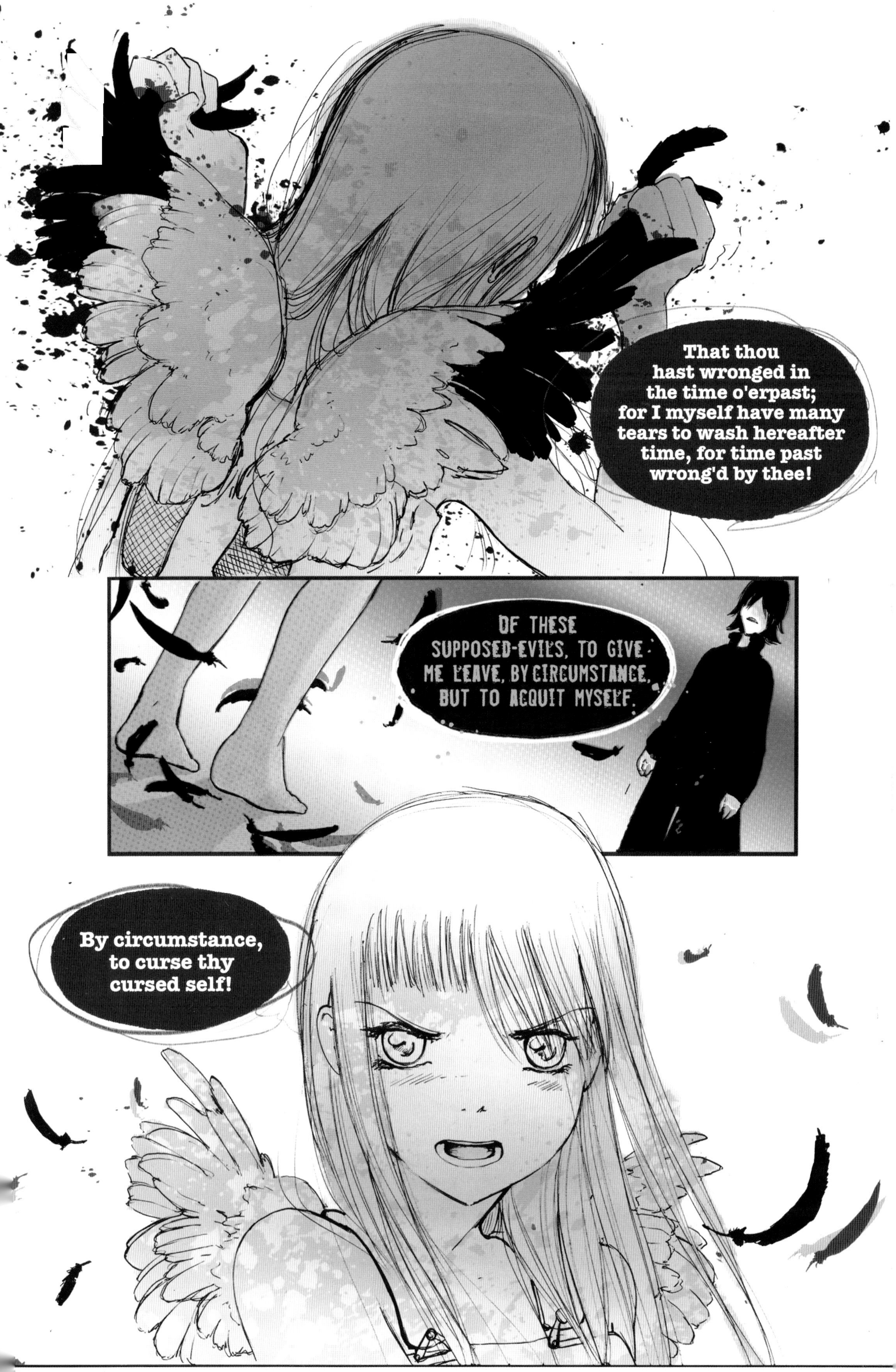
That thou hast wronged in the time o'erpast; for I myself have many tears to wash hereafter time, for time past wrong'd by thee!
OF THESE SUPPOSED-EVILS, TO GIVE ME LEAVE, BY CIRCUMSTANCE, BUT TO ACQUIT MYSELF.
By circumstance, to curse thy cursed self!

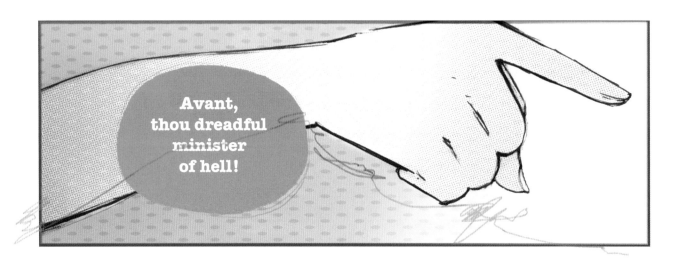

Avant, thou dreadful minister of hell!

Thou hadst but power over her mortal body, her soul thou canst have, therefore be gone.

FAIRER THAN TONGUE CAN NAME THEE, LET ME HAVE SOME PATIENT LEISURE TO EXCUSE MYSELF.

Fouler than heart can think thee, thou canst make no excuse current, but to hang thyself.

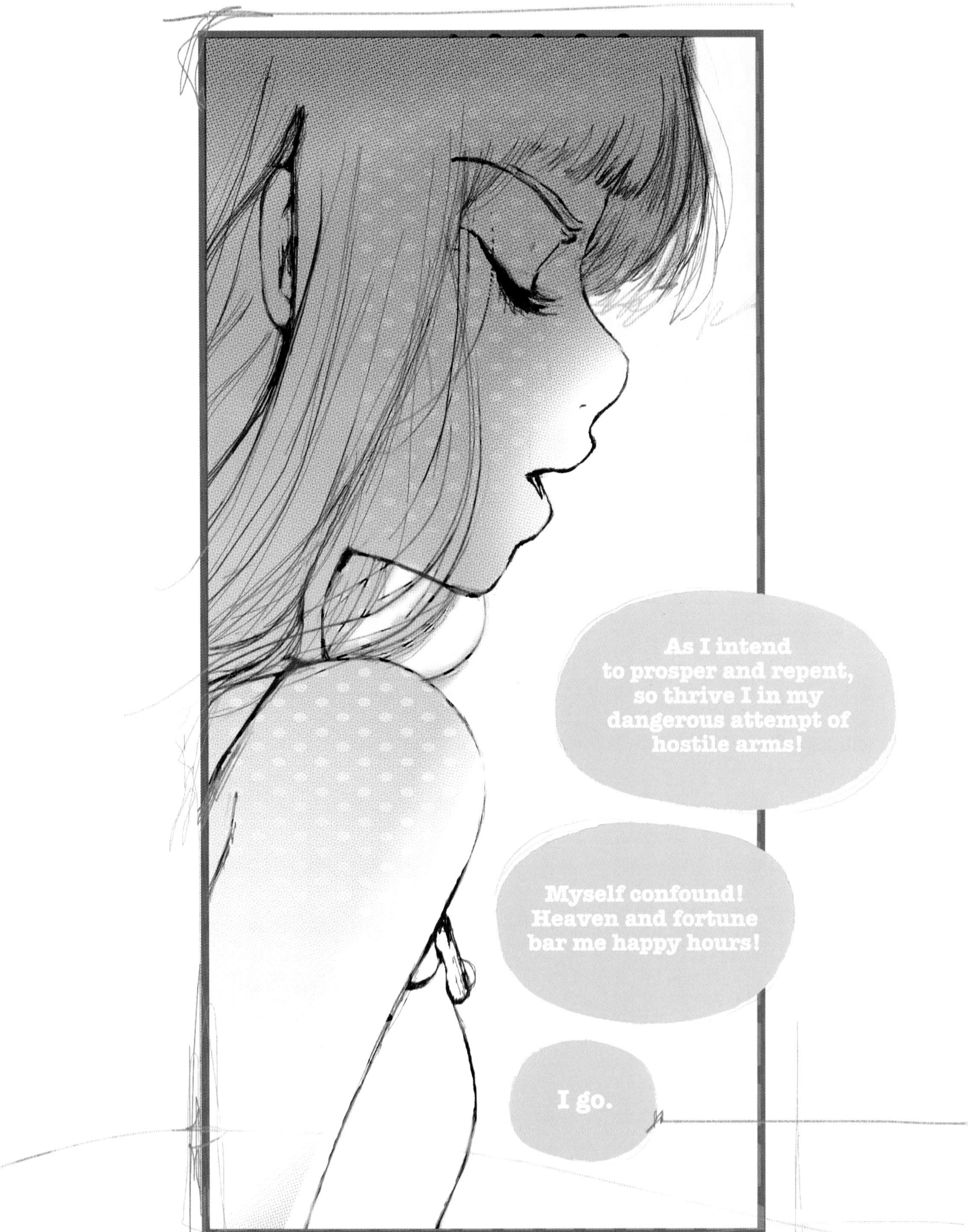
As I intend to prosper and repent, so thrive I in my dangerous attempt of hostile arms!
Myself confound! Heaven and fortune bar me happy hours!
I go.

I CANNOT BLAME HER
SHE HATH TOO MUCH WRONG,
AND I REPENT MY PART THEREOF
THAT I HAVE DONE TO HER.

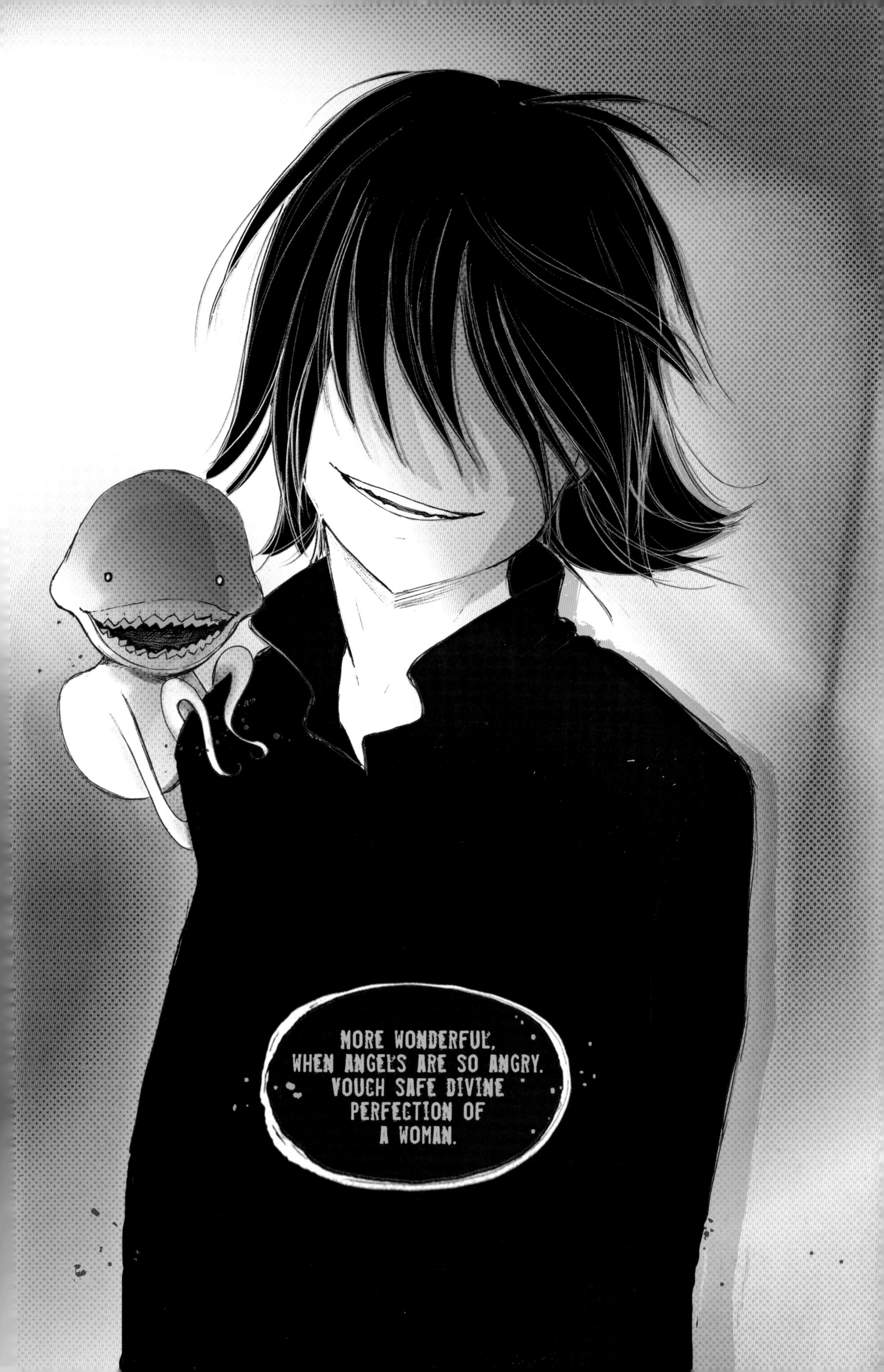
MORE WONDERFUL,
WHEN ANGELS ARE SO ANGRY.
VOUCH SAFE DIVINE
PERFECTION OF
A WOMAN.

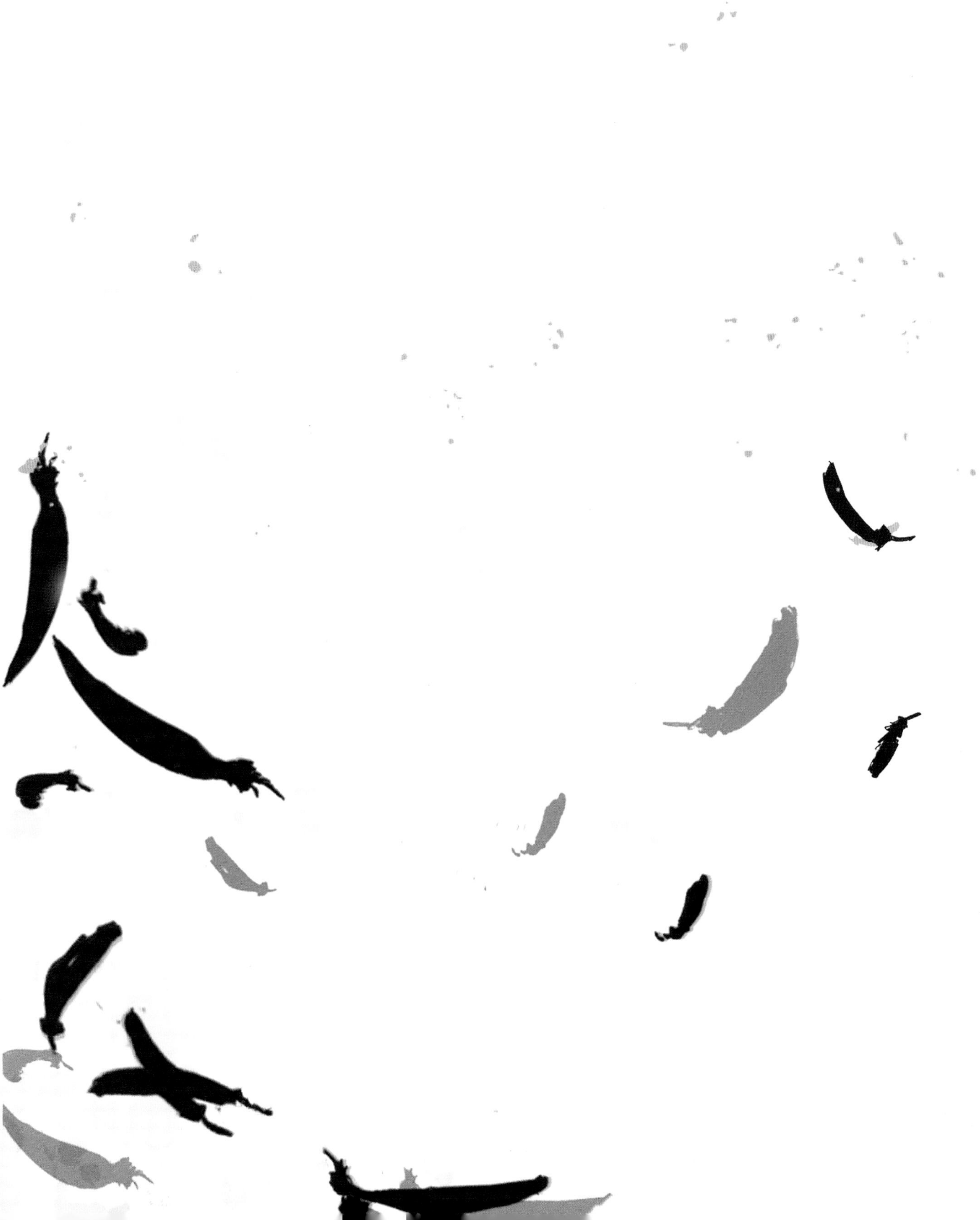

Two loves I have of comfort
and despair,
Which like two spirits do
suggest me still:
The better angel is a man
right fair,
The worser spirit a woman
coloured ill,
To win me soon to hell, my
female evil
Tempteth my better angel
from my side,
And would corrupt my saint
to be a devil,
Wooing his purity with her
foul pride,
And whether that my angel
be turned fiend,
Suspect I may, yet not
directly tell;
But being both from me, both
to each friend,
I guess one angel in
another's hell:
Yet this shall I ne'er know,
but live in doubt,
Till my bad angel fire my
good one out.

CHAPTER 2

WEARY WITH TOIL, I HASTE ME TO MY BED,
THE DEAR REPOSE FOR LIMBS WITH TRAVEL TIRED:
BUT THEN BEGINS A JOURNEY IN MY HEAD,
TO WORK MY MIND, WHEN BODY'S WORK'S EXPIRED:
FOR THEN MY THOUGHTS, FROM FAR WHERE I ABIDE,
INTEND A ZEALOUS PILGRIMAGE TO THEE,
AND KEEP MY DROOPING EYELIDS OPEN WIDE,
LOOKING ON DARKNESS WHICH THE BLIND DO SEE
SAVE THAT MY SOUL'S IMAGINARY SIGHT
PRESENTS THY SHADOW TO MY SIGHTLESS VIEW,
WHICH, LIKE A JEWEL HUNG IN GHASTLY NIGHT,
MAKES BLACK NIGHT BEAUTEOUS AND HER OLD FACE NEW.
LO! THUS, BY DAY MY LIMBS, BY NIGHT MY MIND,
FOR THEE AND FOR MYSELF NO QUIET FIND.

Tanpopo fared on
diligently, now passing
through
uninhabited lands, then
ruins and anon traversing
thirsty wastes and then
mountains which spired
high in air.

Journeying
a whole years space,
til, one morning, when the
day broke, after
she had travelled all night,
behold, Tanpopo found
herself in a land
she knew not . . .

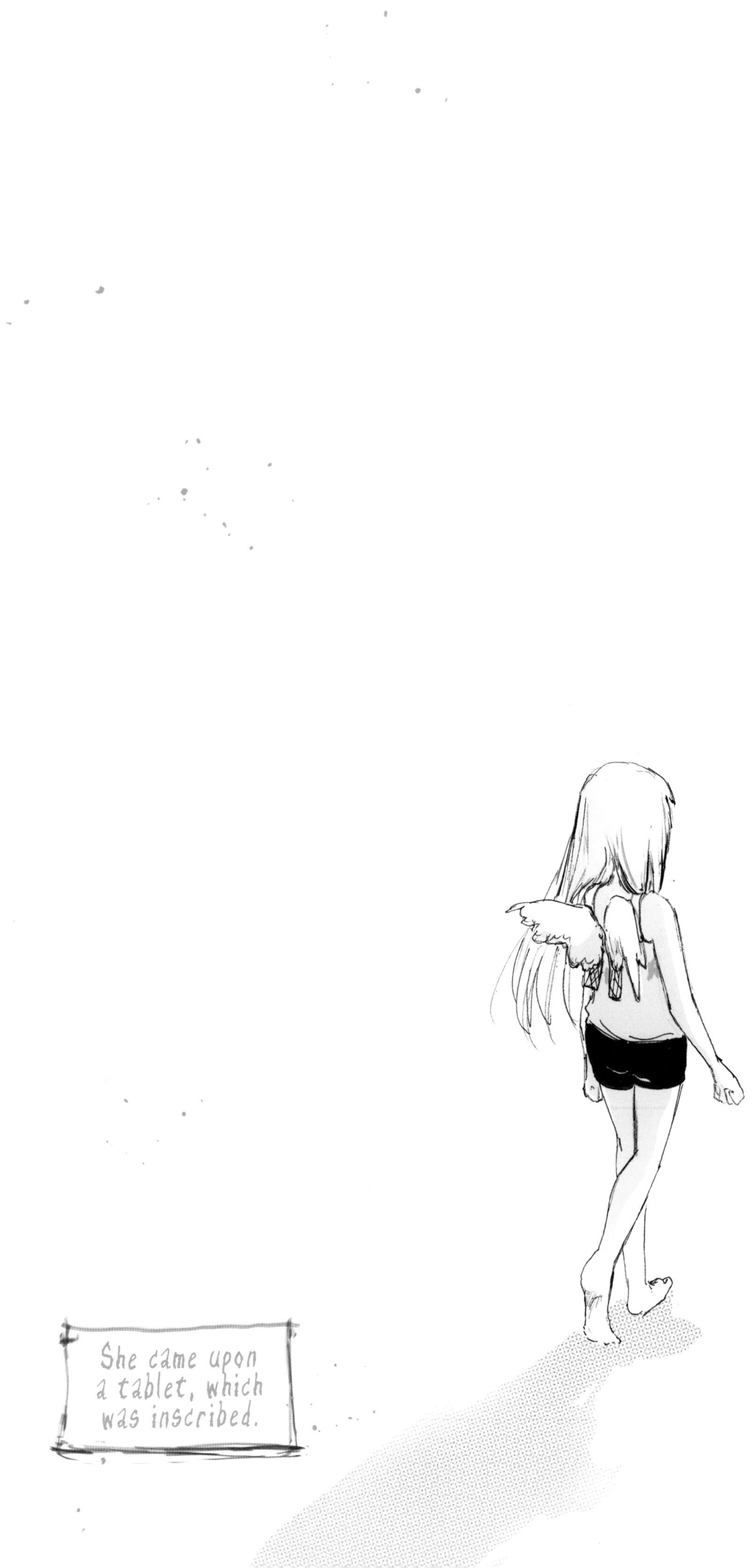
She came upon a tablet, which was inscribed.

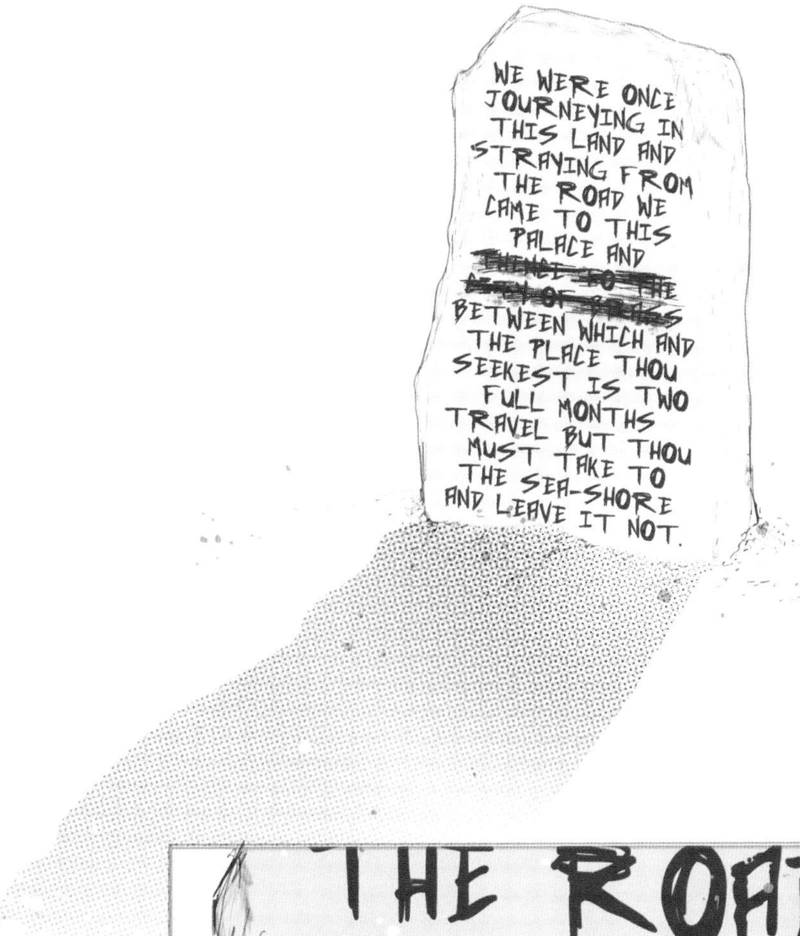
WE WERE ONCE JOURNEYING IN THIS LAND AND STRAYING FROM THE ROAD WE CAME TO THIS PALACE AND [redacted] BETWEEN WHICH AND THE PLACE THOU SEEKEST IS TWO FULL MONTHS TRAVEL BUT THOU MUST TAKE TO THE SEA-SHORE AND LEAVE IT NOT.

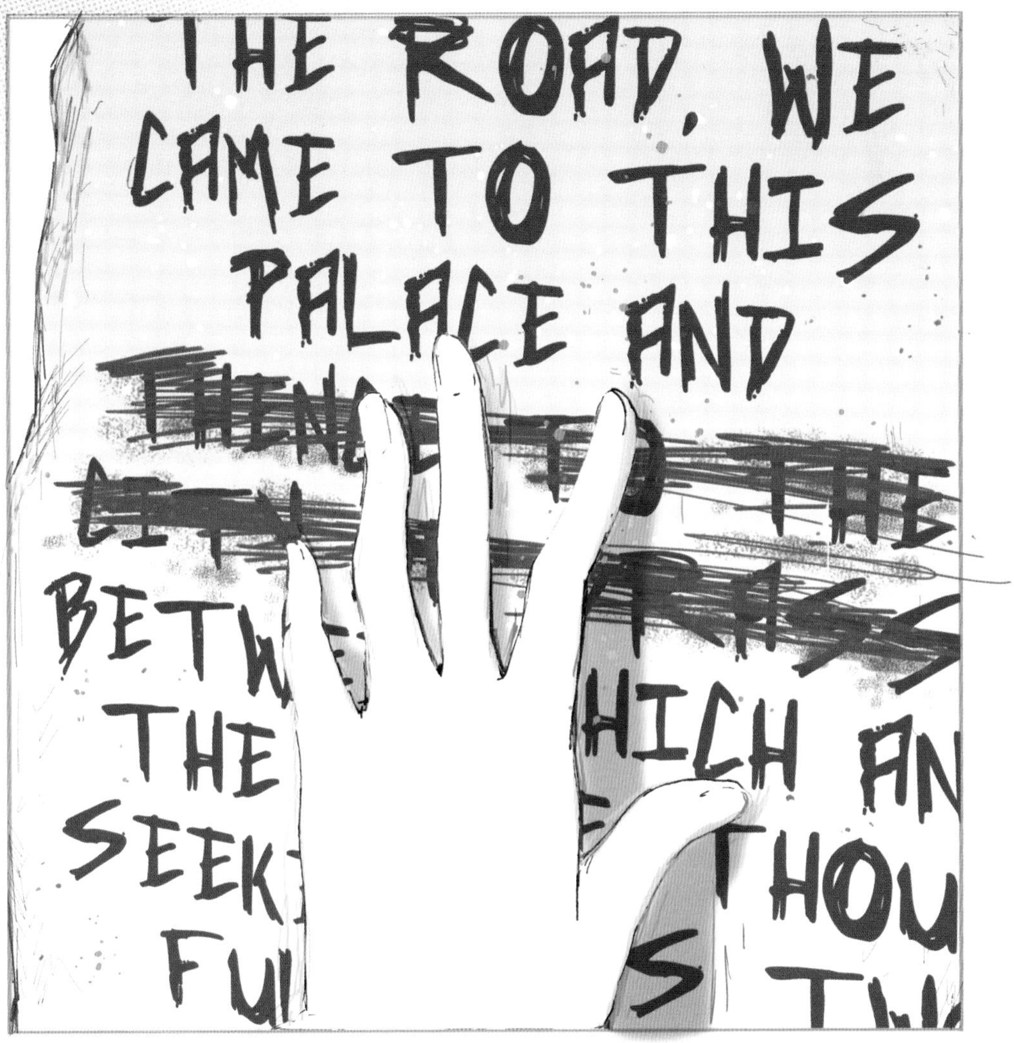
THE ROAD, WE CAME TO THIS PALACE AND [redacted]

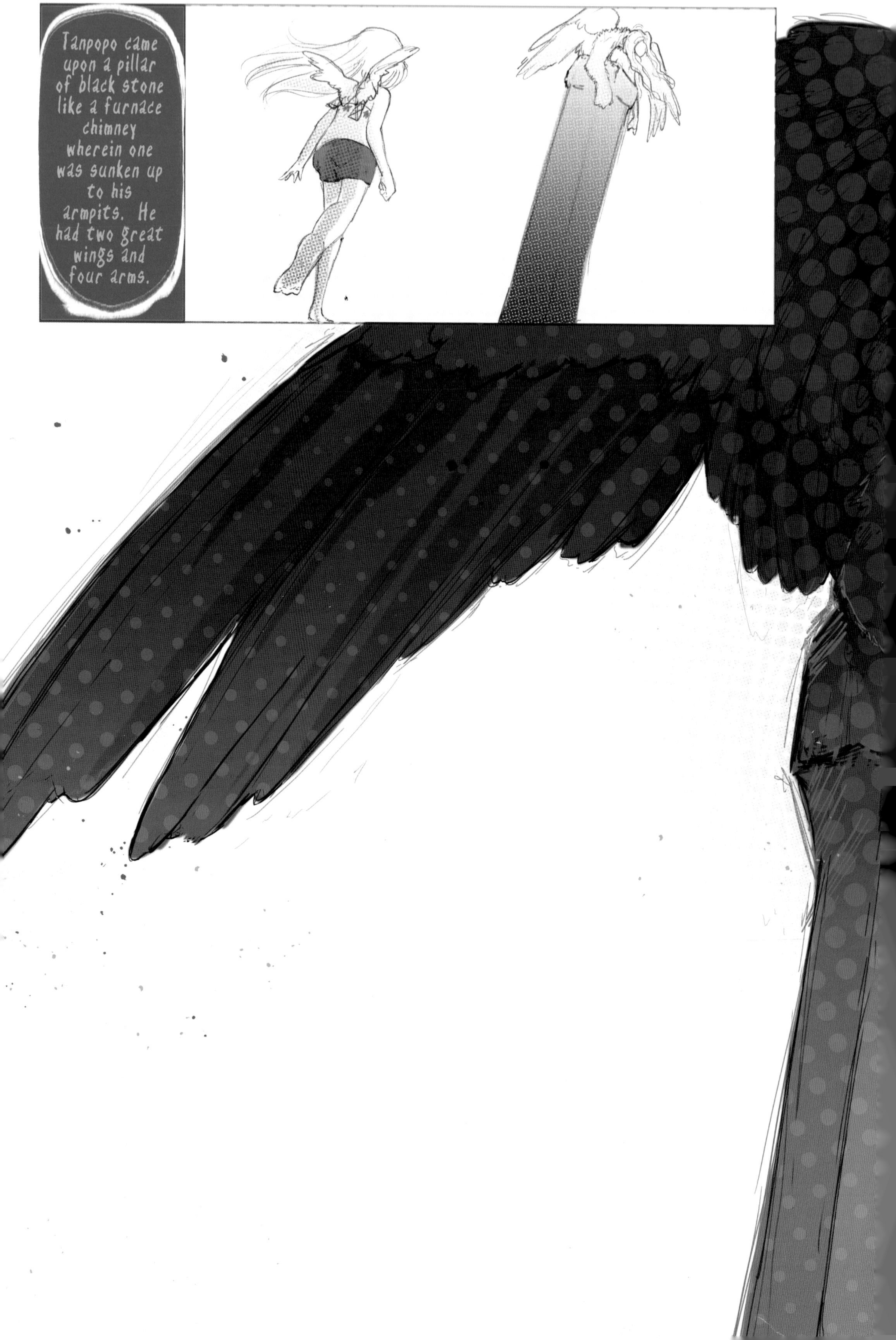
Tanpopo came upon a pillar of black stone like a furnace chimney wherein one was sunken up to his armpits. He had two great wings and four arms.

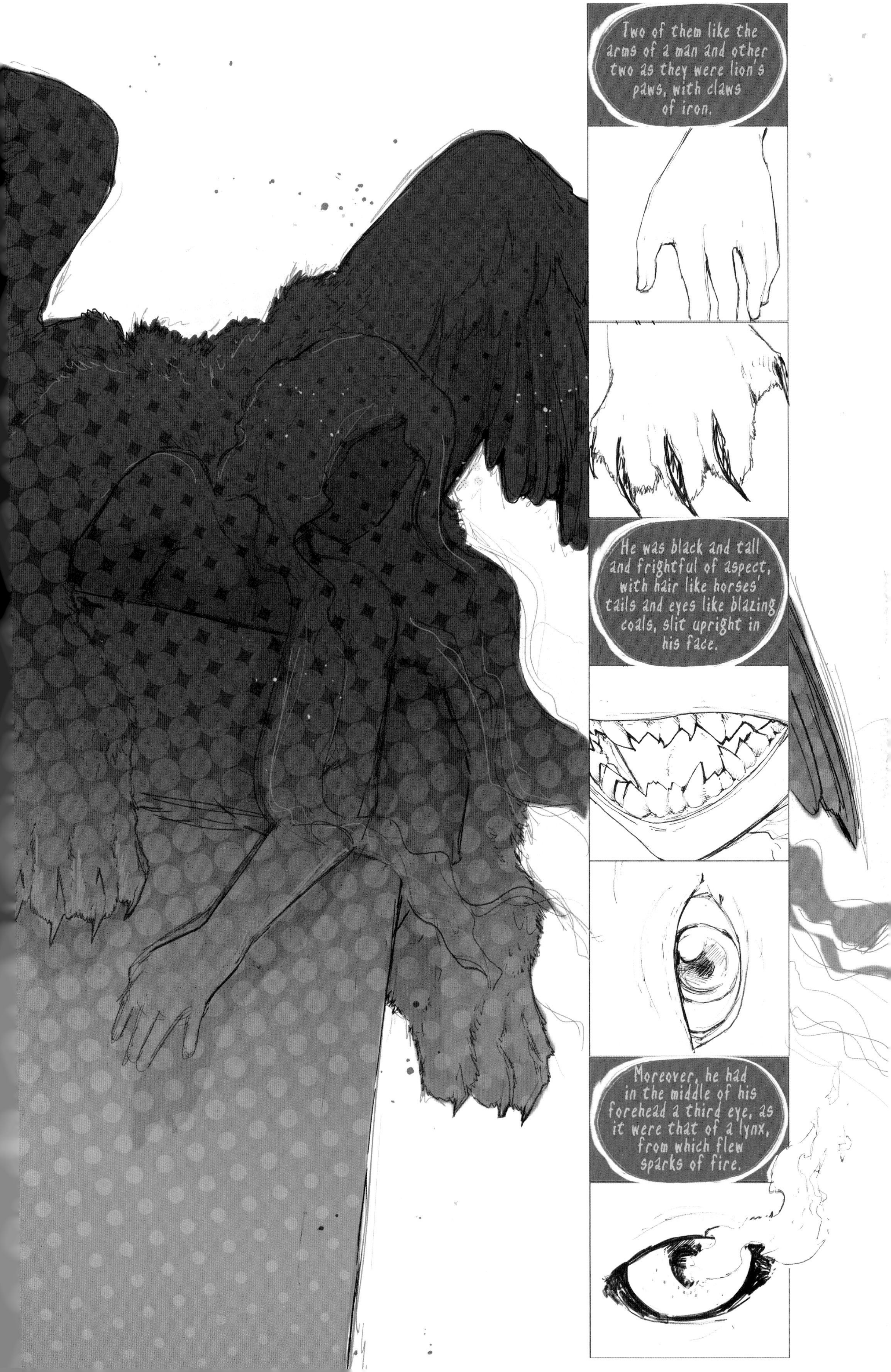
Two of them like the arms of a man and other two as they were lion's paws, with claws of iron.
He was black and tall and frightful of aspect, with hair like horses' tails and eyes like blazing coals, slit upright in his face.
Moreover, he had in the middle of his forehead a third eye, as it were that of a lynx, from which flew sparks of fire.

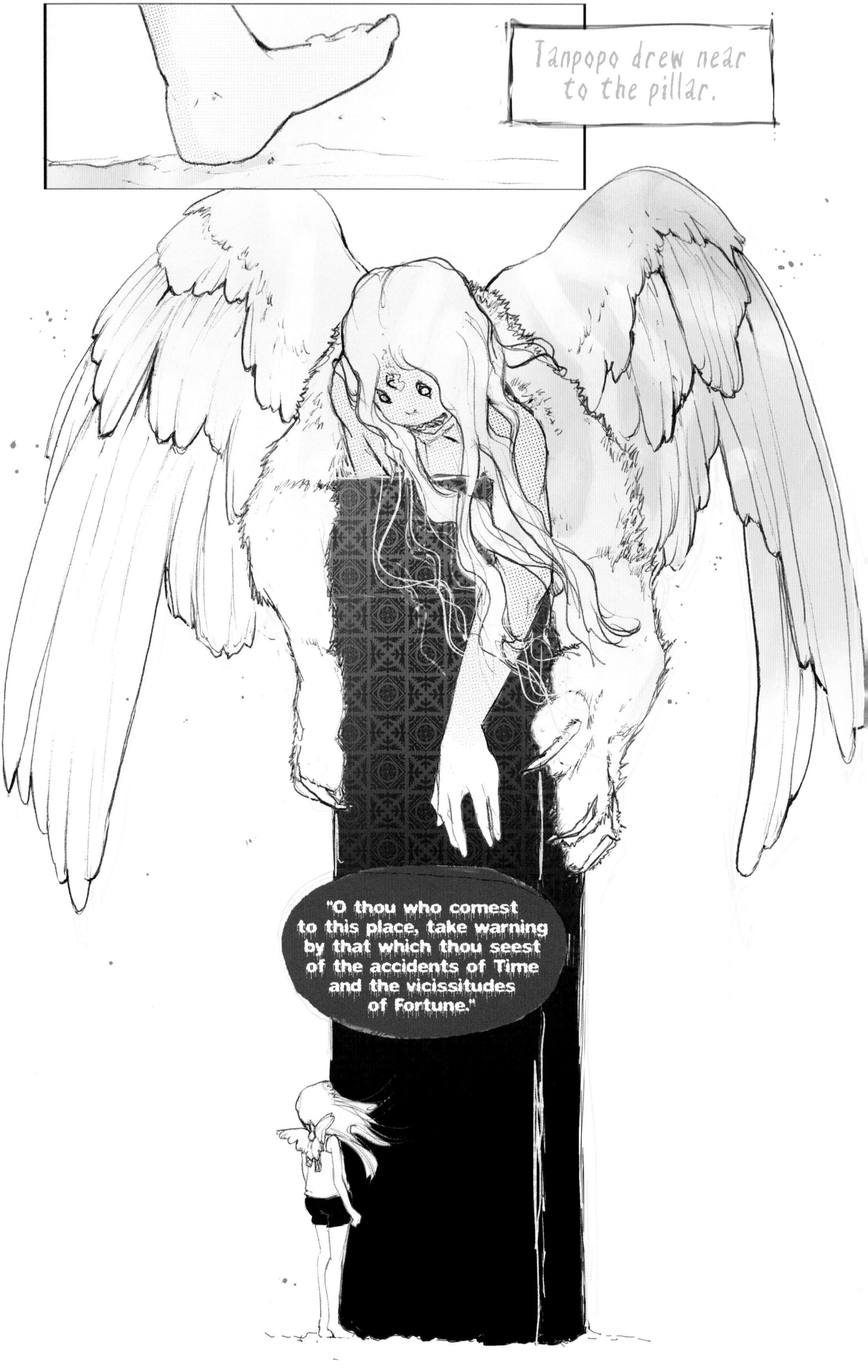
Tanpopo drew near to the pillar.
"O thou who comest to this place, take warning by that which thou seest of the accidents of Time and the vicissitudes of Fortune."

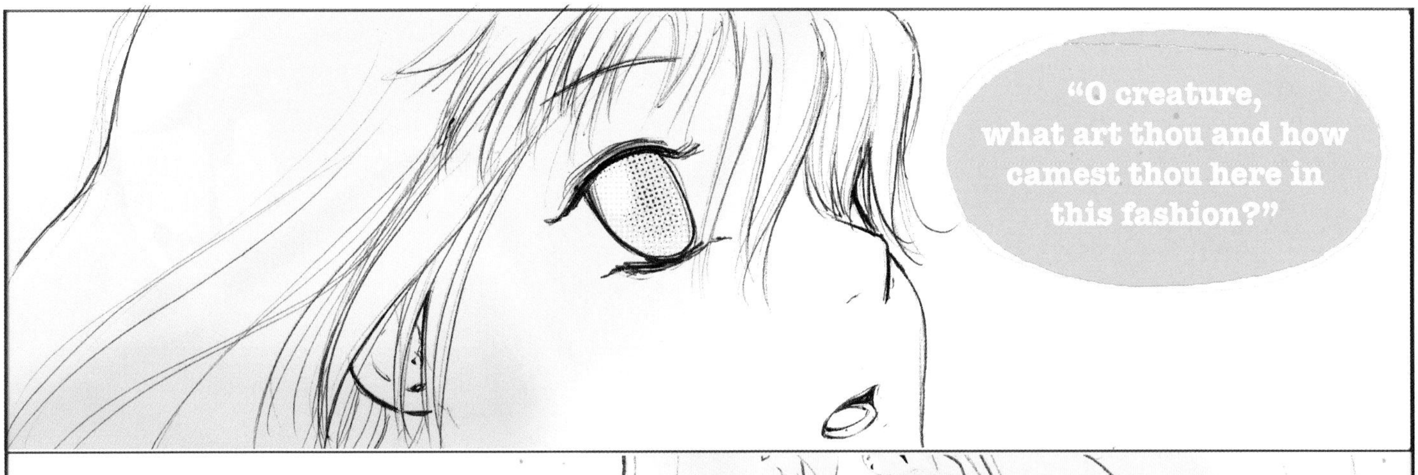
"O creature, what art thou and how camest thou here in this fashion?"
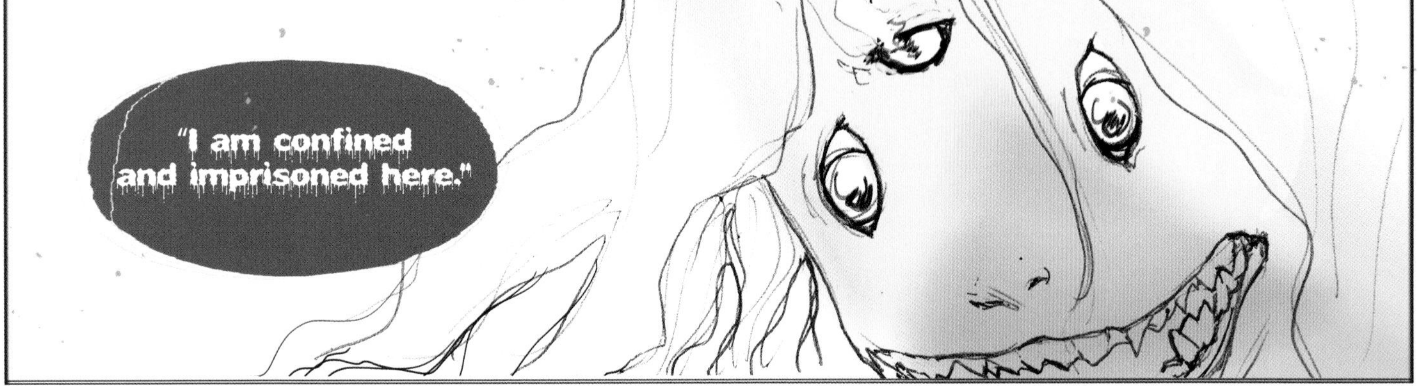
"I am confined and imprisoned here."

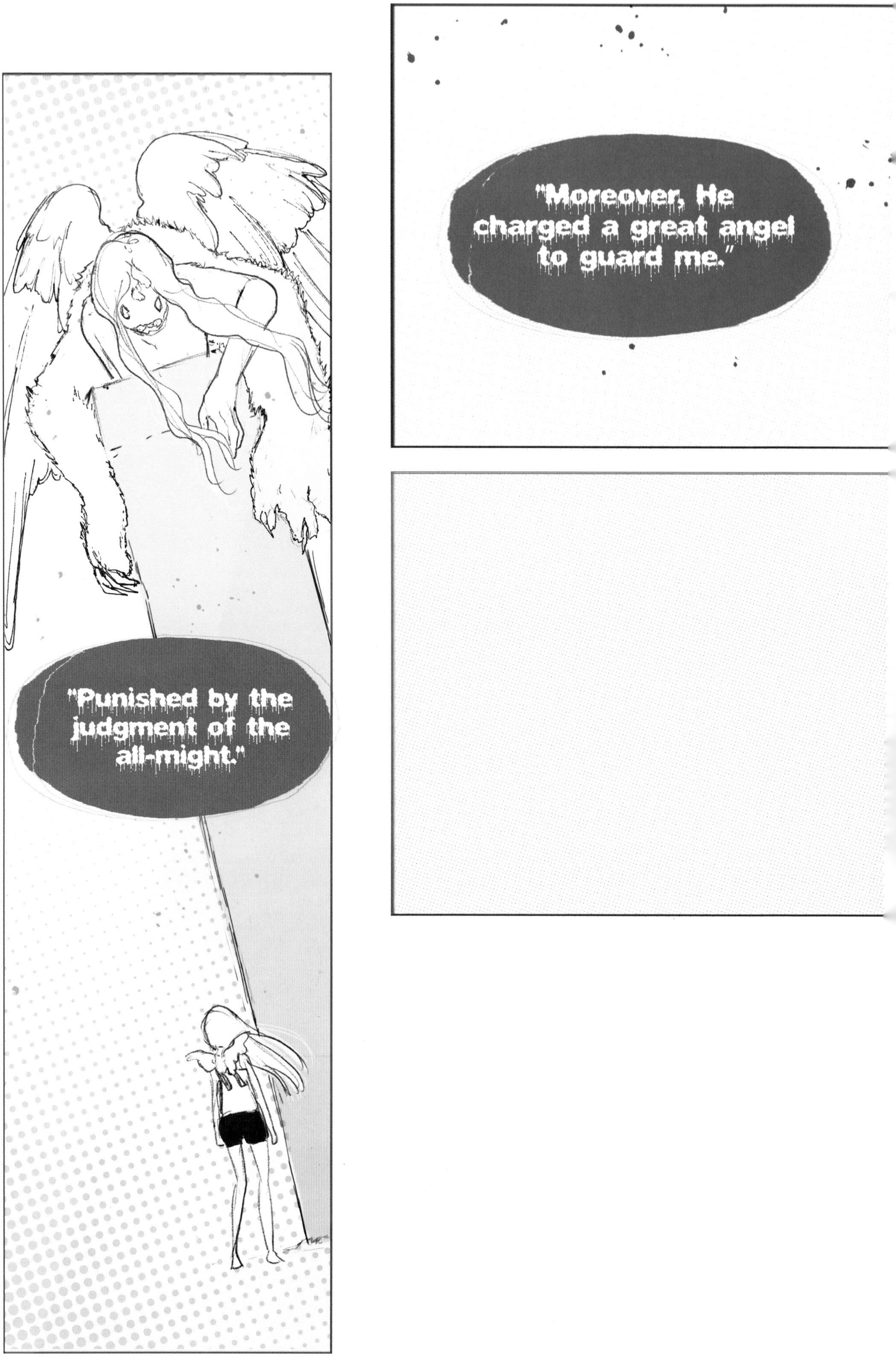
"Moreover, He charged a great angel to guard me."
"Punished by the judgment of the all-might."

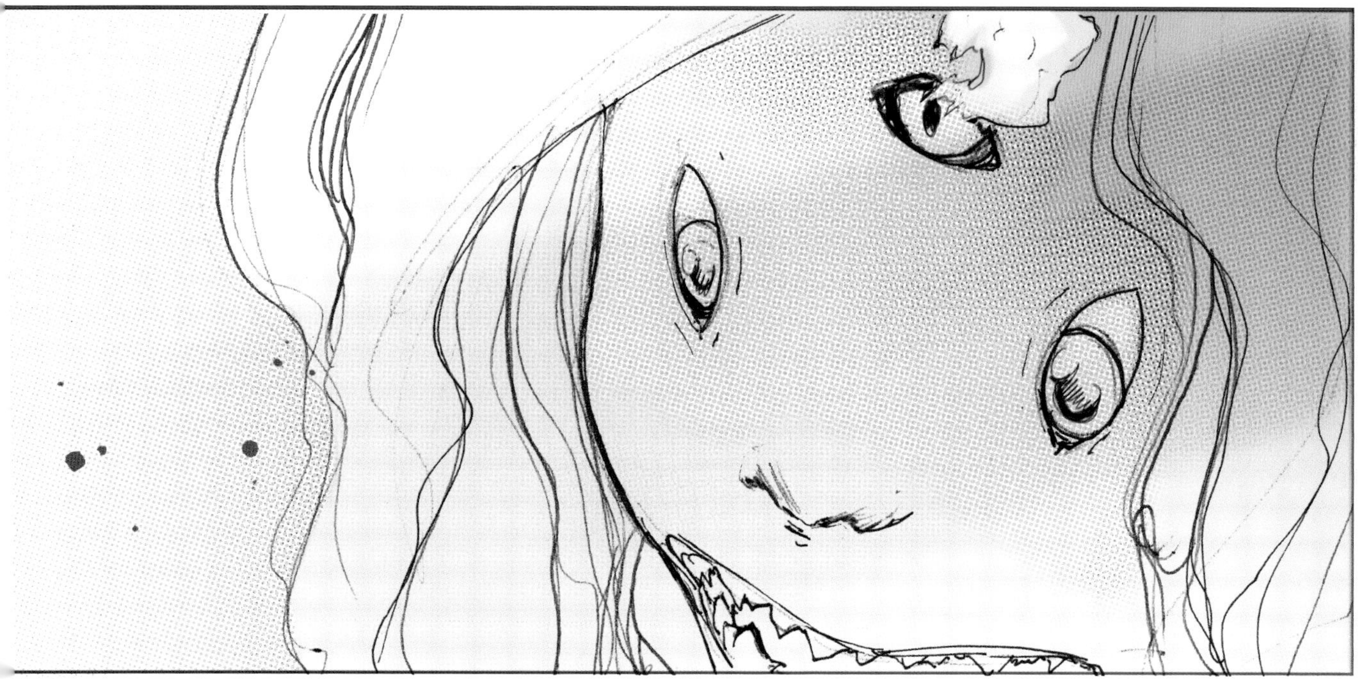

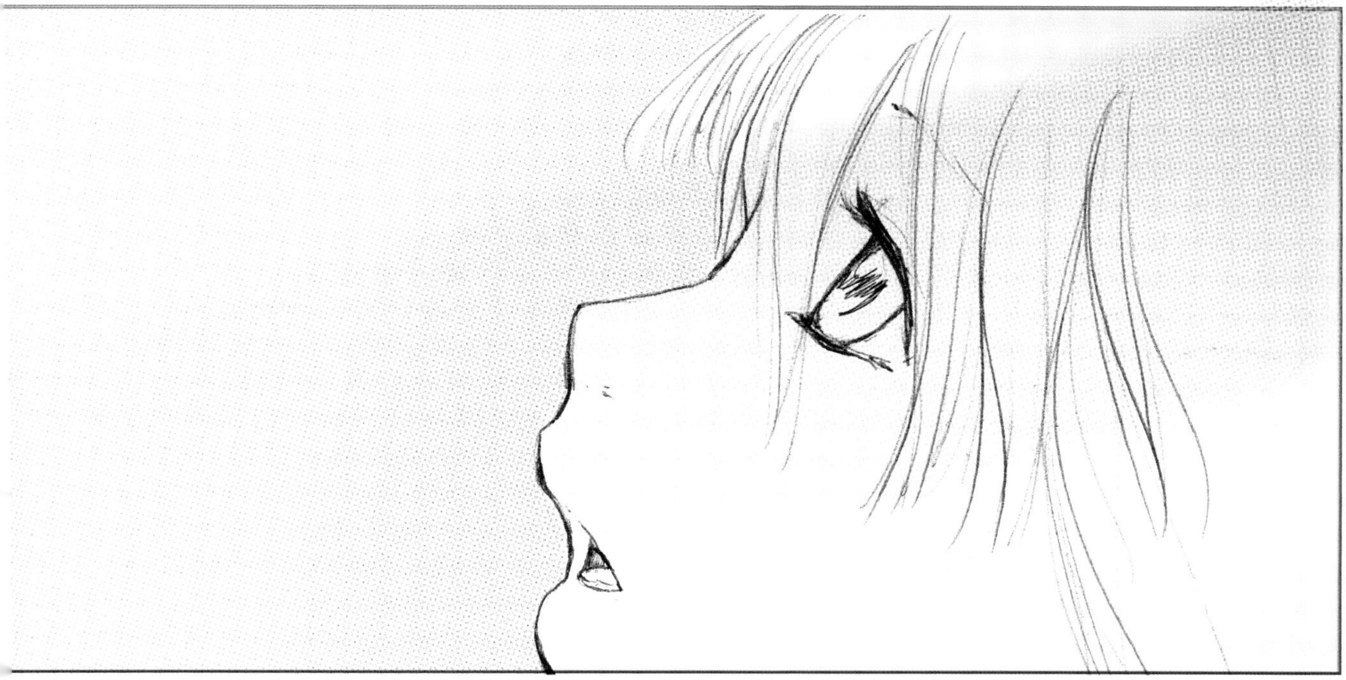

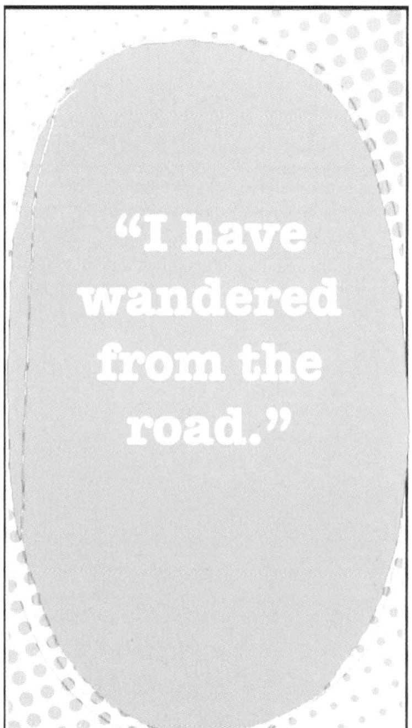
"I have wandered from the road."

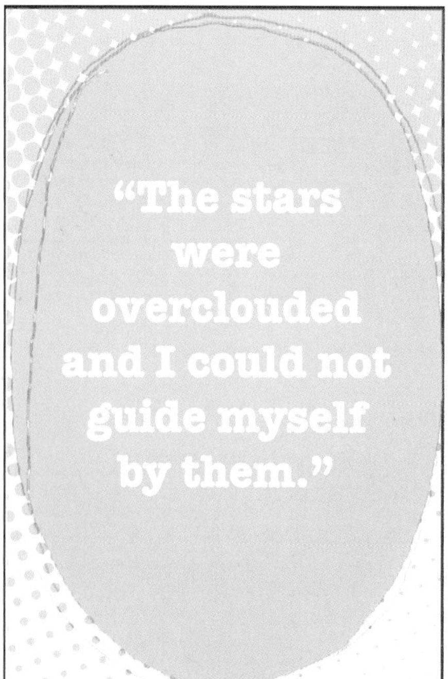
"The stars were overclouded and I could not guide myself by them."

"Where on
earth are
we now?"

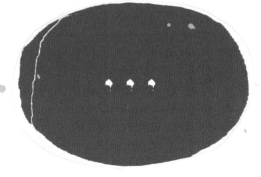

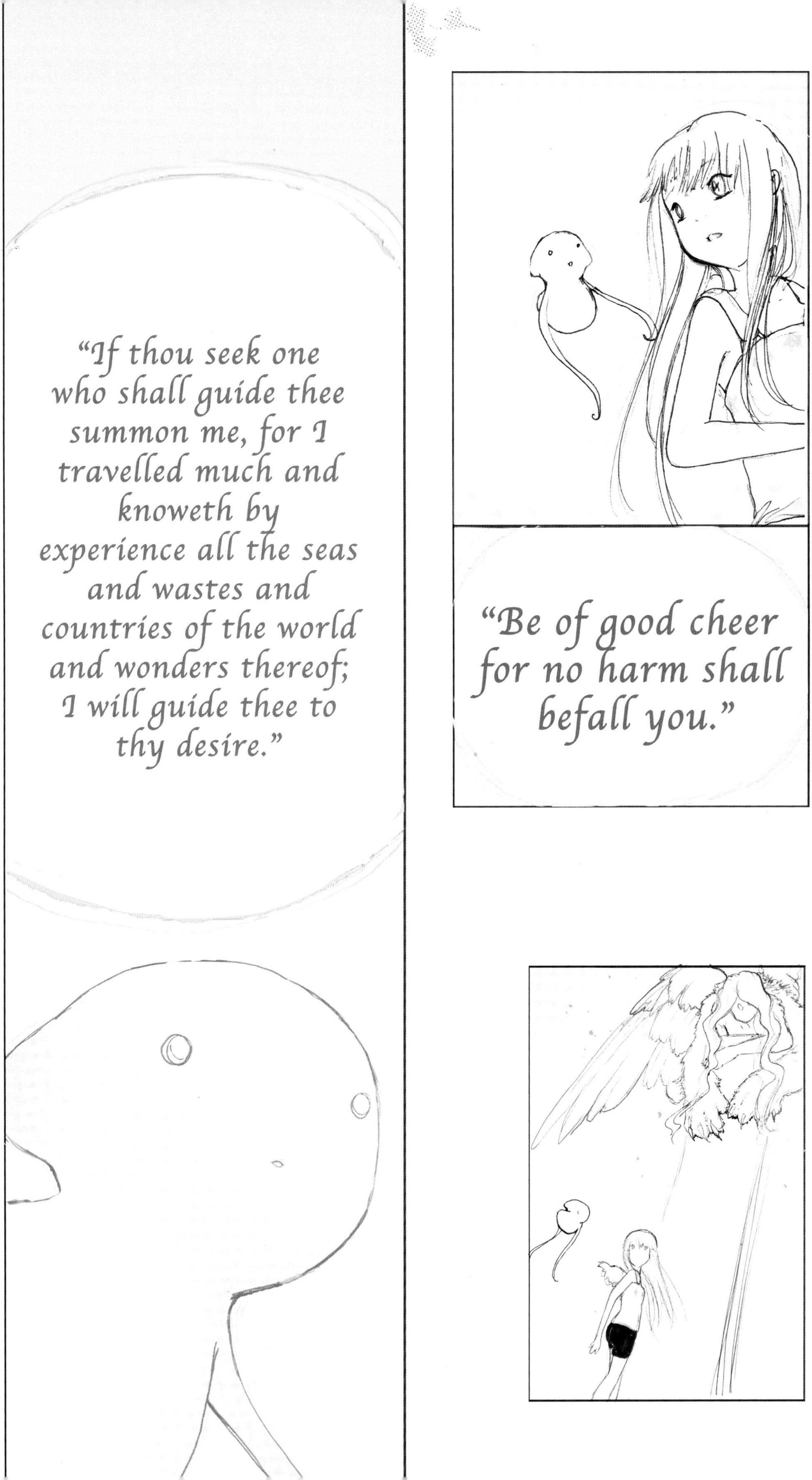
"Be of good cheer for no harm shall befall you."
"If thou seek one who shall guide thee summon me, for I travelled much and knoweth by experience all the seas and wastes and countries of the world and wonders thereof; I will guide thee to thy desire."

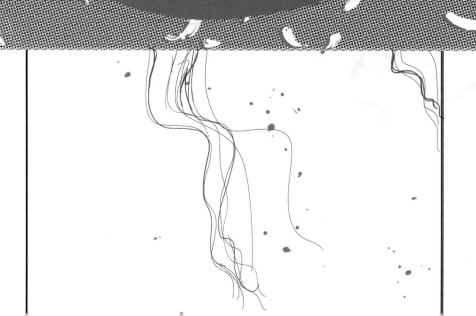

"Wherefore put not thou thy trust therein neither incline thereto, for it betrayeth him who leaneth upon it and who committeth himself in his affairs. Fall not thou into its snares. Be warned by my example!"

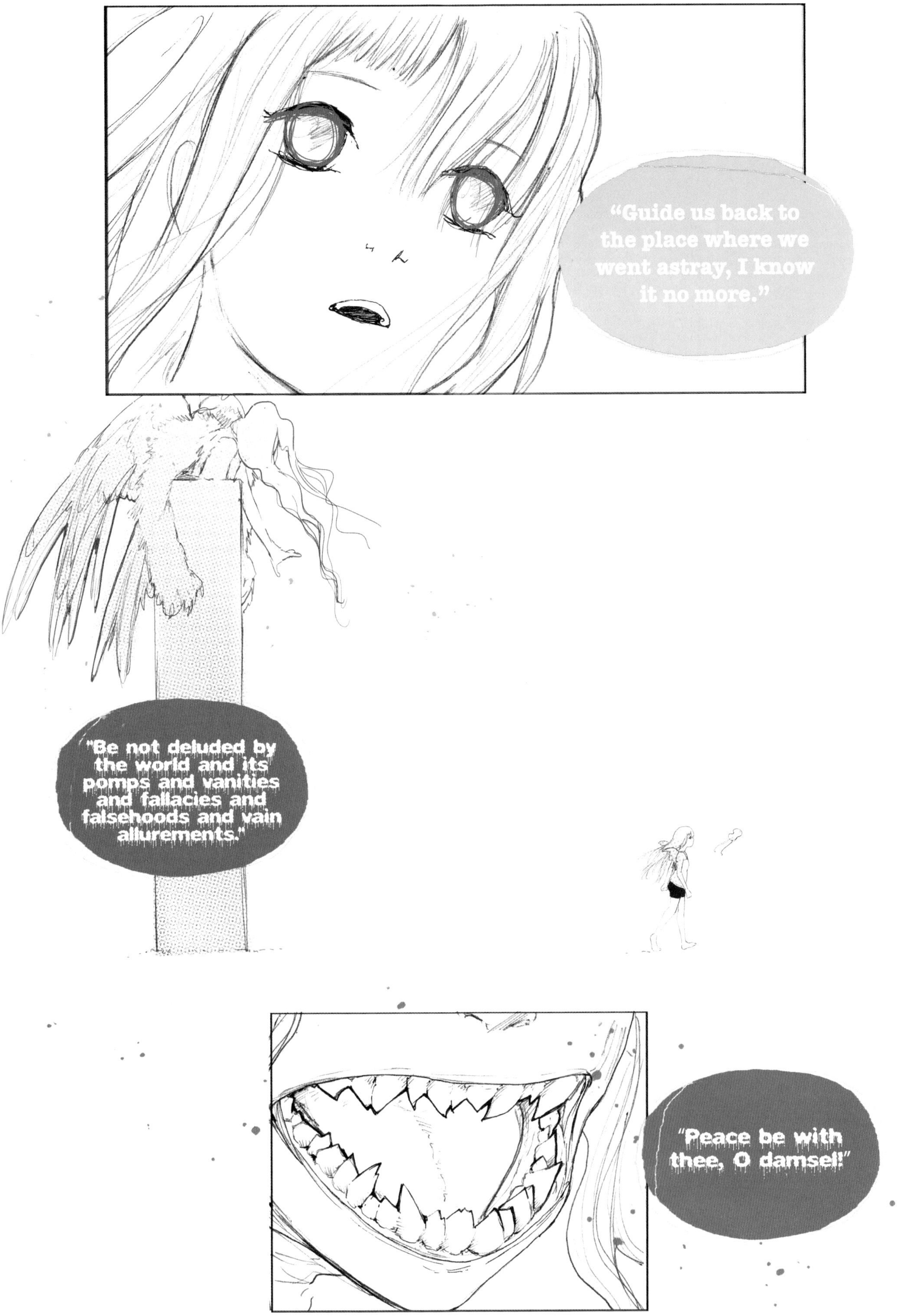
"Guide us back to the place where we went astray, I know it no more."
"Be not deluded by the world and its pomps and vanities and fallacies and falsehoods and vain allurements."
"Peace be with thee, O damsel!"

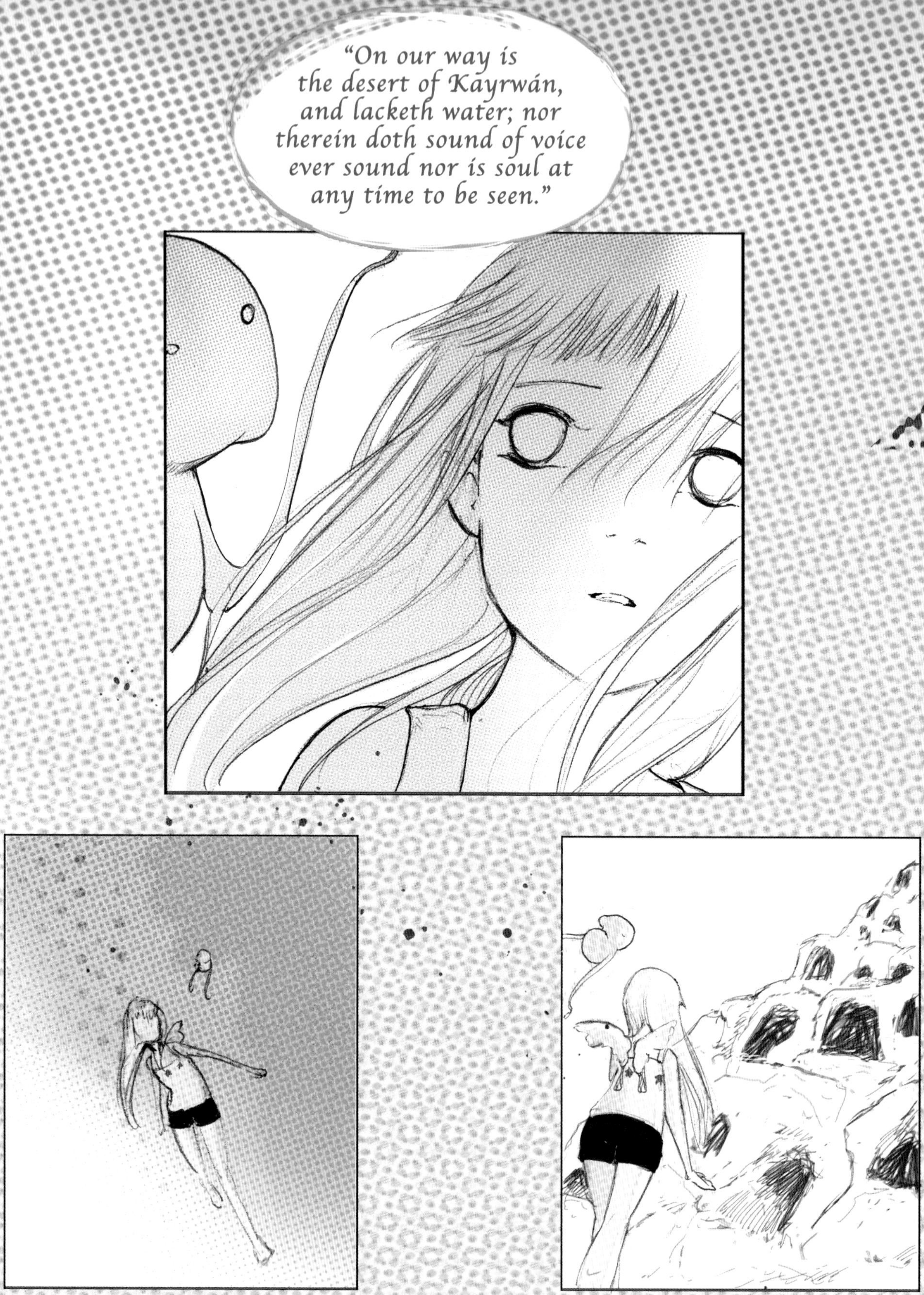
"On our way is the desert of Kayrwán, and lacketh water; nor therein doth sound of voice ever sound nor is soul at any time to be seen."

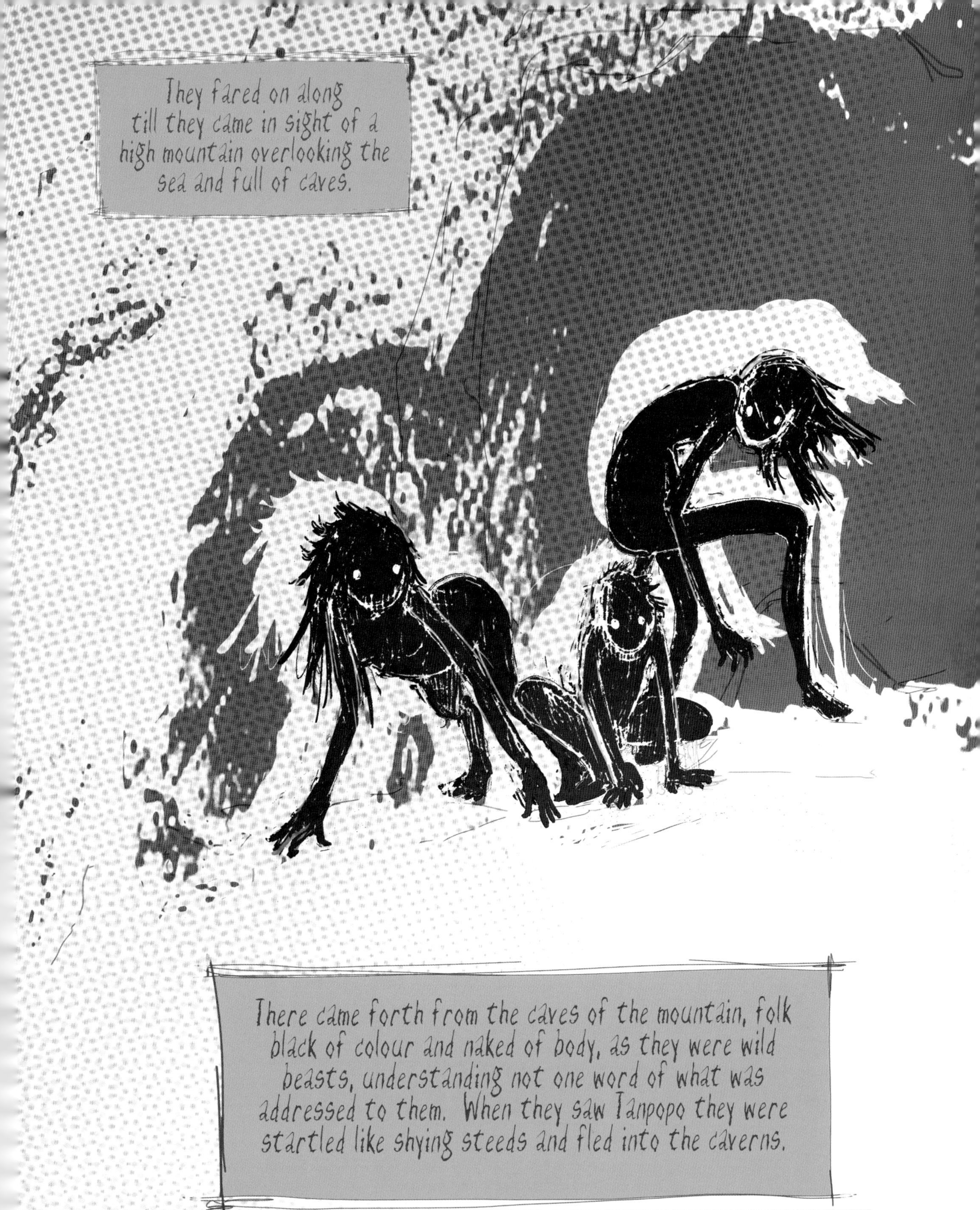
They fared on along till they came in sight of a high mountain overlooking the sea and full of caves.
There came forth from the caves of the mountain, folk black of colour and naked of body, as they were wild beasts, understanding not one word of what was addressed to them. When they saw Tanpopo they were startled like shying steeds and fled into the caverns.
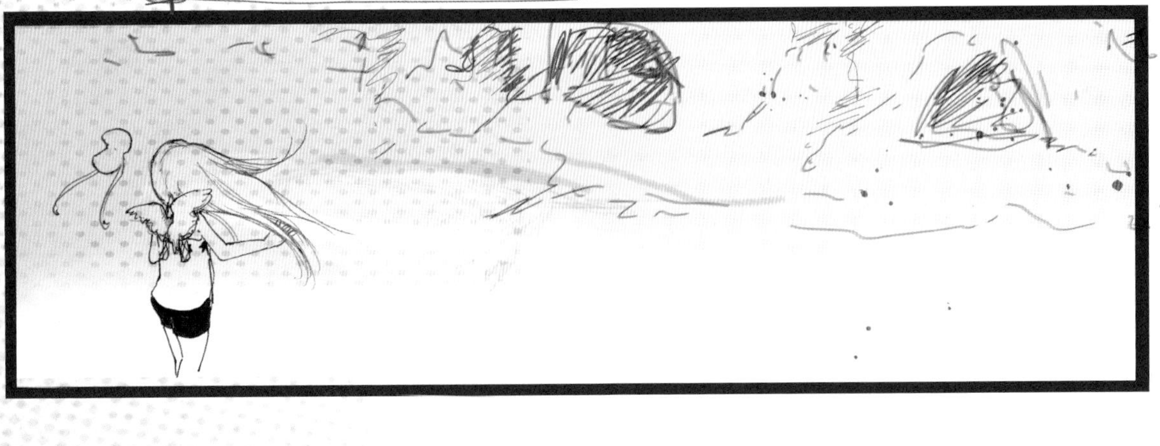

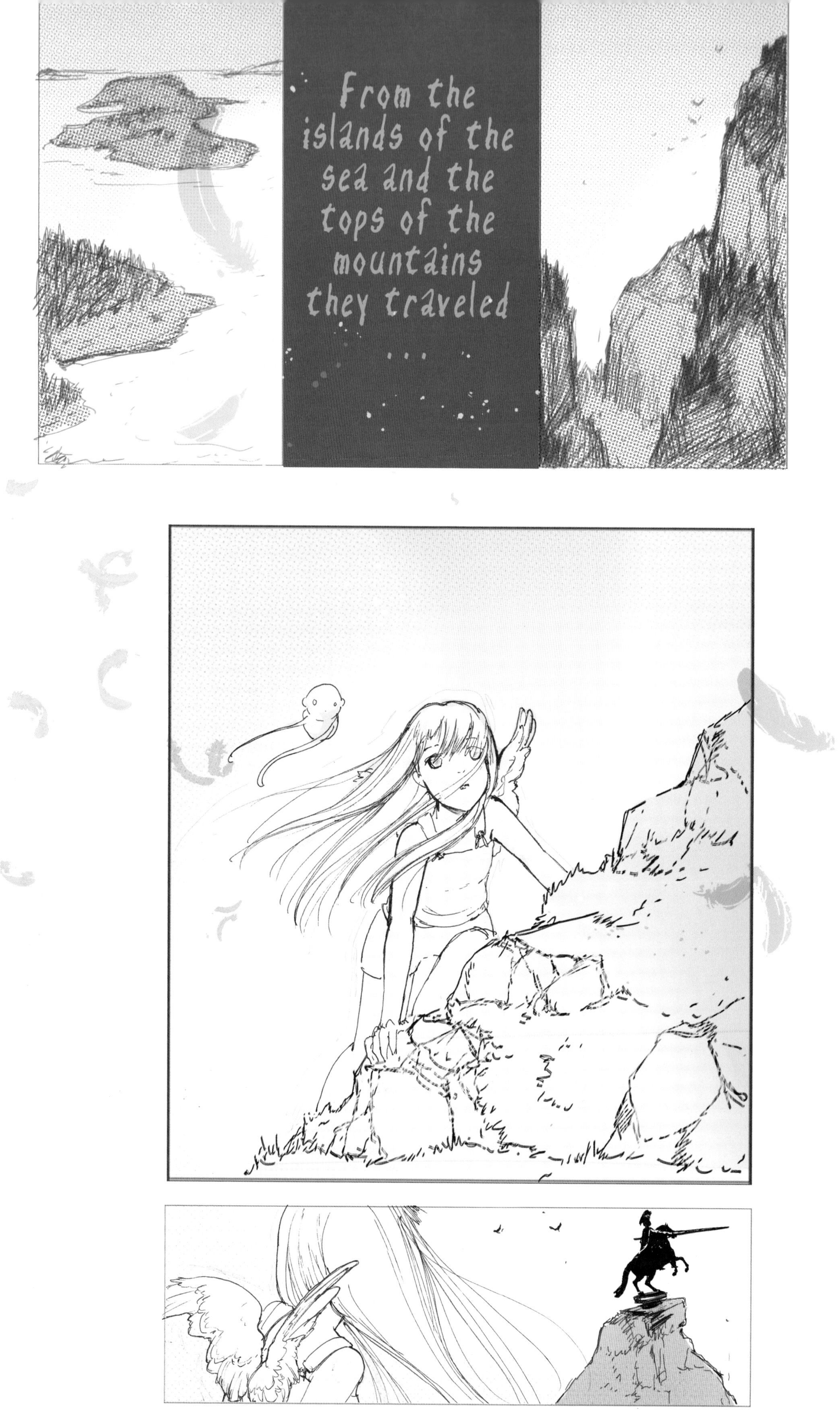
From the islands of the sea and the tops of the mountains they traveled
...

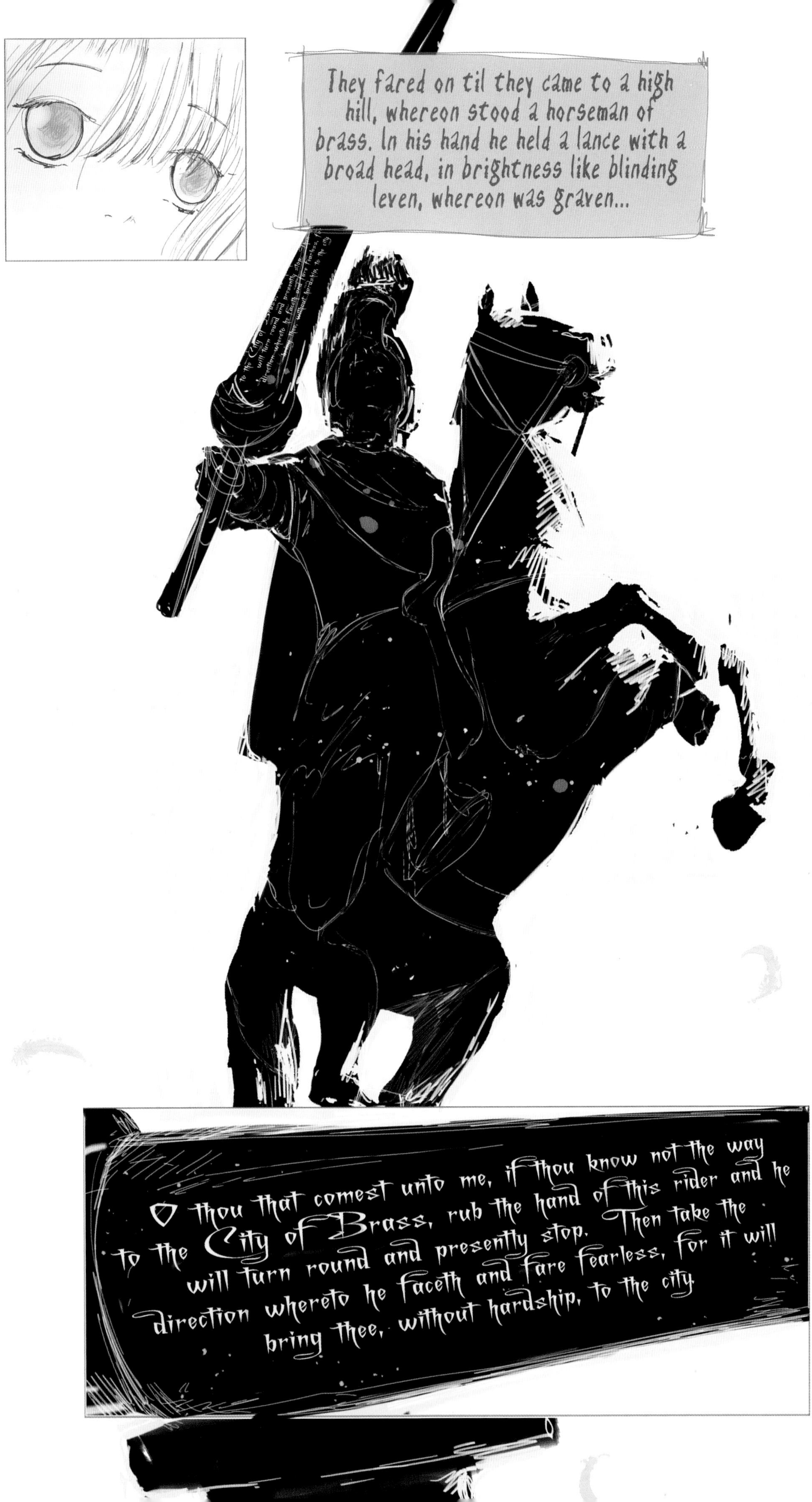
They fared on til they came to a high hill, whereon stood a horseman of brass. In his hand he held a lance with a broad head, in brightness like blinding leven, whereon was graven...
O thou that comest unto me, if thou know not the way to the City of Brass, rub the hand of this rider and he will turn round and presently stop. Then take the direction whereto he faceth and fare fearless, for it will bring thee, without hardship, to the city.

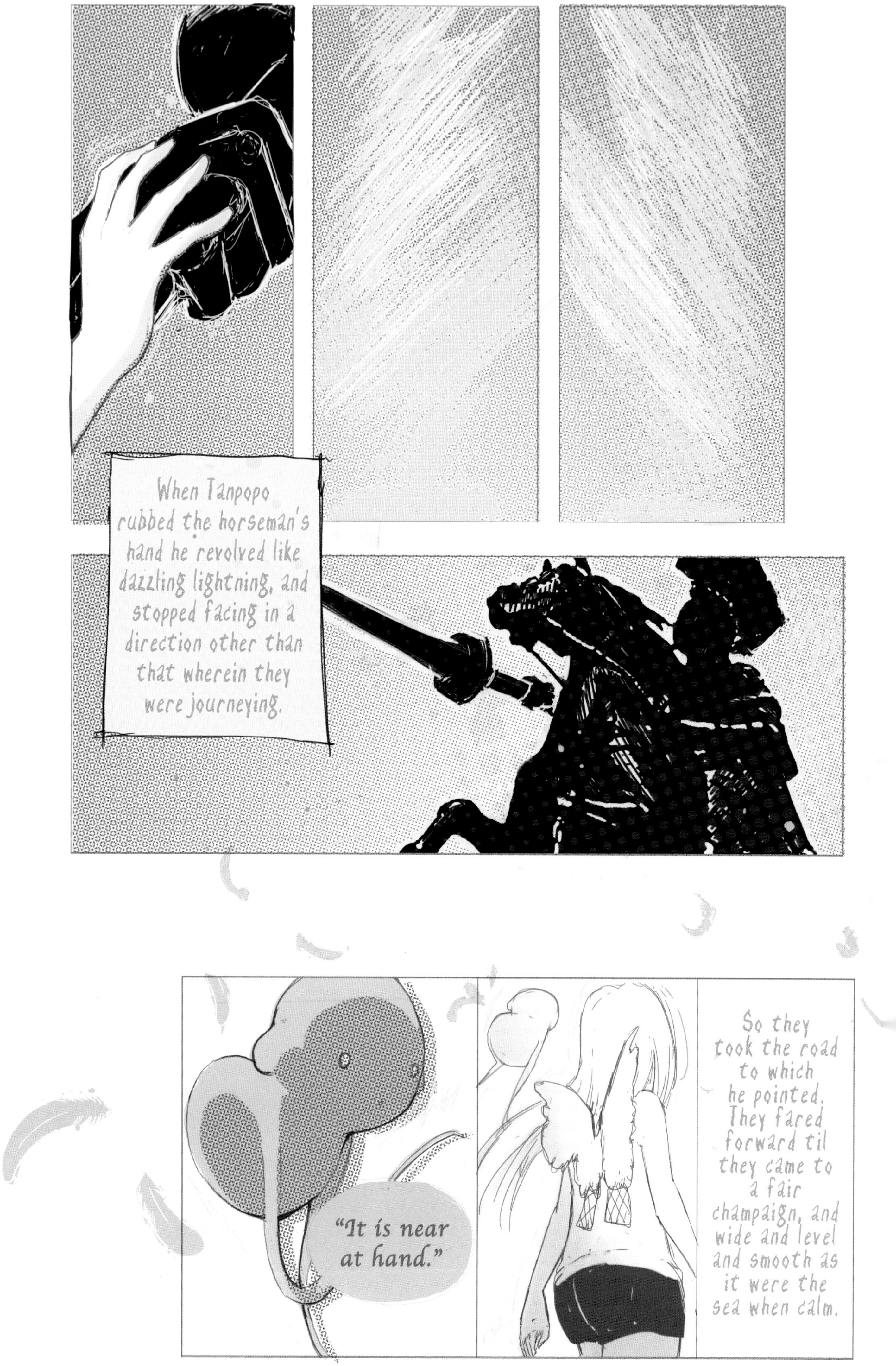
When Tanpopo rubbed the horseman's hand he revolved like dazzling lightning, and stopped facing in a direction other than that wherein they were journeying.
"It is near at hand."
So they took the road to which he pointed. They fared forward til they came to a fair champaign, and wide and level and smooth as it were the sea when calm.

Presently there appeared to them, on the horizon some great thing, high and black, in whose midst was as it were smoke rising to the confines of the sky.

"What is yonder ?"

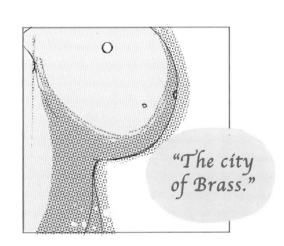

"The city of Brass."

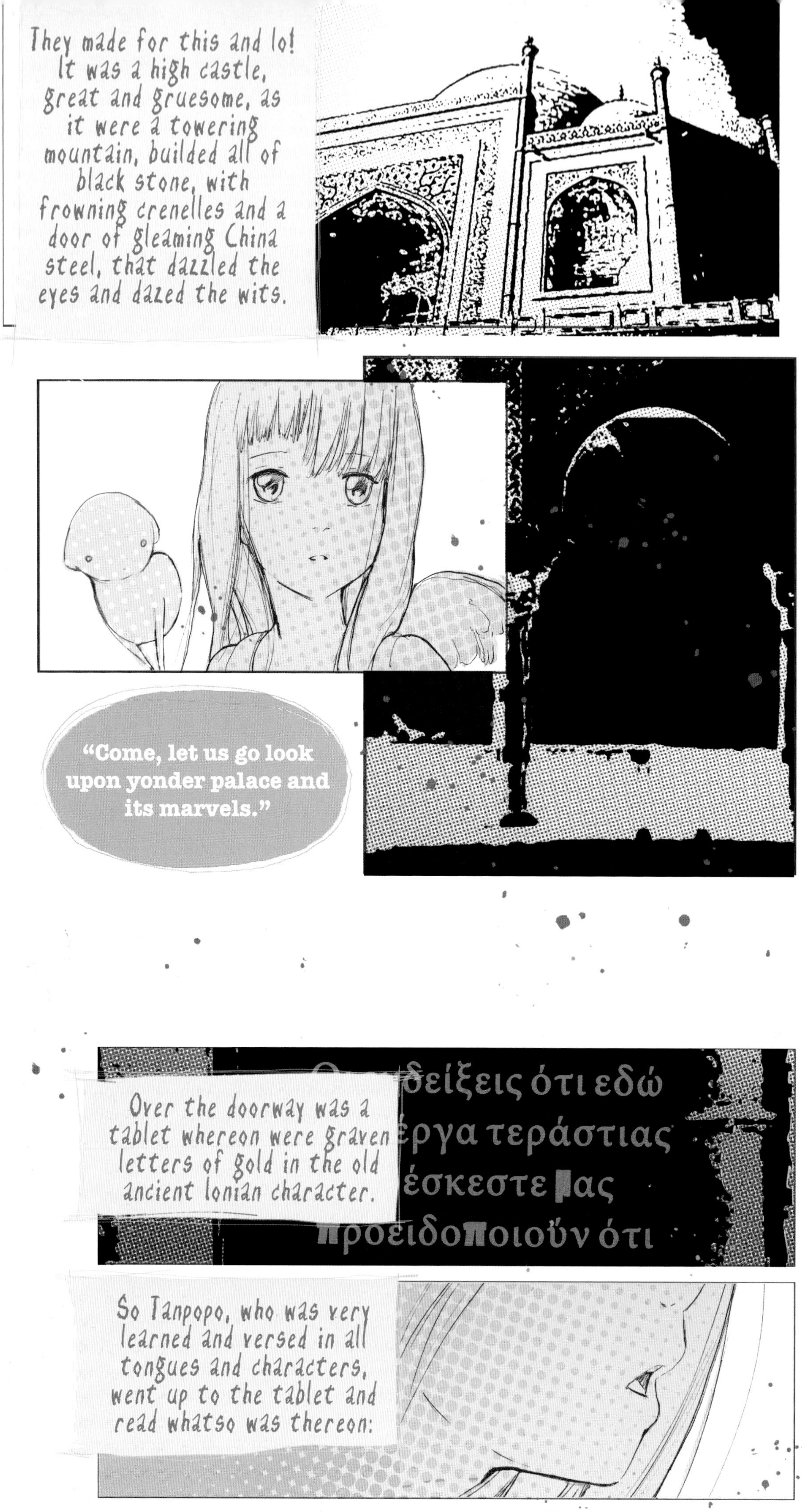
They made for this and lo! It was a high castle, great and gruesome, as it were a towering mountain, builded all of black stone, with frowning crenelles and a door of gleaming China steel, that dazzled the eyes and dazed the wits.
"Come, let us go look upon yonder palace and its marvels."
δείξεις ότι εδώ
τεράστιας
μας
προειδοποιούν ότι
Over the doorway was a tablet whereon were graven letters of gold in the old ancient Ionian character.
So Tanpopo, who was very learned and versed in all tongues and characters, went up to the tablet and read whatso was thereon:

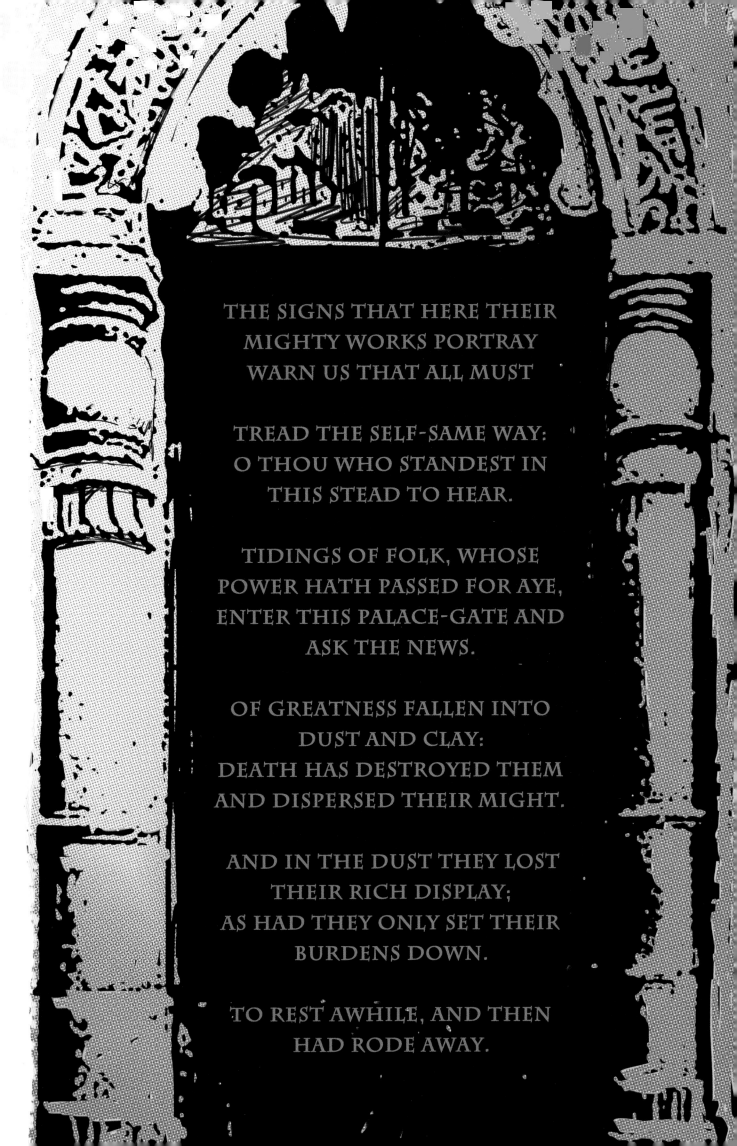

THE SIGNS THAT HERE THEIR
MIGHTY WORKS PORTRAY
WARN US THAT ALL MUST

TREAD THE SELF-SAME WAY:
O THOU WHO STANDEST IN
THIS STEAD TO HEAR.

TIDINGS OF FOLK, WHOSE
POWER HATH PASSED FOR AYE,
ENTER THIS PALACE-GATE AND
ASK THE NEWS.

OF GREATNESS FALLEN INTO
DUST AND CLAY:
DEATH HAS DESTROYED THEM
AND DISPERSED THEIR MIGHT.

AND IN THE DUST THEY LOST
THEIR RICH DISPLAY;
AS HAD THEY ONLY SET THEIR
BURDENS DOWN.

TO REST AWHILE, AND THEN
HAD RODE AWAY.

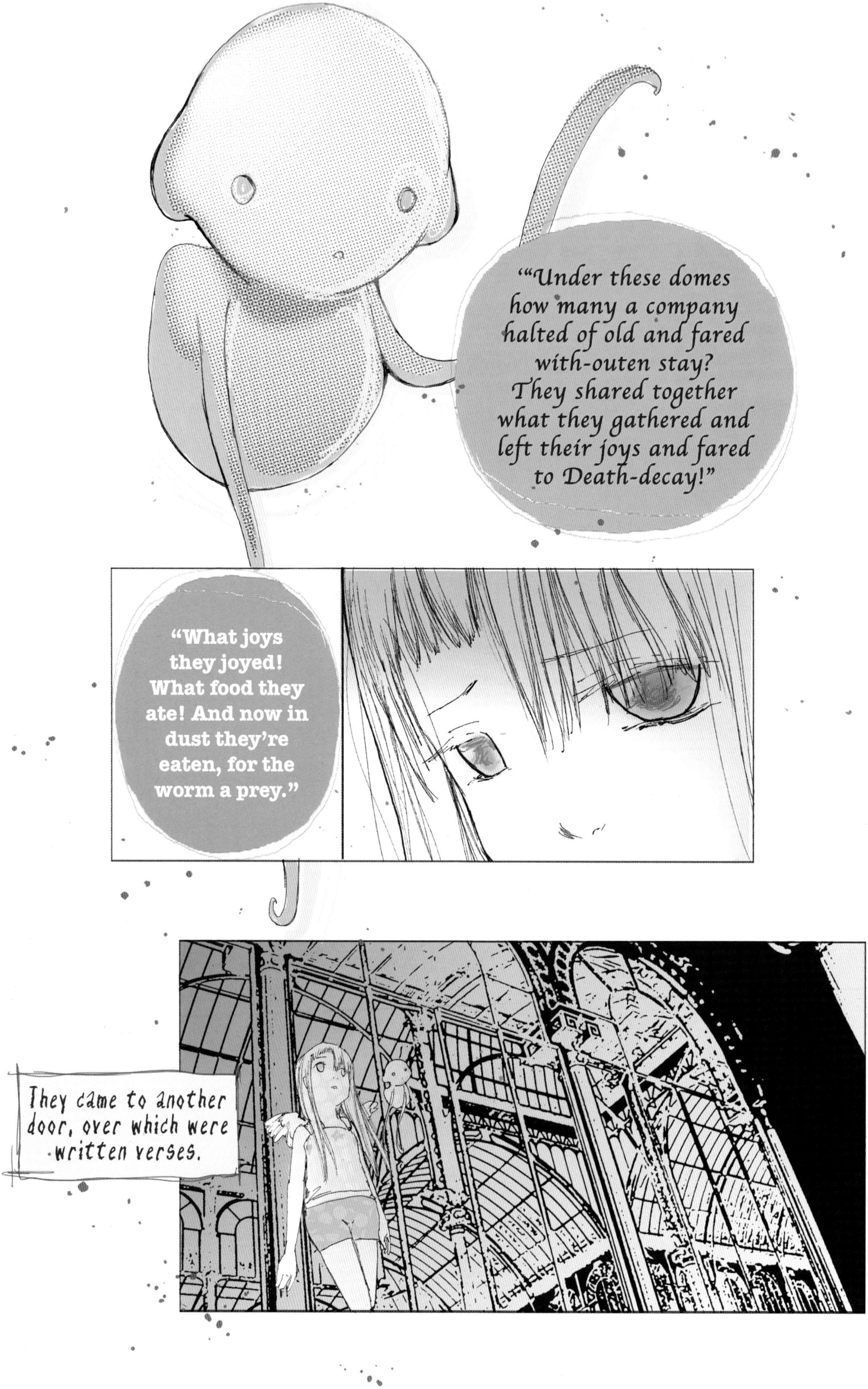
“‘Under these domes how many a company halted of old and fared with-outen stay? They shared together what they gathered and left their joys and fared to Death-decay!”
“What joys they joyed! What food they ate! And now in dust they’re eaten, for the worm a prey.”
They came to another door, over which were written verses.

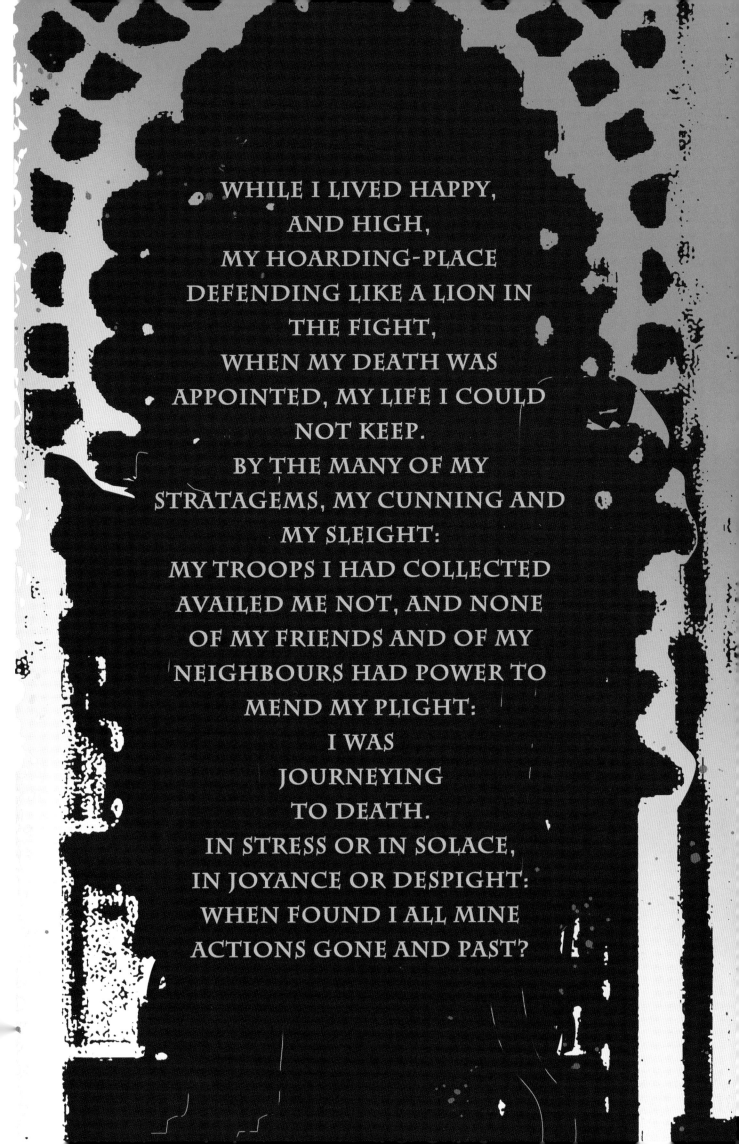

WHILE I LIVED HAPPY,
AND HIGH,
MY HOARDING-PLACE
DEFENDING LIKE A LION IN
THE FIGHT,
WHEN MY DEATH WAS
APPOINTED, MY LIFE I COULD
NOT KEEP.
BY THE MANY OF MY
STRATAGEMS, MY CUNNING AND
MY SLEIGHT:
MY TROOPS I HAD COLLECTED
AVAILED ME NOT, AND NONE
OF MY FRIENDS AND OF MY
NEIGHBOURS HAD POWER TO
MEND MY PLIGHT:
I WAS
JOURNEYING
TO DEATH.
IN STRESS OR IN SOLACE,
IN JOYANCE OR DESPIGHT:
WHEN FOUND I ALL MINE
ACTIONS GONE AND PAST?

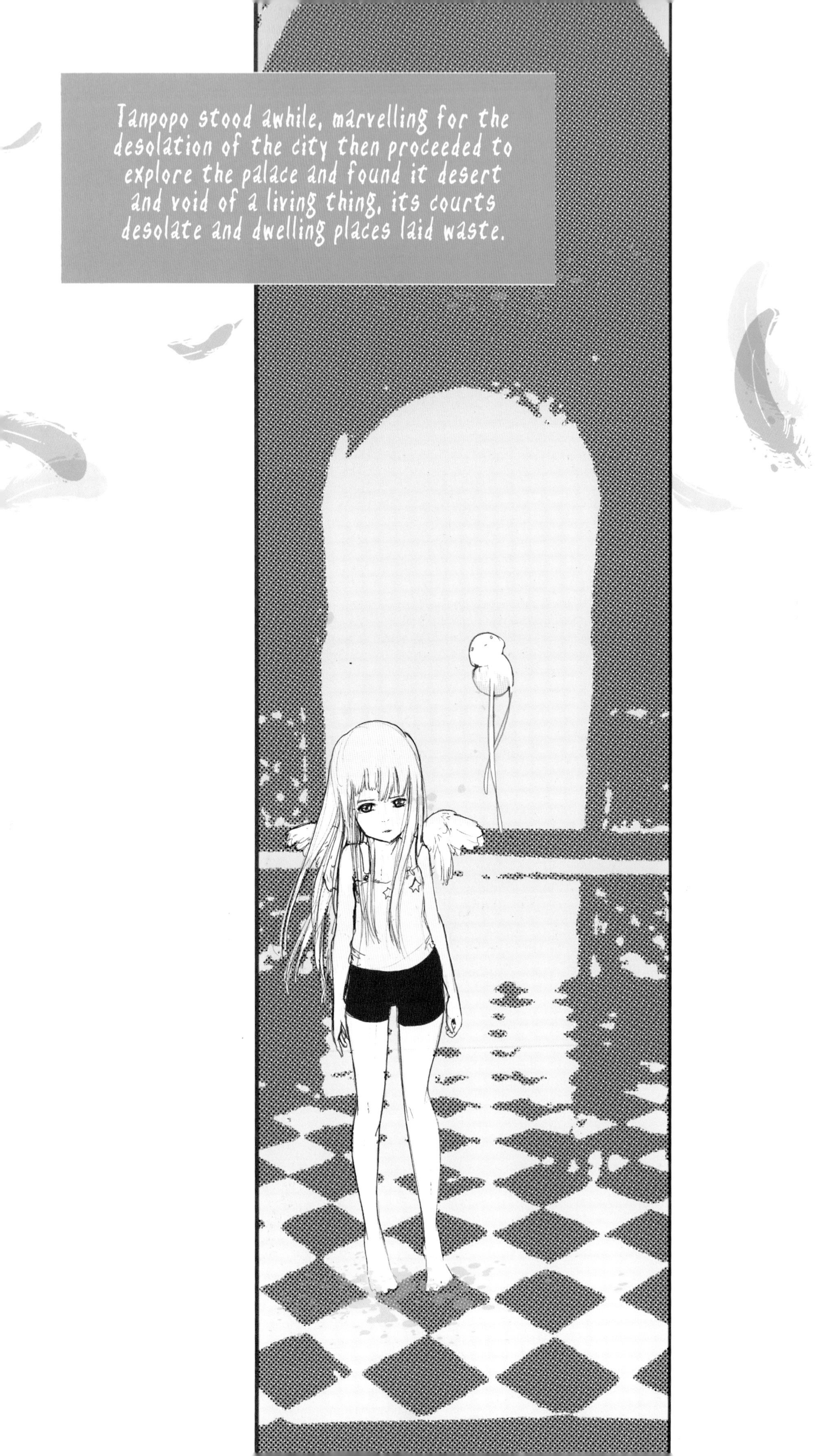
Tanpopo stood awhile, marvelling for the desolation of the city then proceeded to explore the palace and found it desert and void of a living thing, its courts desolate and dwelling places laid waste.

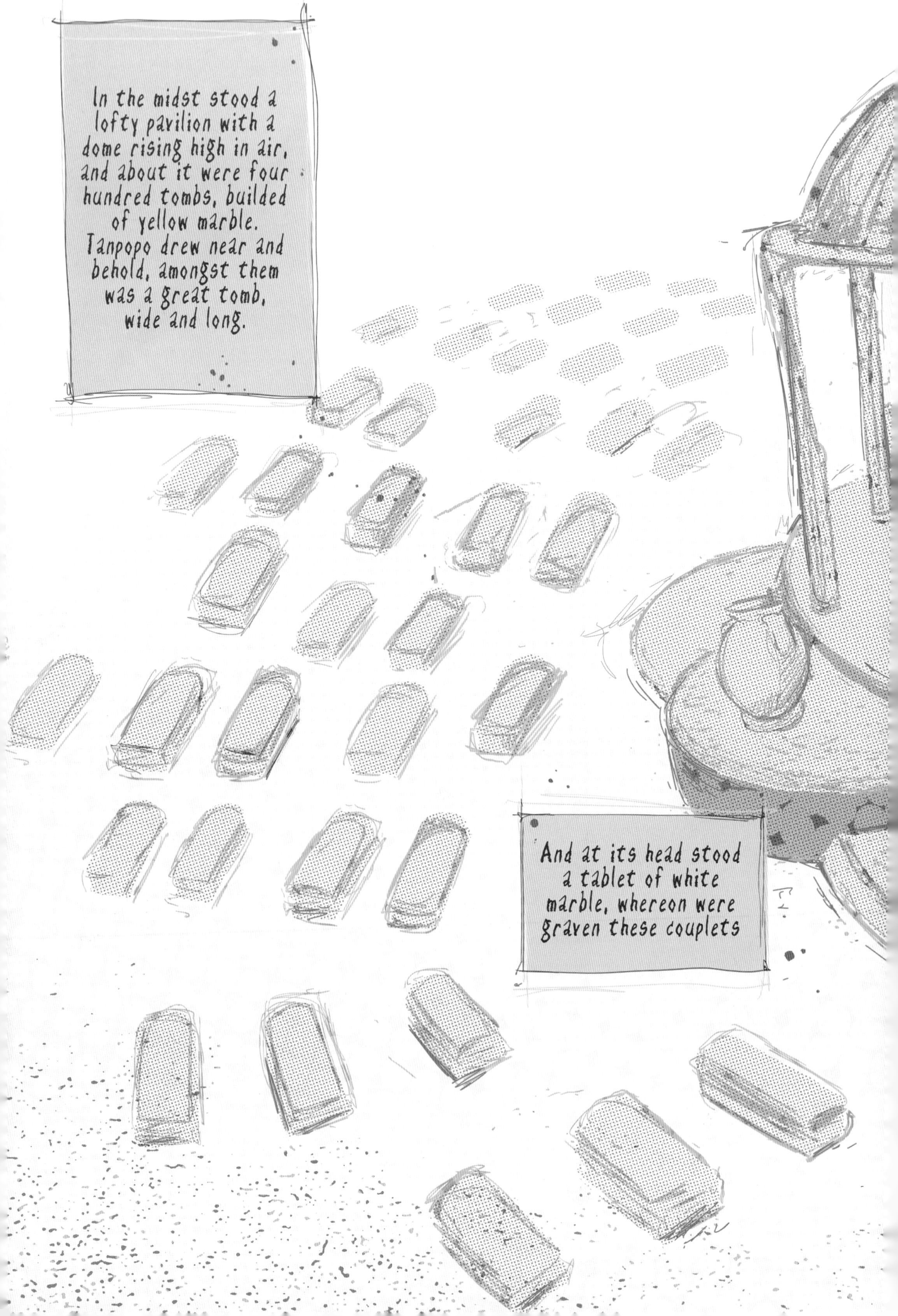
In the midst stood a lofty pavilion with a dome rising high in air, and about it were four hundred tombs, builded of yellow marble. Tanpopo drew near and behold, amongst them was a great tomb, wide and long.
And at its head stood a tablet of white marble, whereon were graven these couplets

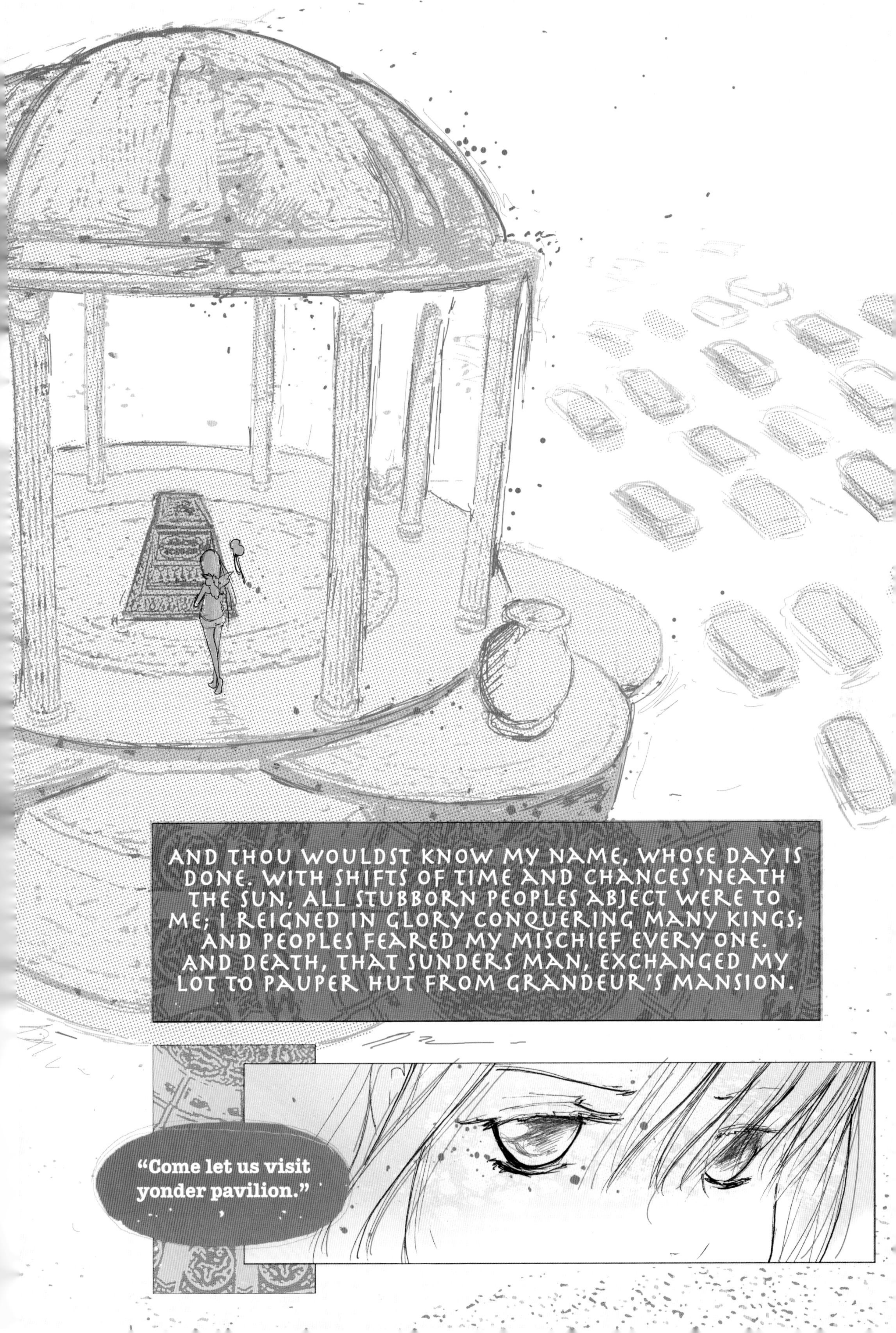
AND THOU WOULDST KNOW MY NAME, WHOSE DAY IS DONE. WITH SHIFTS OF TIME AND CHANCES 'NEATH THE SUN, ALL STUBBORN PEOPLES ABJECT WERE TO ME; I REIGNED IN GLORY CONQUERING MANY KINGS; AND PEOPLES FEARED MY MISCHIEF EVERY ONE. AND DEATH, THAT SUNDERS MAN, EXCHANGED MY LOT TO PAUPER HUT FROM GRANDEUR'S MANSION.
"Come let us visit yonder pavilion."

They went about the highways and byways of the palace, viewing its sitting-chambers and pleasaunces they came upon a table of yellow onyx.

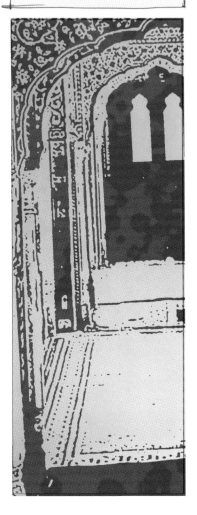

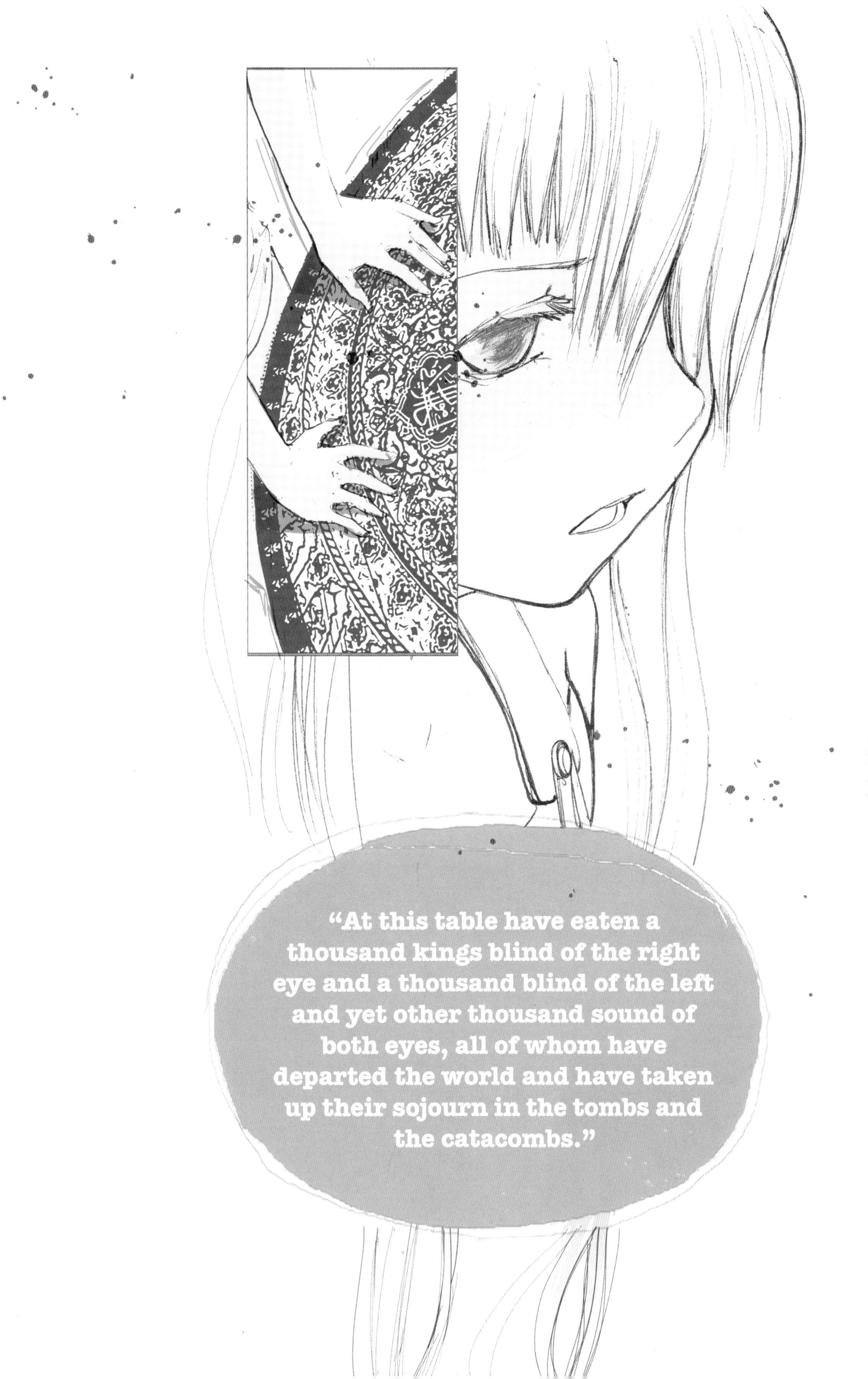
"At this table have eaten a thousand kings blind of the right eye and a thousand blind of the left and yet other thousand sound of both eyes, all of whom have departed the world and have taken up their sojourn in the tombs and the catacombs."

"Consider thou, Tanpopo, what these places to thee showed. Consider how this people their palaces adorned and in dust have been pledged for the seeds they sowed."
"They built but their building availed them not, nor saved their lives nor day of Destiny forslowed. How often did they hope for what things were undecreed and passed unto their tombs before Hope the bounty showed?!"

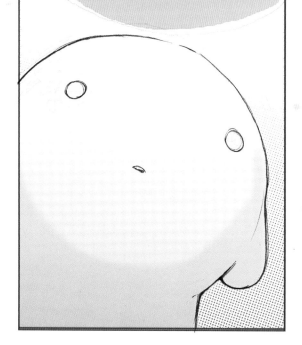

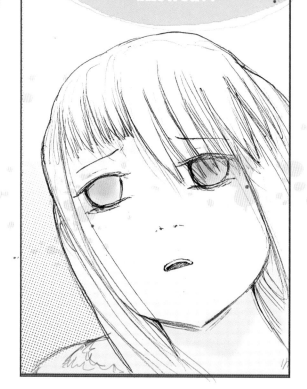

Tanpopo chanced to look aside and caught sight of tablets of white marble afar off. So she drew near them and examining the inscriptions, found that they contained matter of admonition and warning and instances and restraint to those of understanding.

PEOPLED LEFT THEY E'ER AND AYE!

THEY'RE TOMBED YET PLEDGED TO ACTIONS PAST AWAY AND AFTER DEATH UPON THEM CAME DECAY.

WHERE ARE THEIR TROOPS? THEY FAILED TO WARD AND GUARD! WHERE ARE THE WEALTH AND HOARDS IN TREASURIES LAY?

NOR WEALTH NOR REFUGE COULD THEIR

Tanpopo was hurt to her heart and loathed her life for what she saw of the slaughtering places of the folk.

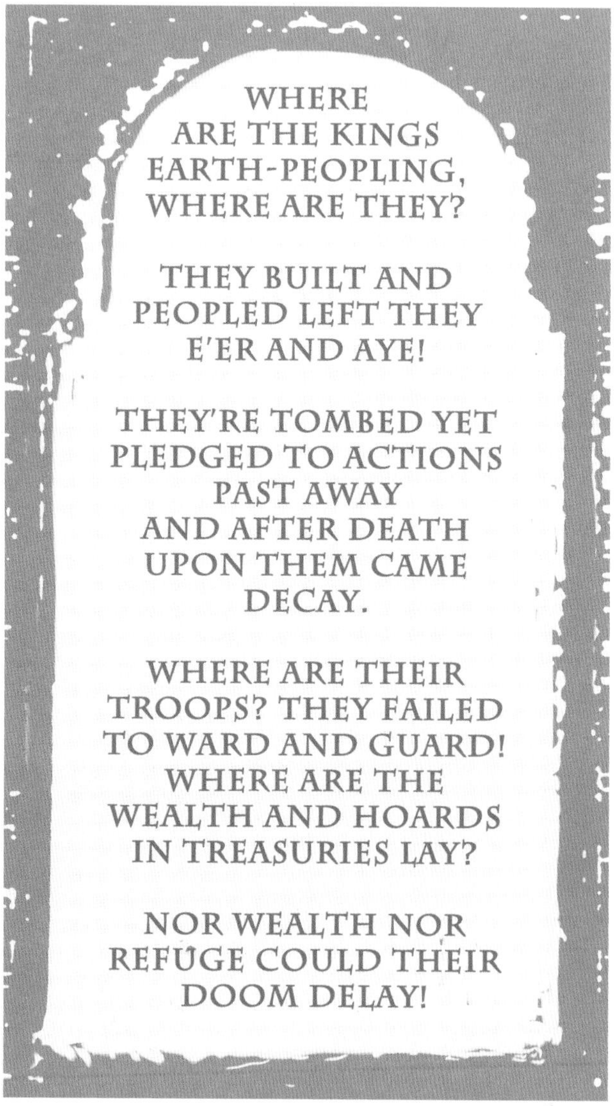
WHERE ARE THE KINGS EARTH-PEOPLING, WHERE ARE THEY?
THEY BUILT AND PEOPLED LEFT THEY E'ER AND AYE!
THEY'RE TOMBED YET PLEDGED TO ACTIONS PAST AWAY AND AFTER DEATH UPON THEM CAME DECAY.
WHERE ARE THEIR TROOPS? THEY FAILED TO WARD AND GUARD! WHERE ARE THE WEALTH AND HOARDS IN TREASURIES LAY?
NOR WEALTH NOR REFUGE COULD THEIR DOOM DELAY!

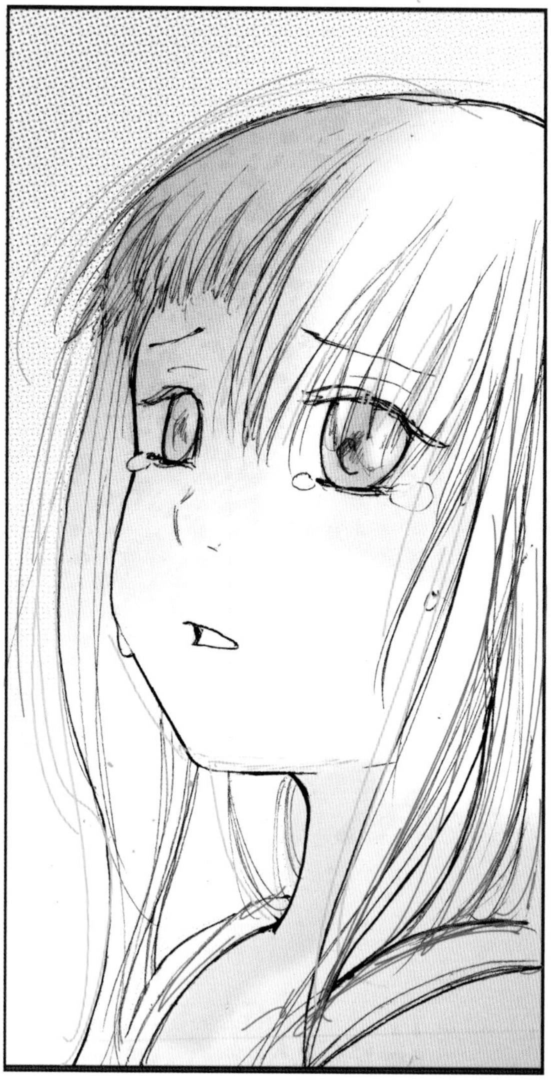

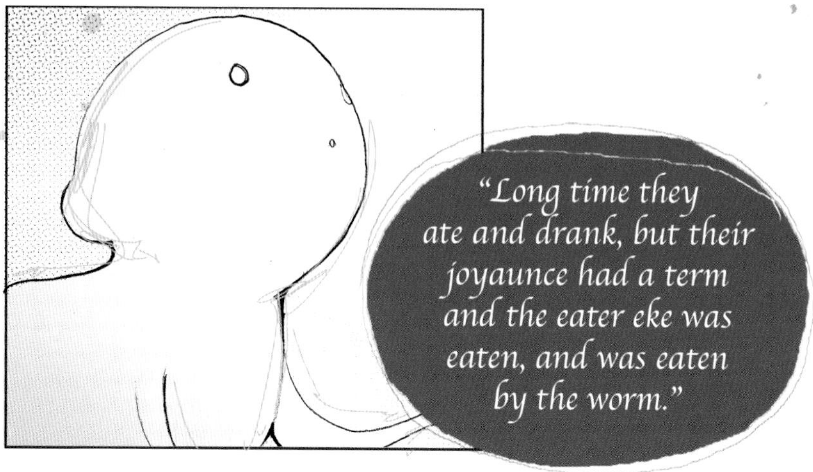
"Long time they ate and drank, but their joyaunce had a term and the eater eke was eaten, and was eaten by the worm."

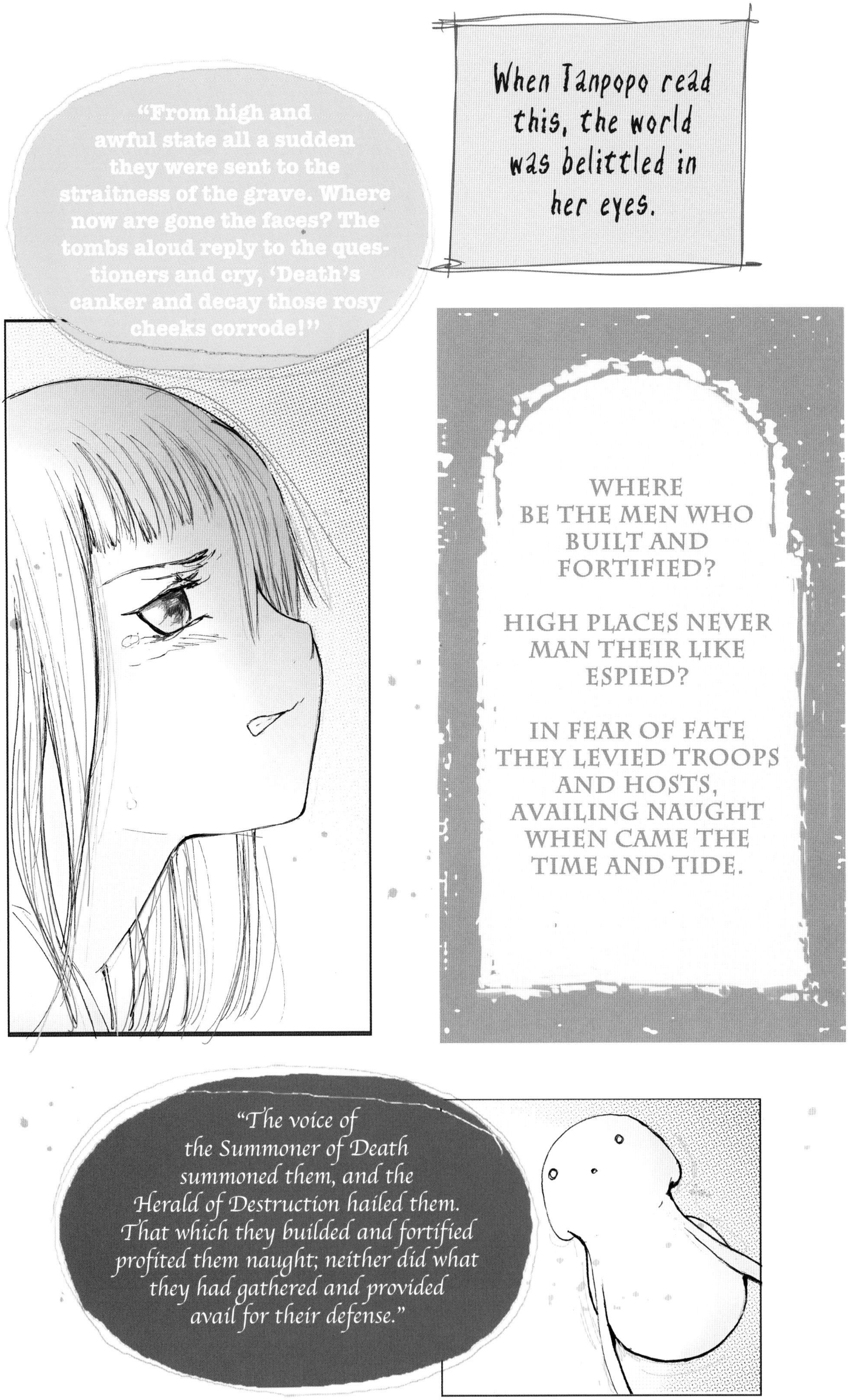

When Tanpopo read this, the world was belittled in her eyes.
"From high and awful state all a sudden they were sent to the straitness of the grave. Where now are gone the faces? The tombs aloud reply to the questioners and cry, 'Death's canker and decay those rosy cheeks corrode!'"
WHERE BE THE MEN WHO BUILT AND FORTIFIED?
HIGH PLACES NEVER MAN THEIR LIKE ESPIED?
IN FEAR OF FATE THEY LEVIED TROOPS AND HOSTS, AVAILING NAUGHT WHEN CAME THE TIME AND TIDE.
"The voice of the Summoner of Death summoned them, and the Herald of Destruction hailed them. That which they builded and fortified profited them naught; neither did what they had gathered and provided avail for their defense."

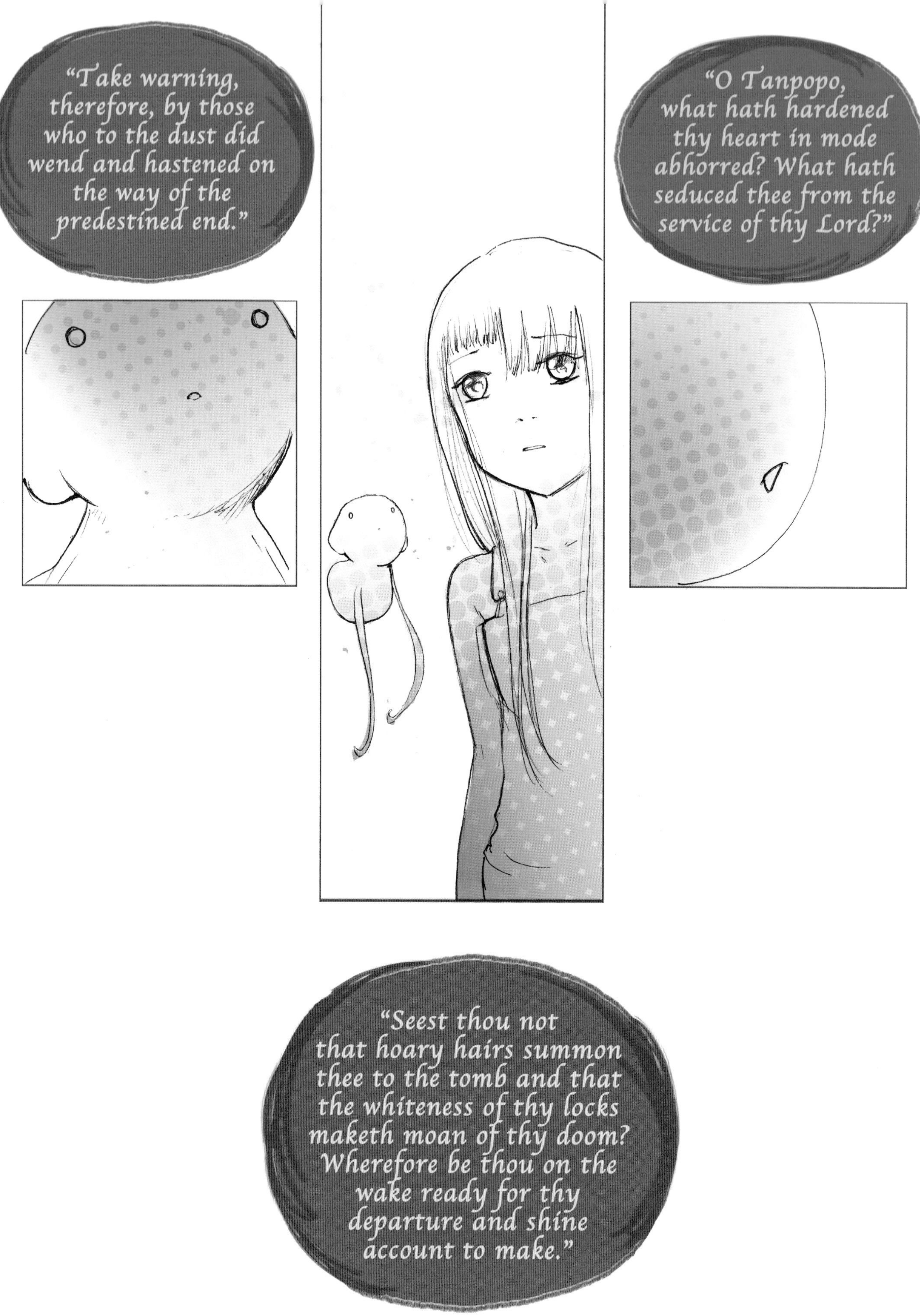
"O Tanpopo, what hath hardened thy heart in mode abhorred? What hath seduced thee from the service of thy Lord?"
"Take warning, therefore, by those who to the dust did wend and hastened on the way of the predestined end."
"Seest thou not that hoary hairs summon thee to the tomb and that the whiteness of thy locks maketh moan of thy doom? Wherefore be thou on the wake ready for thy departure and shine account to make."

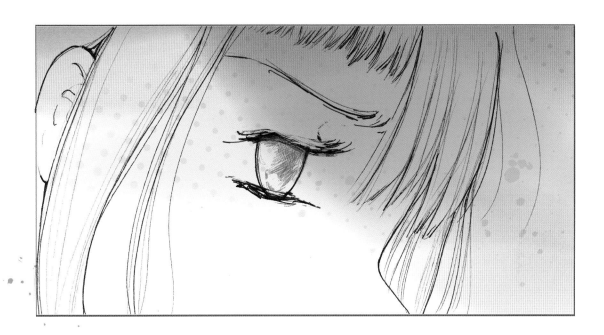

"What I left,
I left it for
nobility of soul."

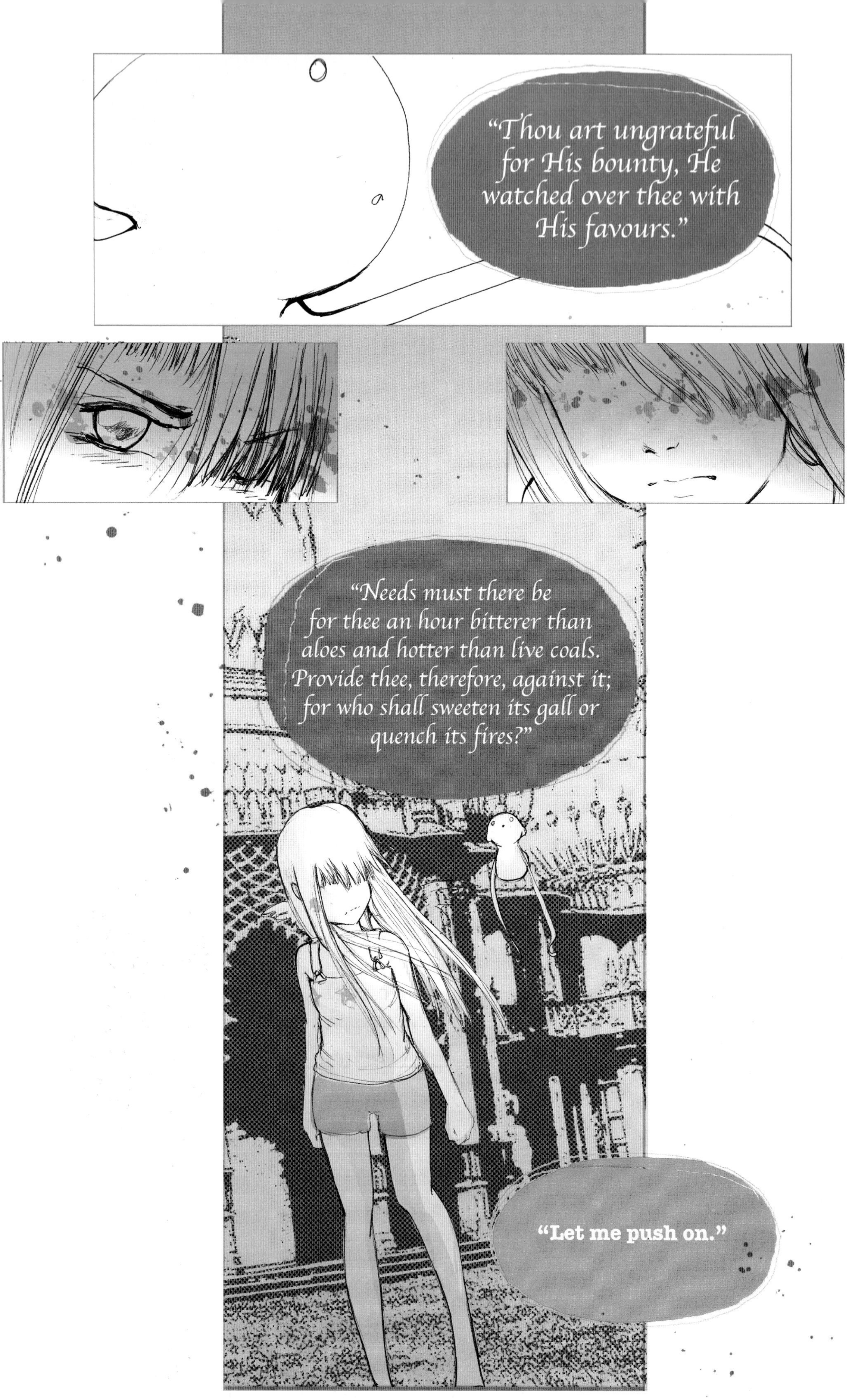
"Thou art ungrateful for His bounty, He watched over thee with His favours."
"Needs must there be for thee an hour bitterer than aloes and hotter than live coals. Provide thee, therefore, against it; for who shall sweeten its gall or quench its fires?"
"Let me push on."

"O Tanpopo, let not thy days delude thee, and know that death to thee cometh and upon thy shoulder sitteth. Down is the curtain of His protection over thee. Thou wastest the sweet of thy life and the joyance of hours. Give ear to me and put thy trust in the Lord of Lords. Know that in the world is no stability, it is as a spider's web and all that is therein shall die and cease to be."

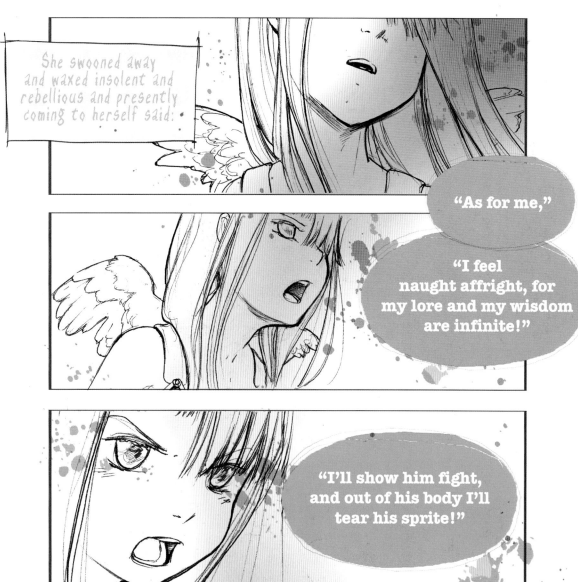

She swooned away and waxed insolent and rebellious and presently coming to herself said:

"As for me,"

"I feel naught affright, for my lore and my wisdom are infinite!"

"I'll show him fight, and out of his body I'll tear his sprite!"

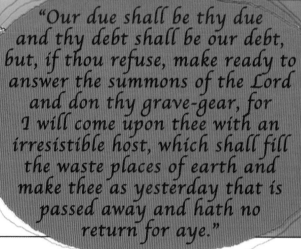

"Our due shall be thy due and thy debt shall be our debt, but, if thou refuse, make ready to answer the summons of the Lord and don thy grave-gear, for I will come upon thee with an irresistible host, which shall fill the waste places of earth and make thee as yesterday that is passed away and hath no return for aye."

"Wherefor I'm pledged and by my sin undone. If he say, fight him, fight him, and if not, NOT!"

"THEN FEAR, O HUMAN, WHO BY A BRINK DOST RANGE,"

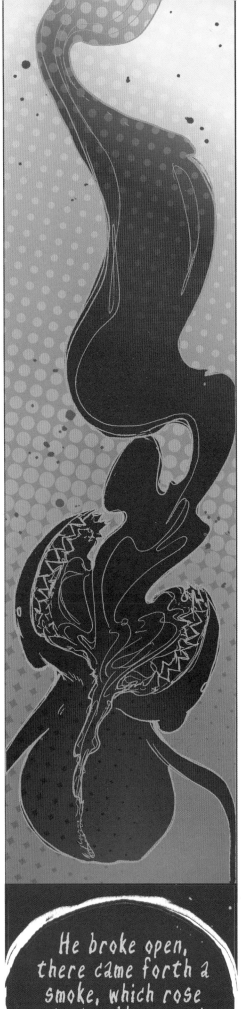

He broke open, there came forth a smoke, which rose twisting blue to the zenith.

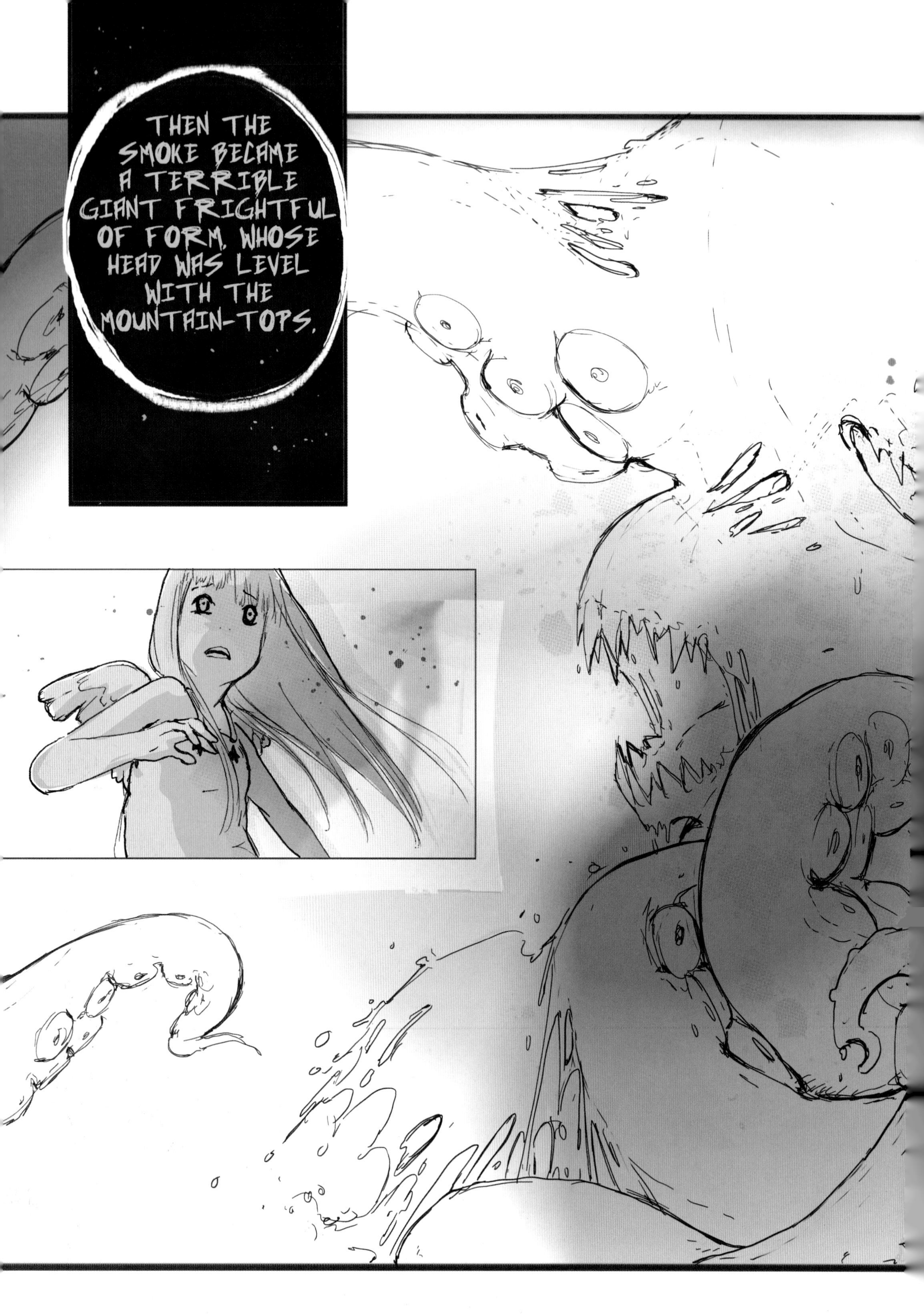
THEN THE SMOKE BECAME A TERRIBLE GIANT FRIGHTFUL OF FORM, WHOSE HEAD WAS LEVEL WITH THE MOUNTAIN-TOPS.

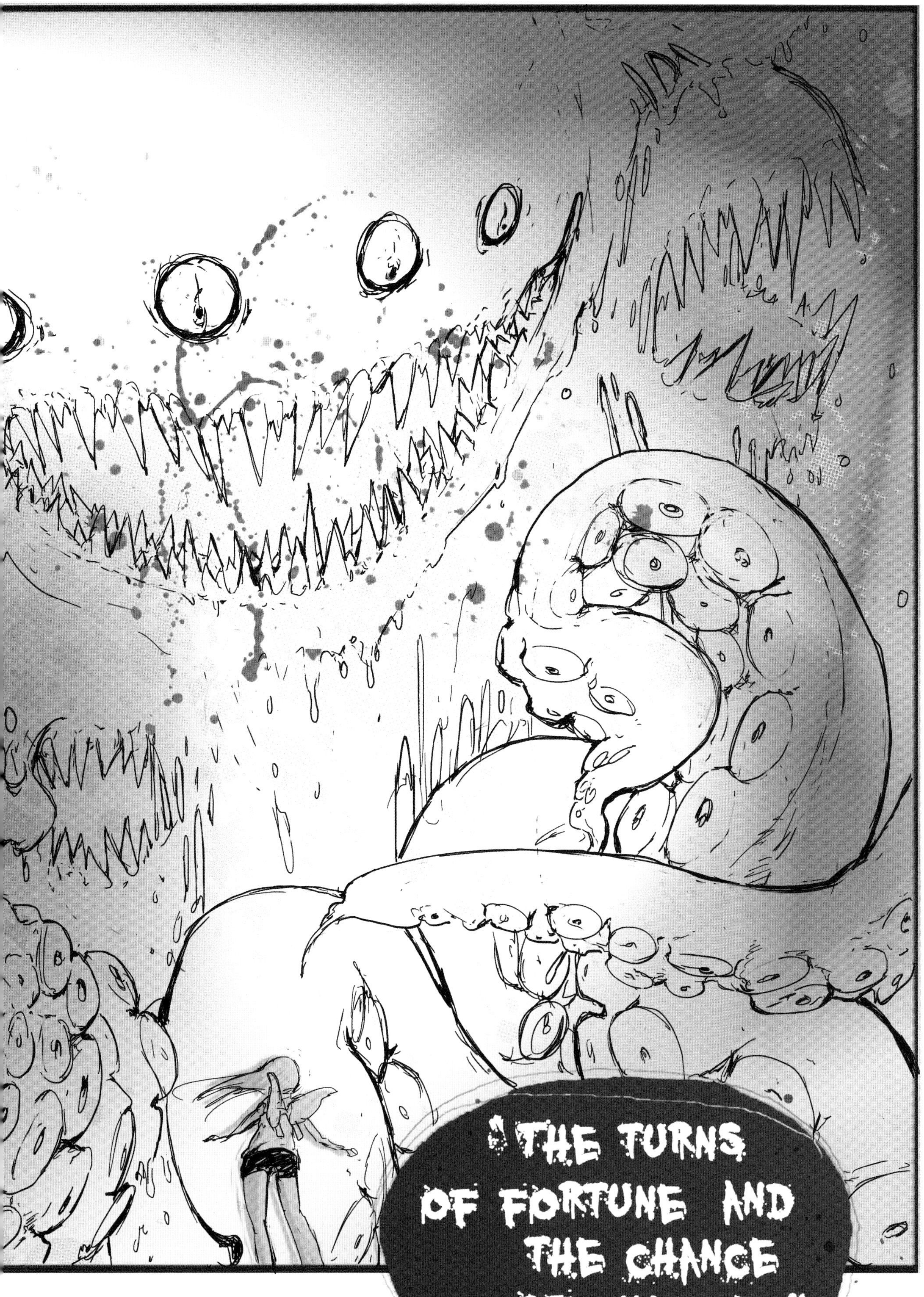
"THE TURNS OF FORTUNE AND THE CHANCE OF CHANGE."

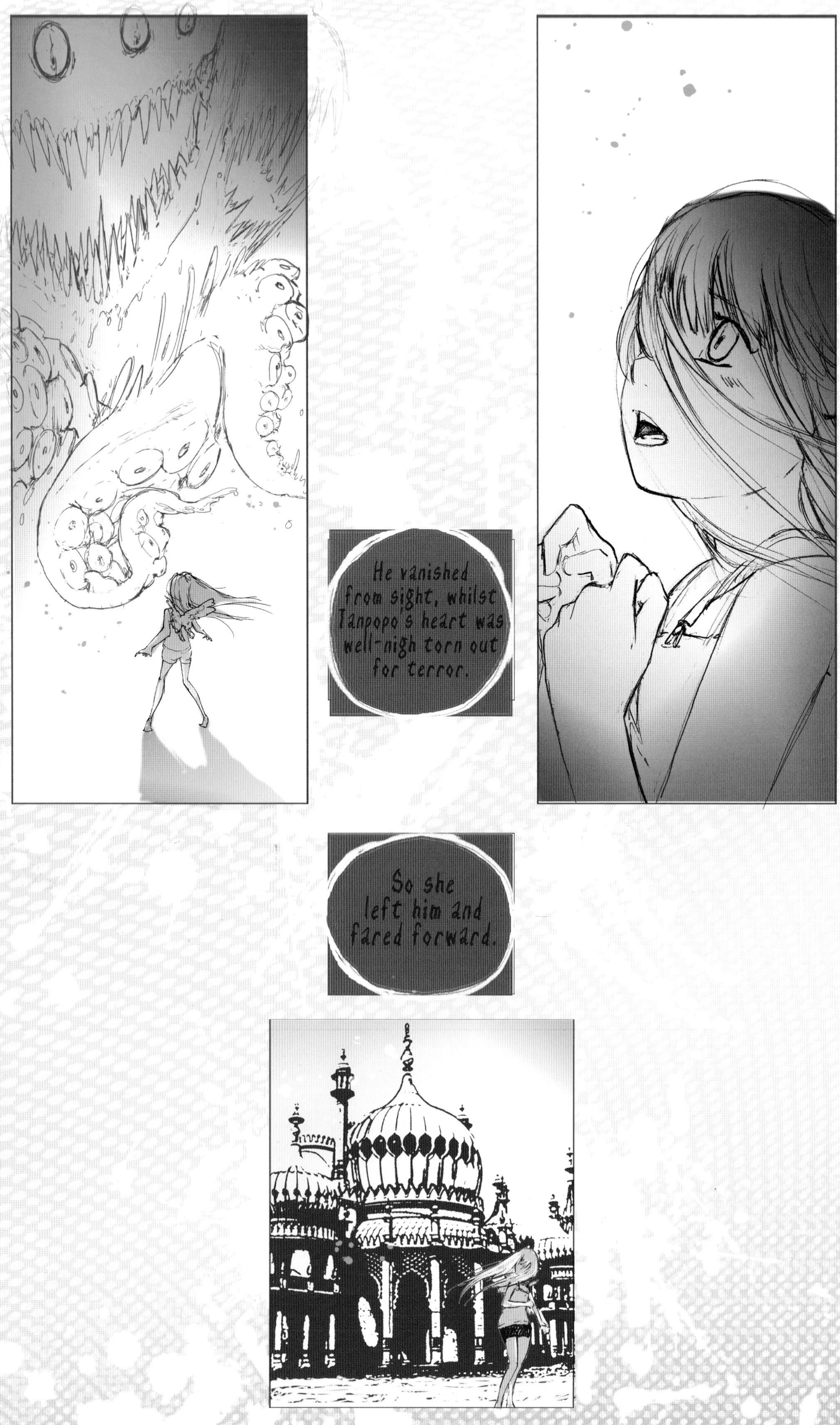
He vanished from sight, whilst Tanpopo's heart was well-nigh torn out for terror.
So she left him and fared forward.

Til there appeared to her afar off a great blackness and therein two fires facing each other.

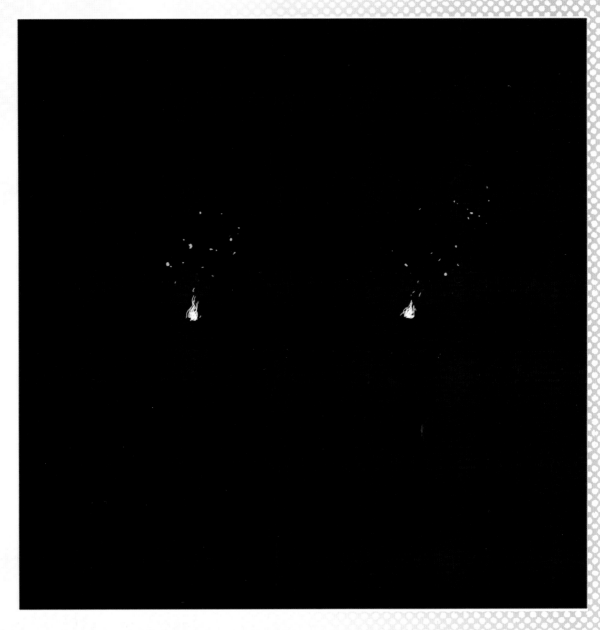

"When found I all mine actions gone and past?"

CHAPTER 3

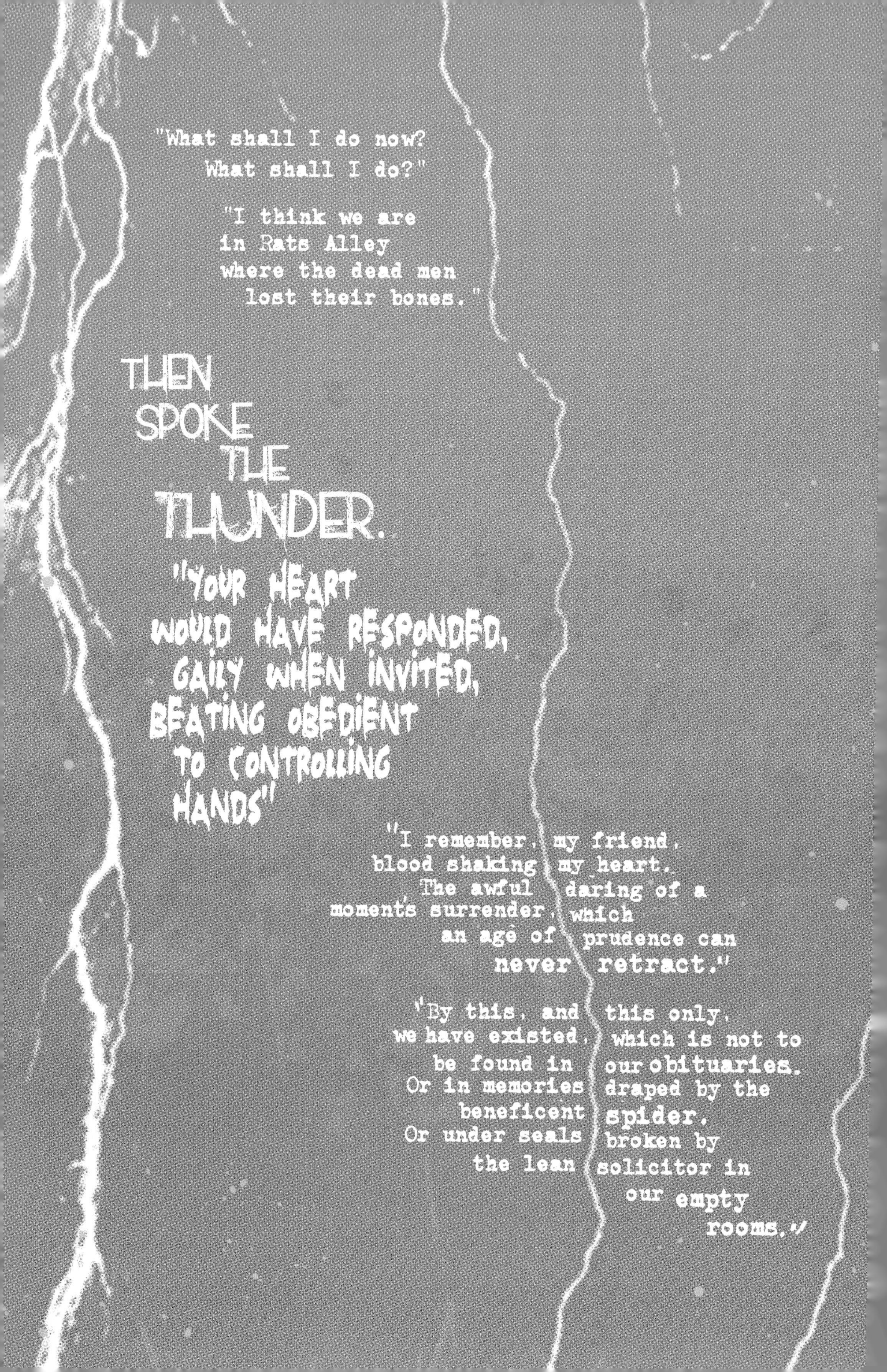
"What shall I do now? What shall I do?"
"I think we are in Rats Alley where the dead men lost their bones."
THEN SPOKE THE THUNDER.
"YOUR HEART WOULD HAVE RESPONDED, GAILY WHEN INVITED, BEATING OBEDIENT TO CONTROLLING HANDS"
"I remember, my friend, blood shaking my heart. The awful daring of a moment's surrender, which an age of prudence can never retract."
"By this, and this only, we have existed, which is not to be found in our obituaries. Or in memories draped by the beneficent spider. Or under seals broken by the lean solicitor in our empty rooms."

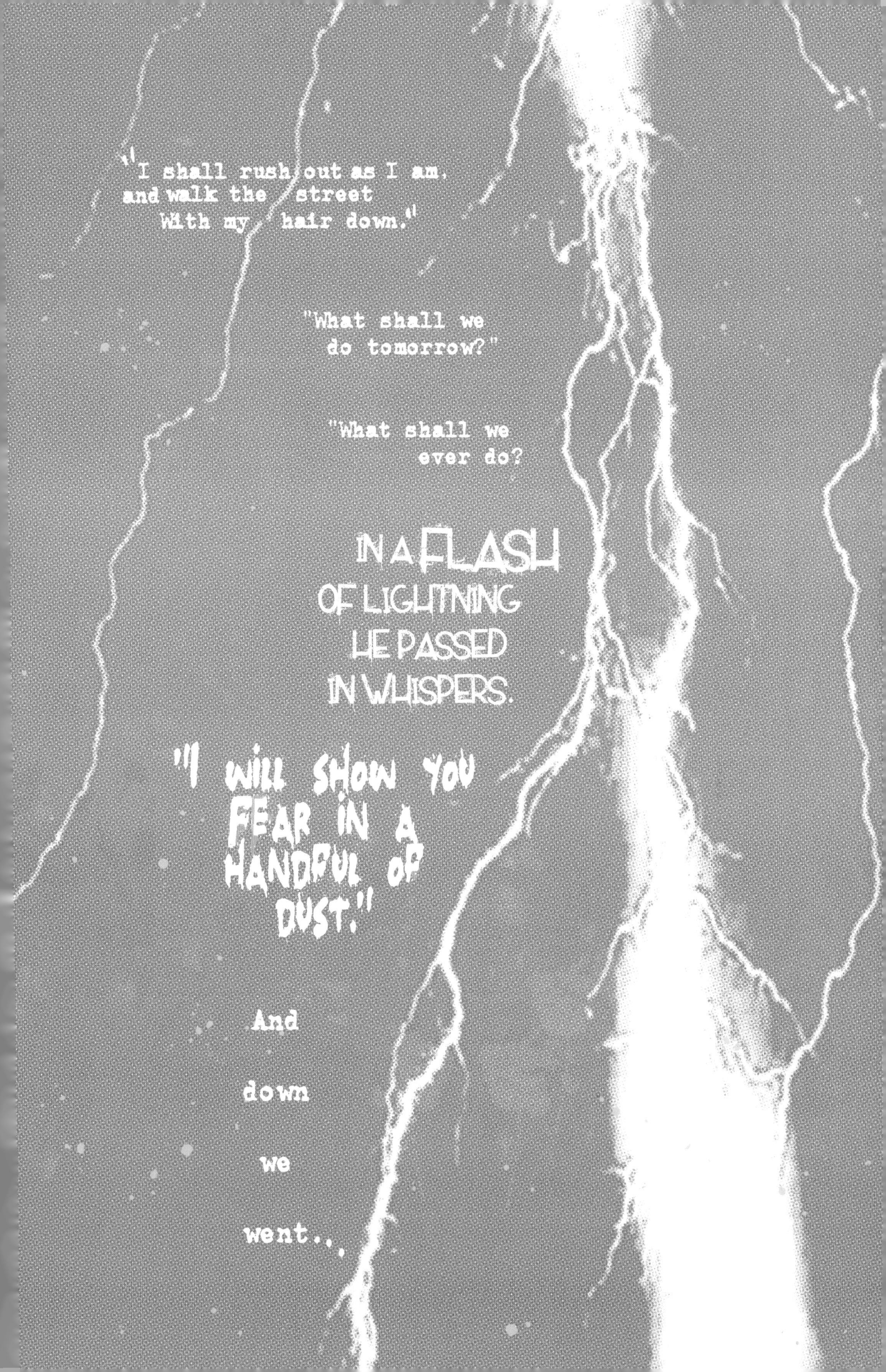
"I shall rush out as I am, and walk the street With my hair down."
"What shall we do tomorrow?"
"What shall we ever do?
IN A FLASH OF LIGHTNING HE PASSED IN WHISPERS.
"I WILL SHOW YOU FEAR IN A HANDFUL OF DUST."
And down we went...

There are chords in the hearts of the most reckless which cannot be touched without emotion...

The thought came stealthily, and it seemed long before it attained full appreciation.

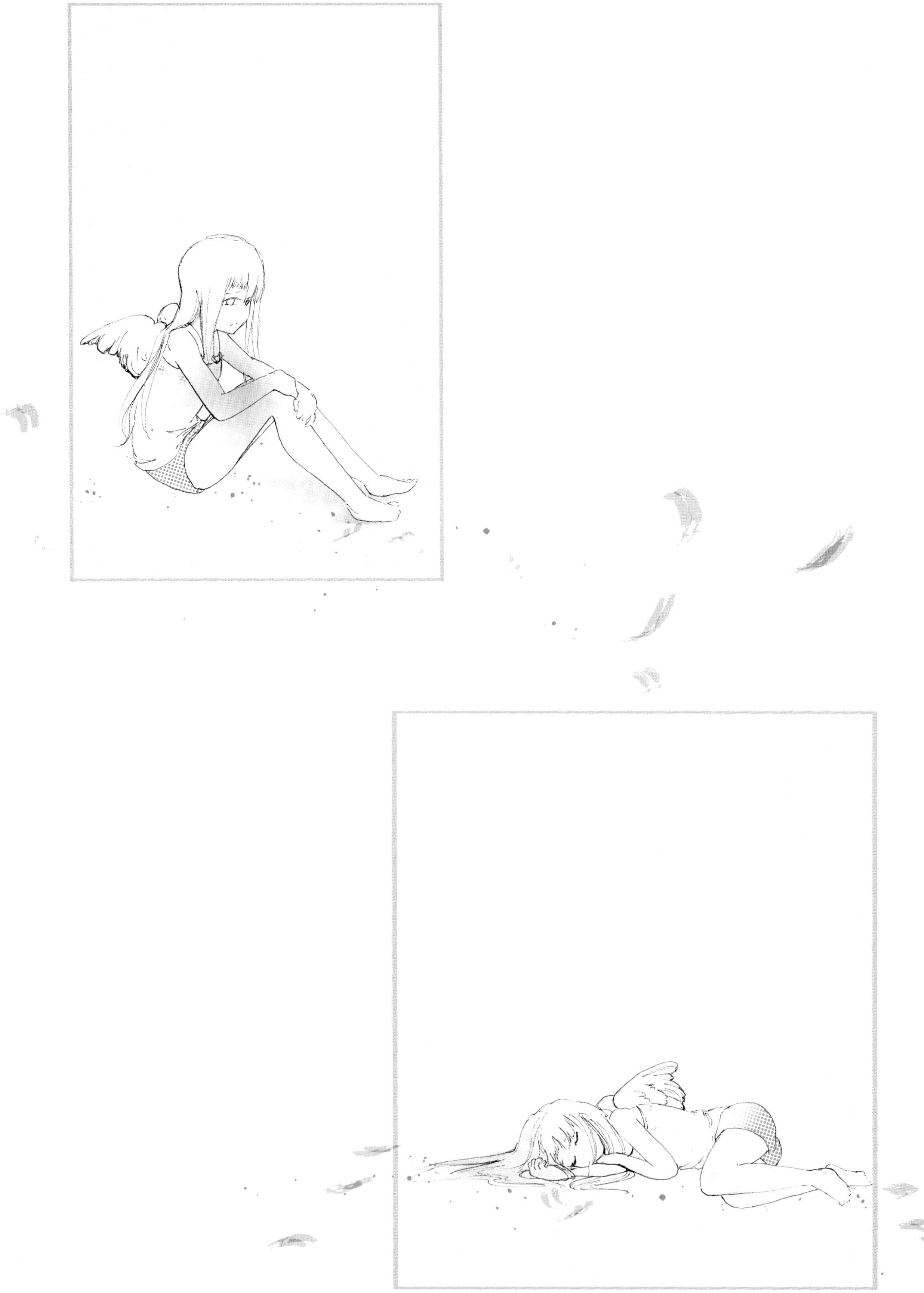

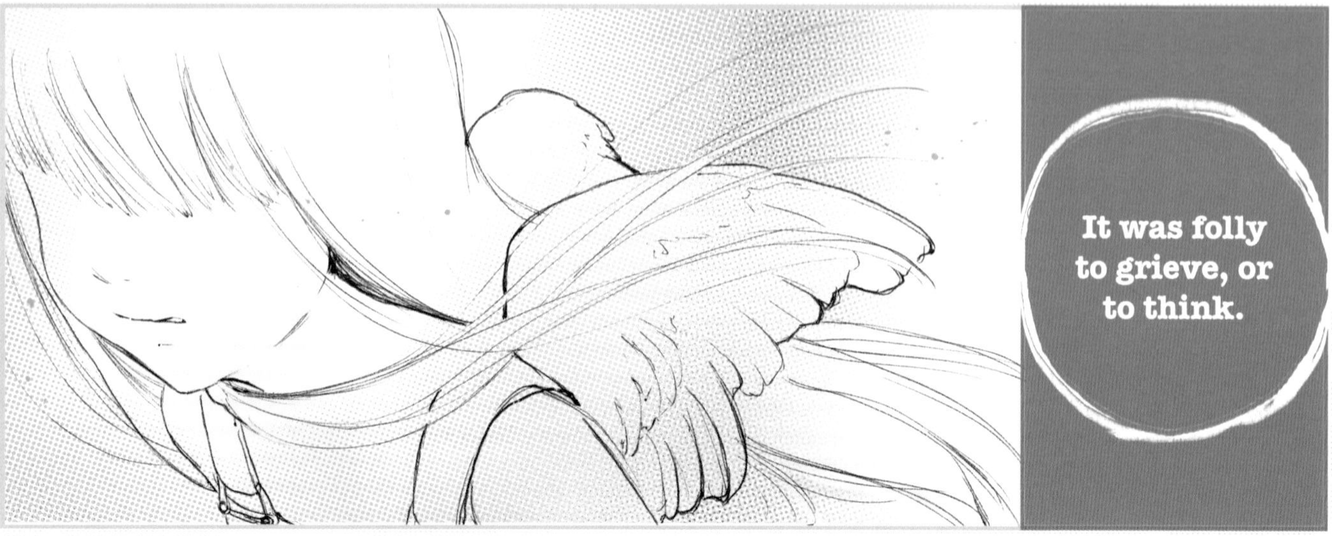
It was folly to grieve, or to think.
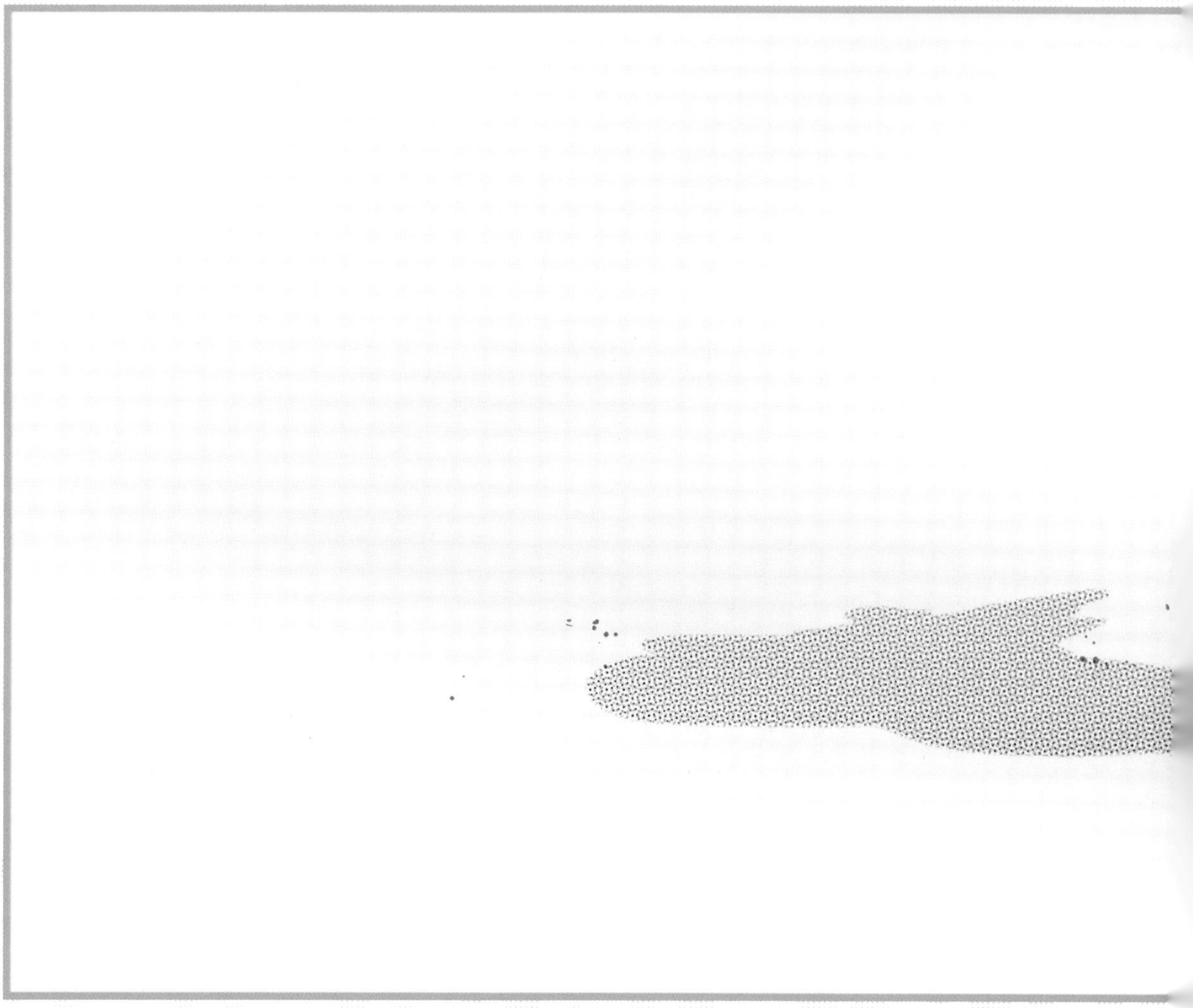

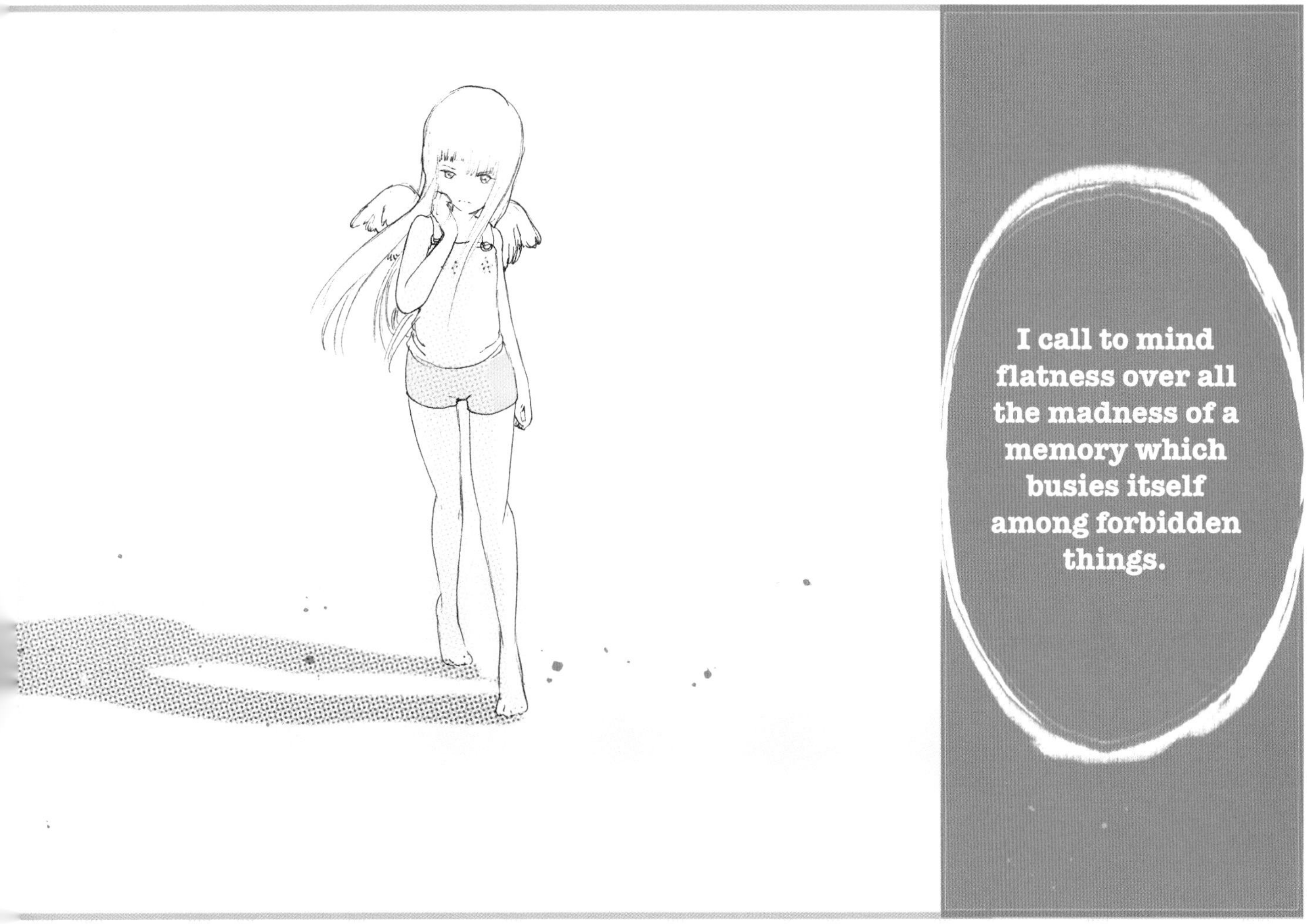
I call to mind flatness over all the madness of a memory which busies itself among forbidden things.
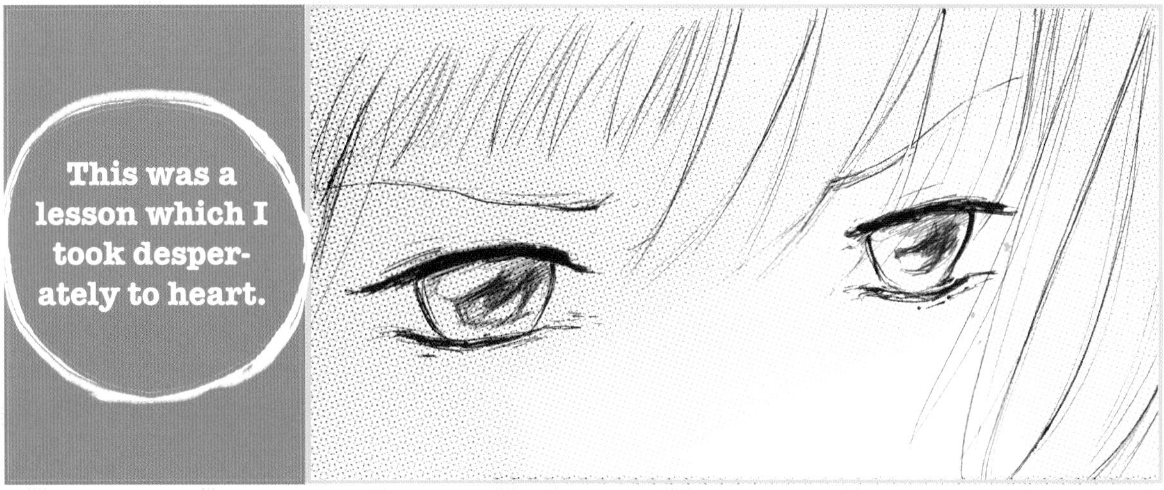
This was a lesson which I took desper-ately to heart.

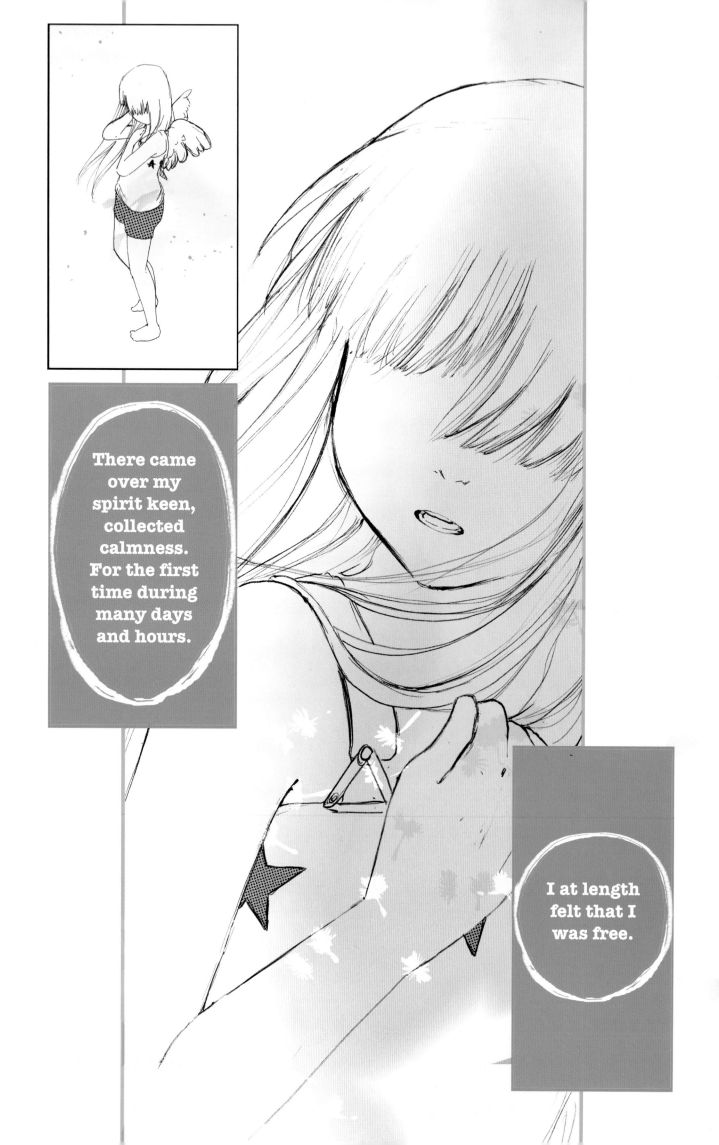

There came over my spirit keen, collected calmness. For the first time during many days and hours.

I at length felt that I was free.

With that
thought I
rolled my eyes
around.

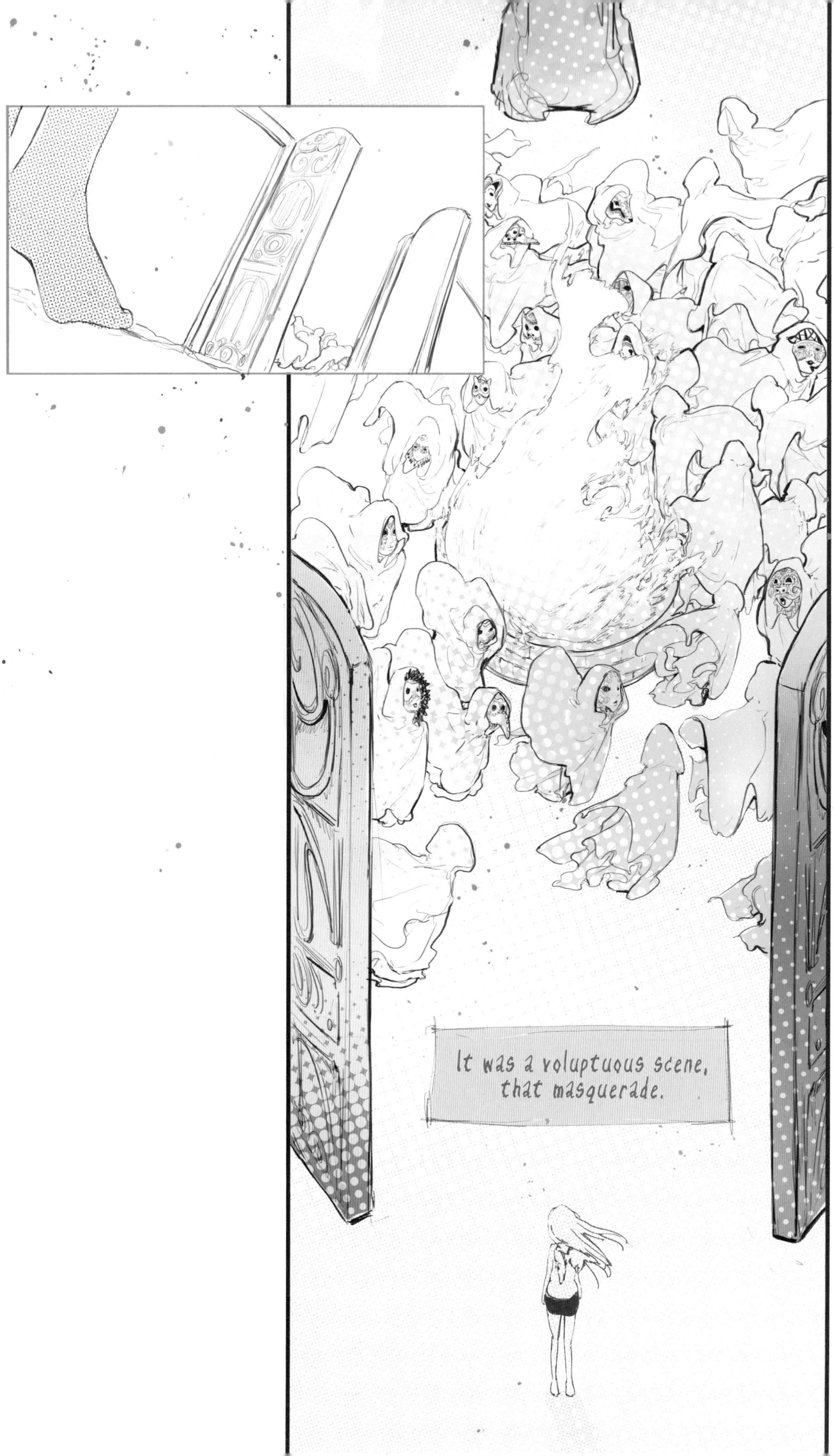
It was a voluptuous scene, that masquerade.

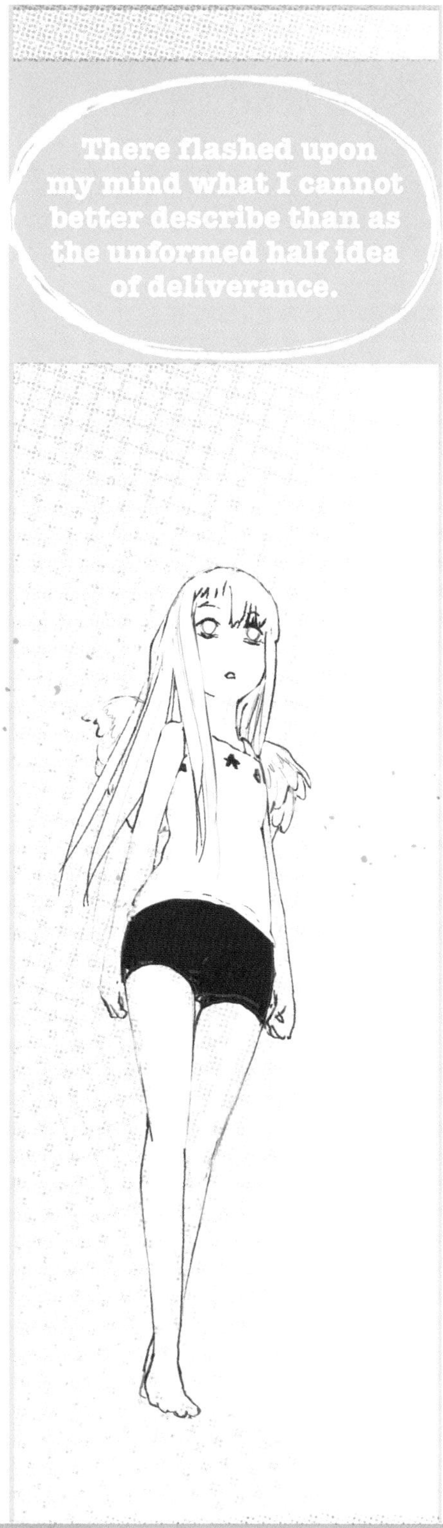
There flashed upon my mind what I cannot better describe than as the unformed half idea of deliverance.

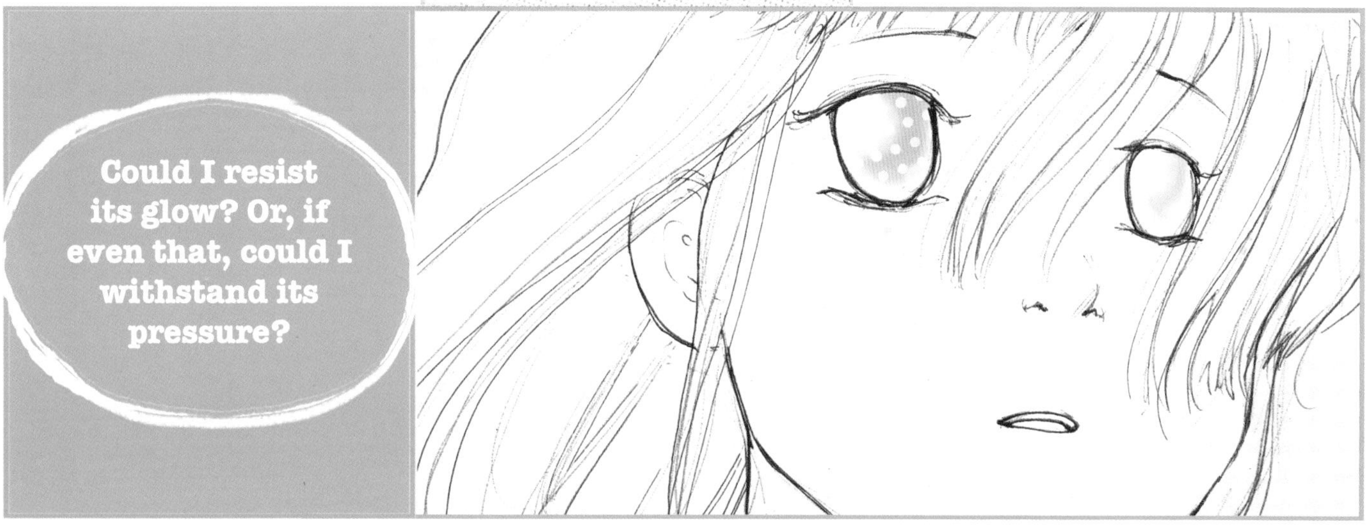
Could I resist its glow? Or, if even that, could I withstand its pressure?

It was hope that prompted the nerve to quiver. With a more than human resolution she continued.

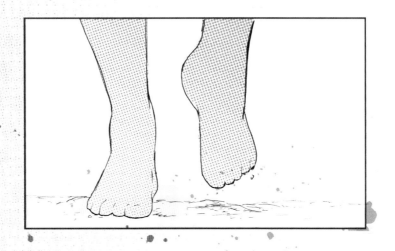

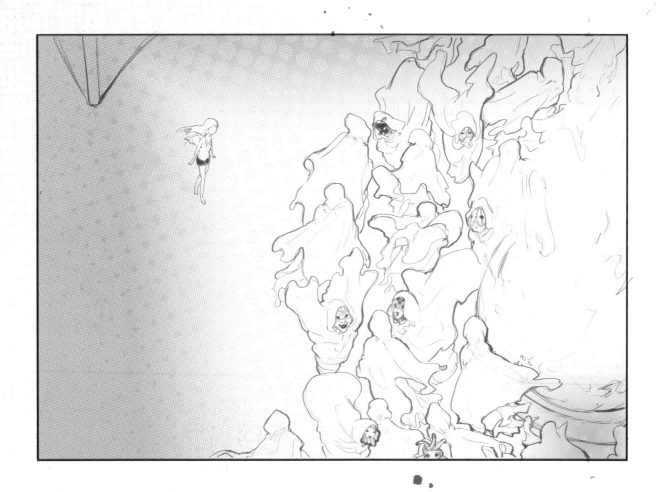

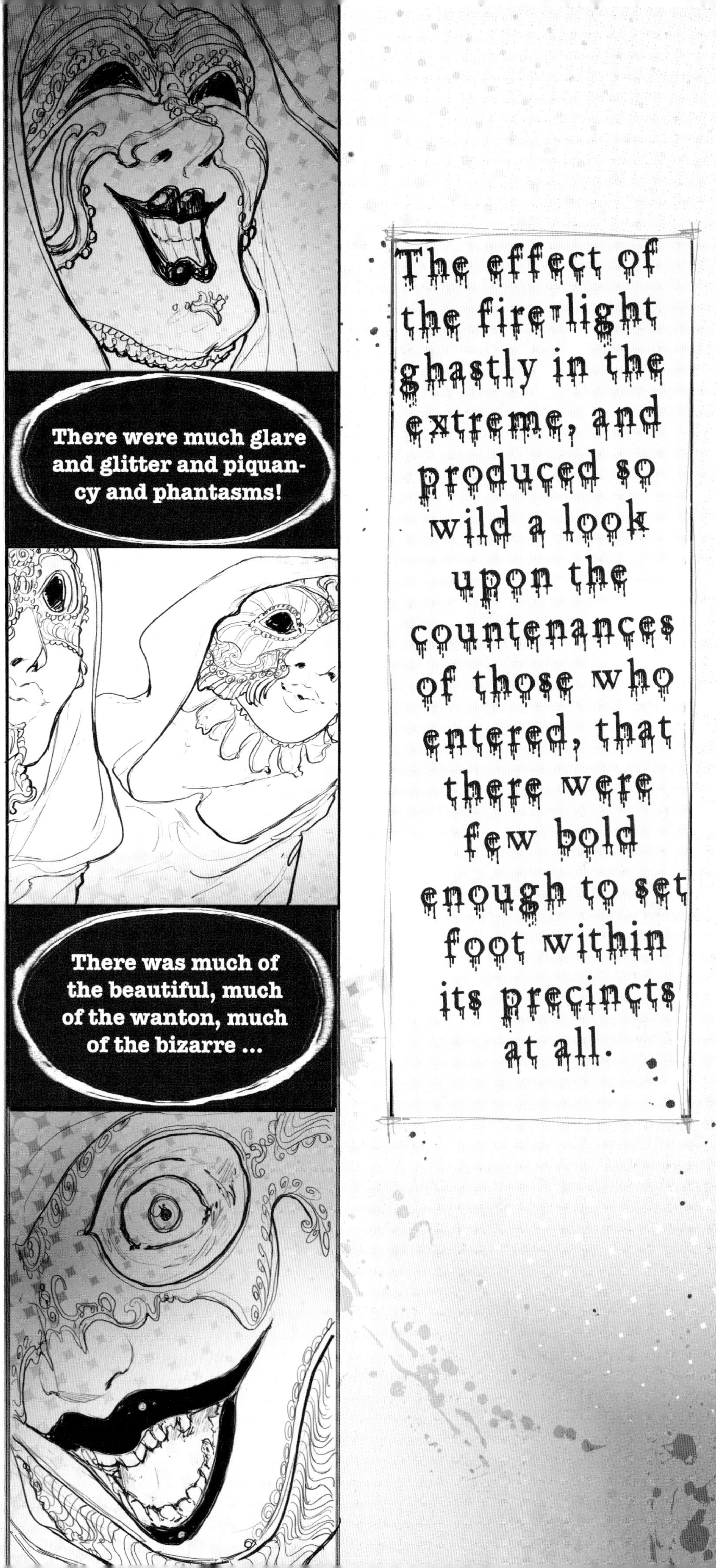
The effect of the fire-light ghastly in the extreme, and produced so wild a look upon the countenances of those who entered, that there were few bold enough to set foot within its precincts at all.
There were much glare and glitter and piquancy and phantasms!
There was much of the beautiful, much of the wanton, much of the bizarre ...

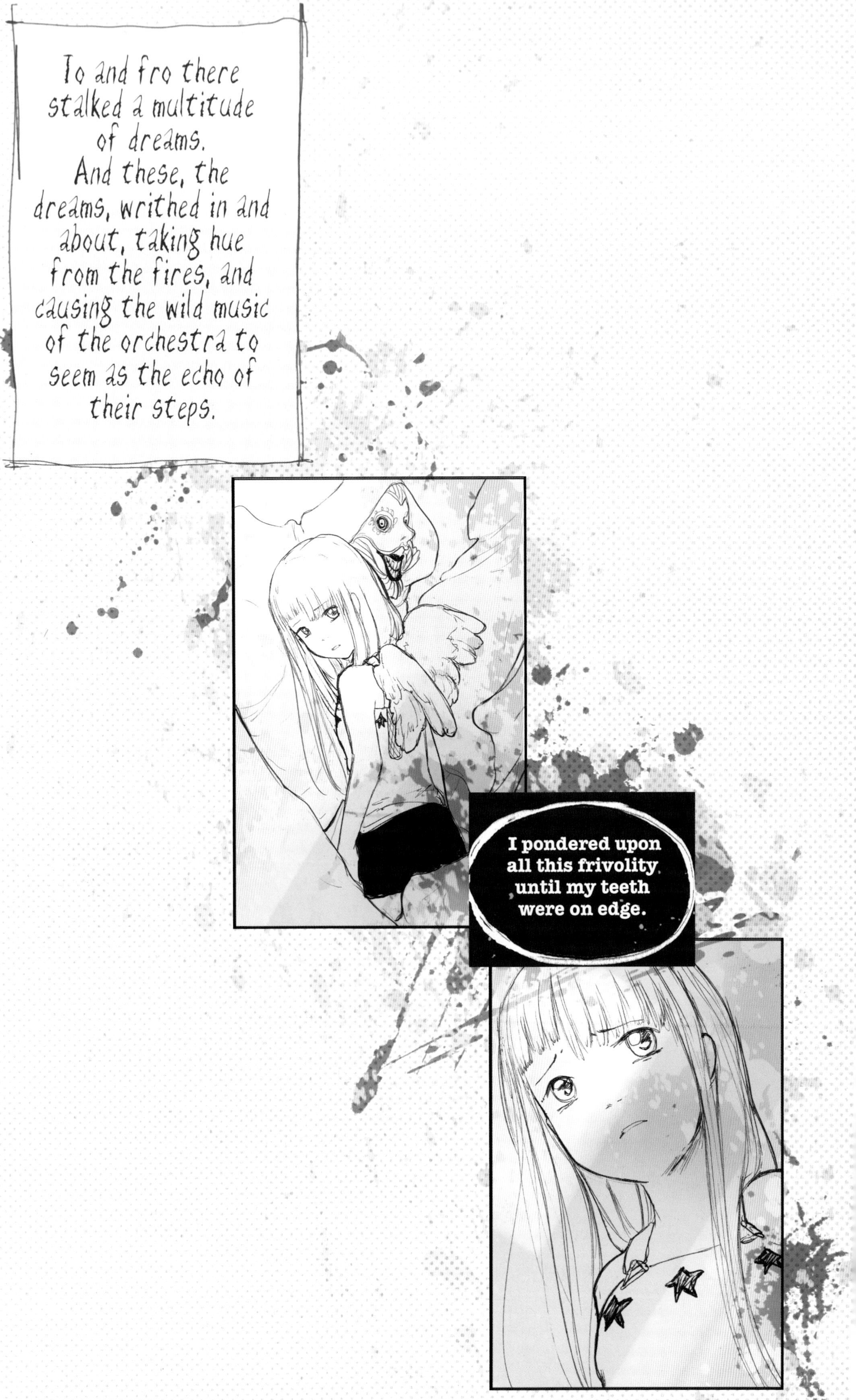
To and fro there stalked a multitude of dreams. And these, the dreams, writhed in and about, taking hue from the fires, and causing the wild music of the orchestra to seem as the echo of their steps.
I pondered upon all this frivolity until my teeth were on edge.

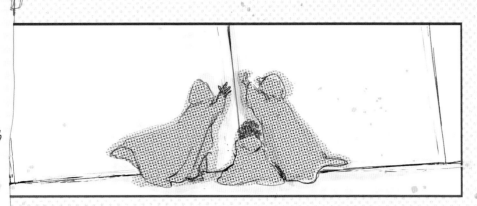

The cortiers, welded the bolts. They resolved to leave means of neither ingress or egress to the sudden impulses of despair or of frenzy from within.

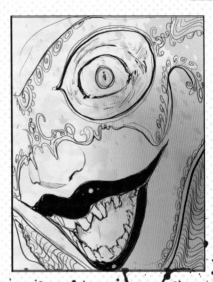

There were arabesque figures with unsuited limbs.

THERE WERE DELIRIOUS FANCIES SUCH AS A MADMAN FASHIONS.

THEY WERE GROTESQUE.

SOMETHING OF THE TERRIBLE, AND NOT A LITTLE OF THAT WHICH MIGHT HAVE EXCITED DISGUST.

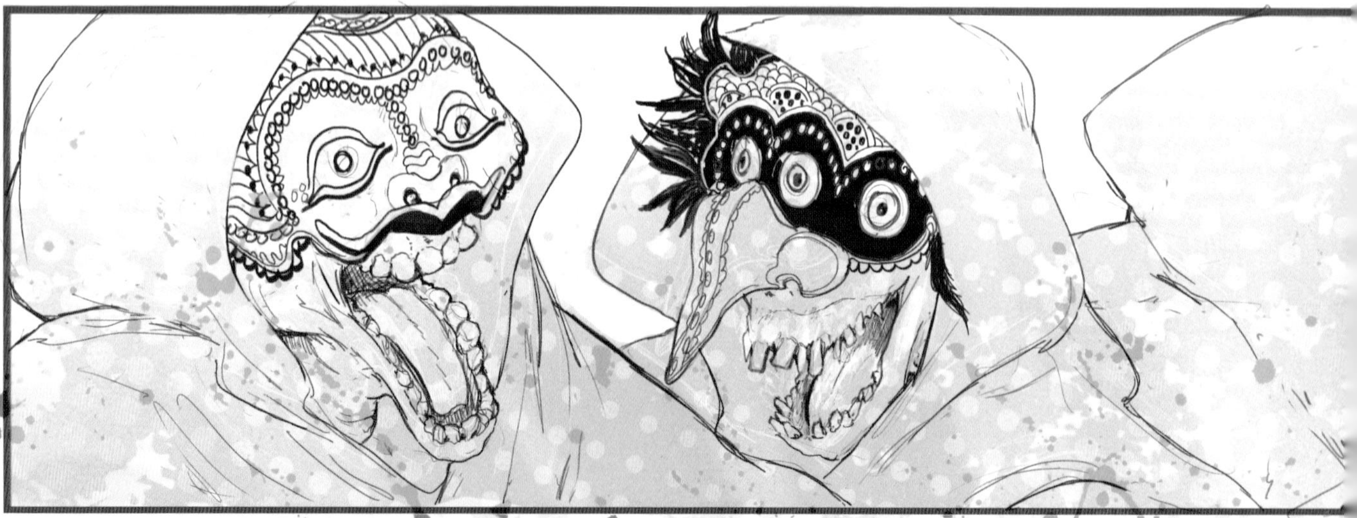

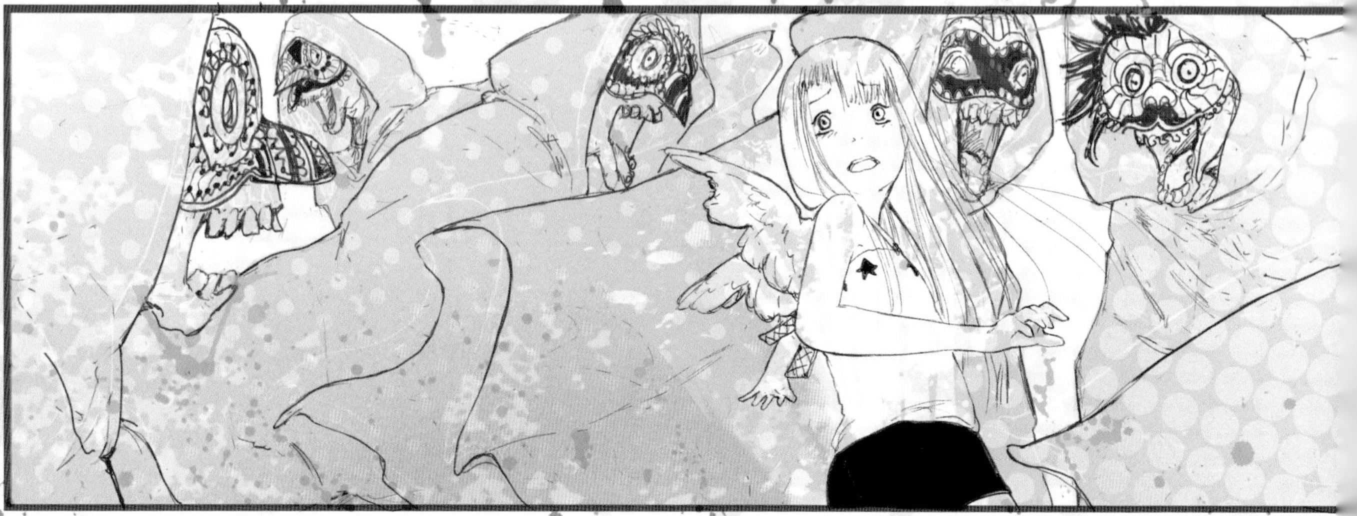

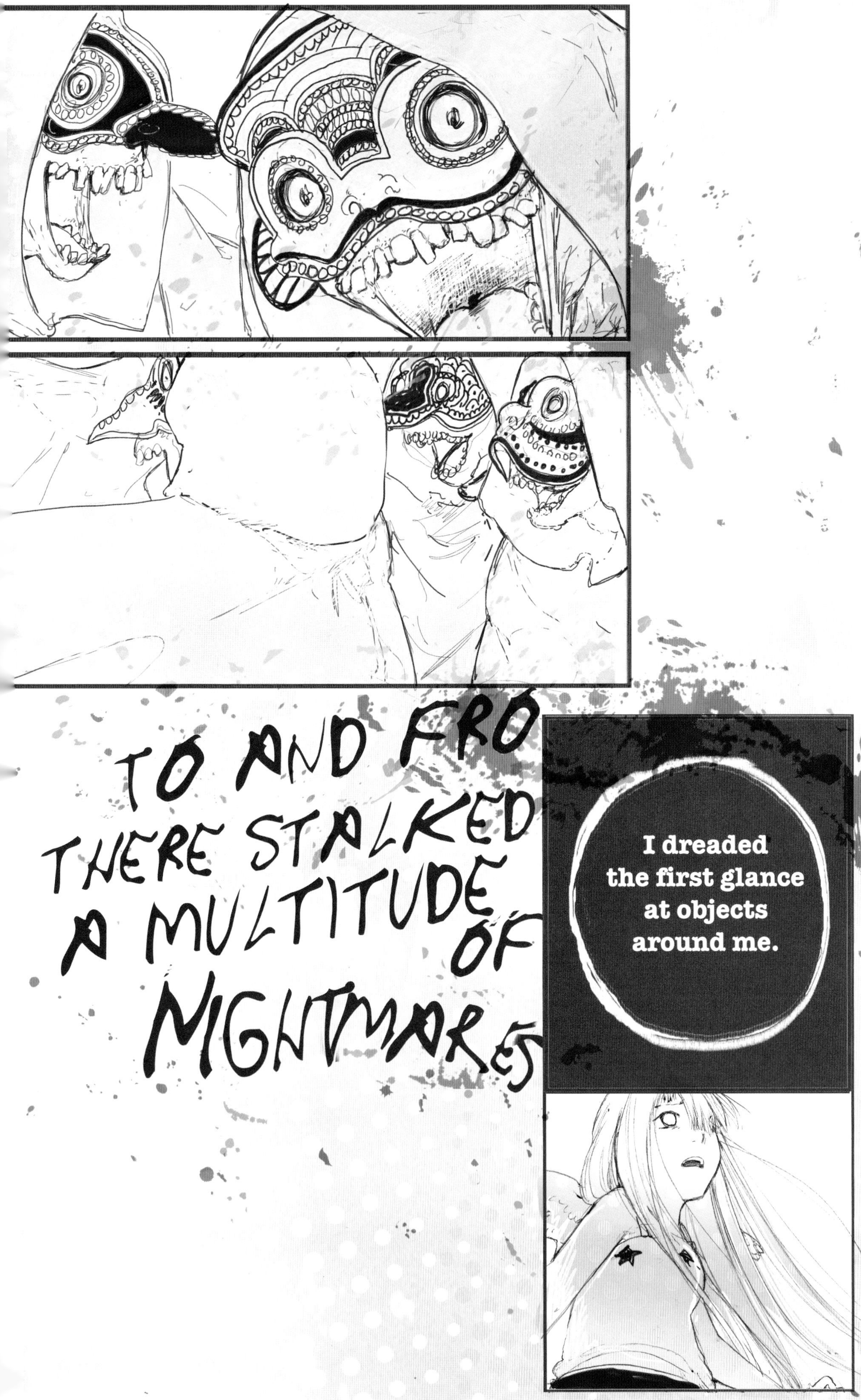
I dreaded the first glance at objects around me.
TO AND FRO THERE STALKED A MULTITUDE OF NIGHTMARES

I shrank back!
I dared not go
farther than this.

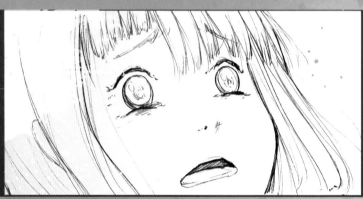

Eyes,
of a wild and
ghastly vivacity,
glared upon me in a
thousand directions,
where none had been
visible before, and
gleamed with the
lurid lustre of a fire
that I could not force
my imagination to
regard as
unreal.

There stood against
the western wall,
a gigantic clock of ebony.

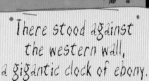

Its pendulum swung to
and fro with a dull,
heavy, monotonous

CLANG!

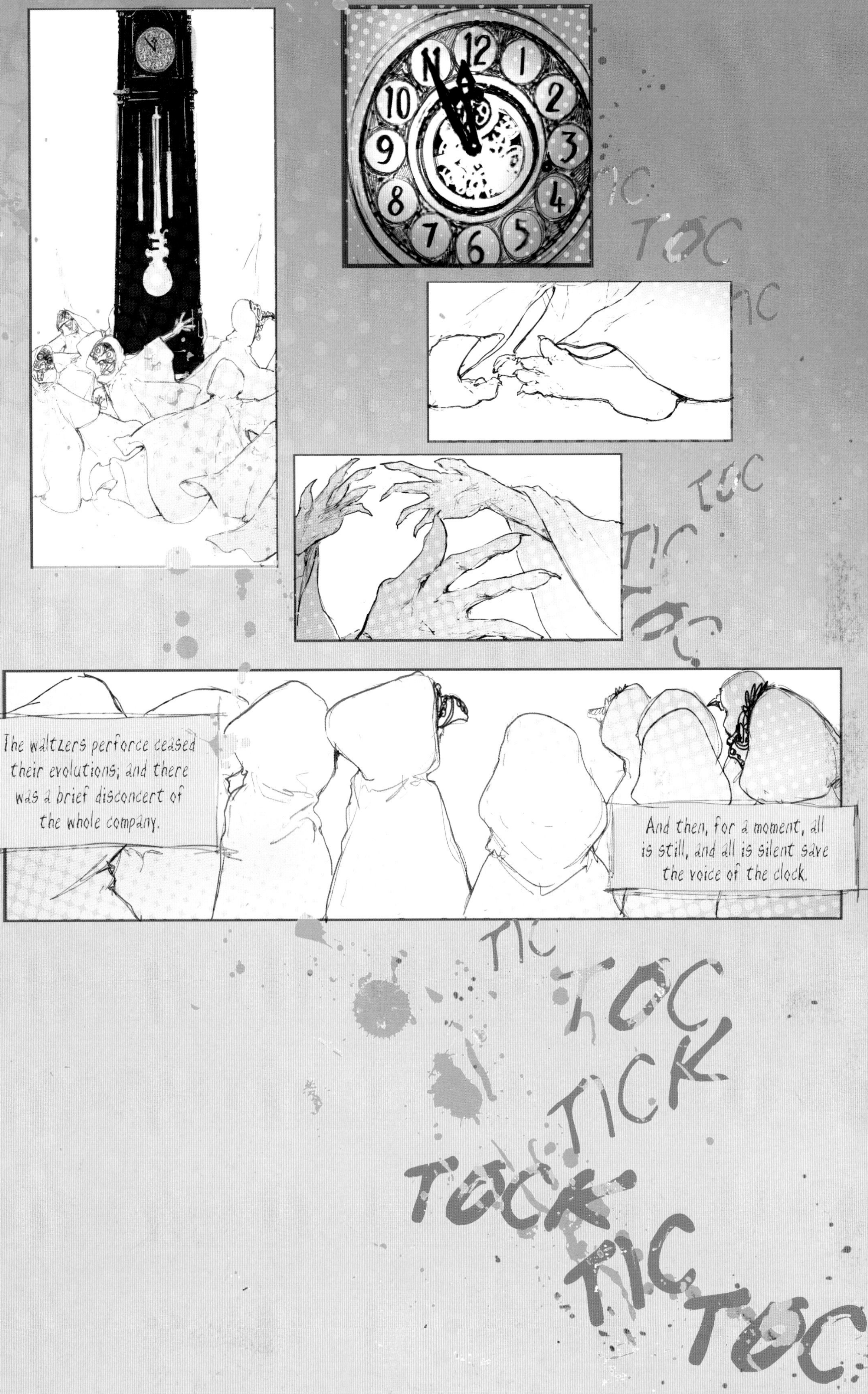
TIC
TOC
TIC
TOC
TIC
TOC
The waltzers perforce ceased their evolutions; and there was a brief disconcert of the whole company.
And then, for a moment, all is still, and all is silent save the voice of the clock.
TIC
TOC
TICK
TOCK
TIC
TOC

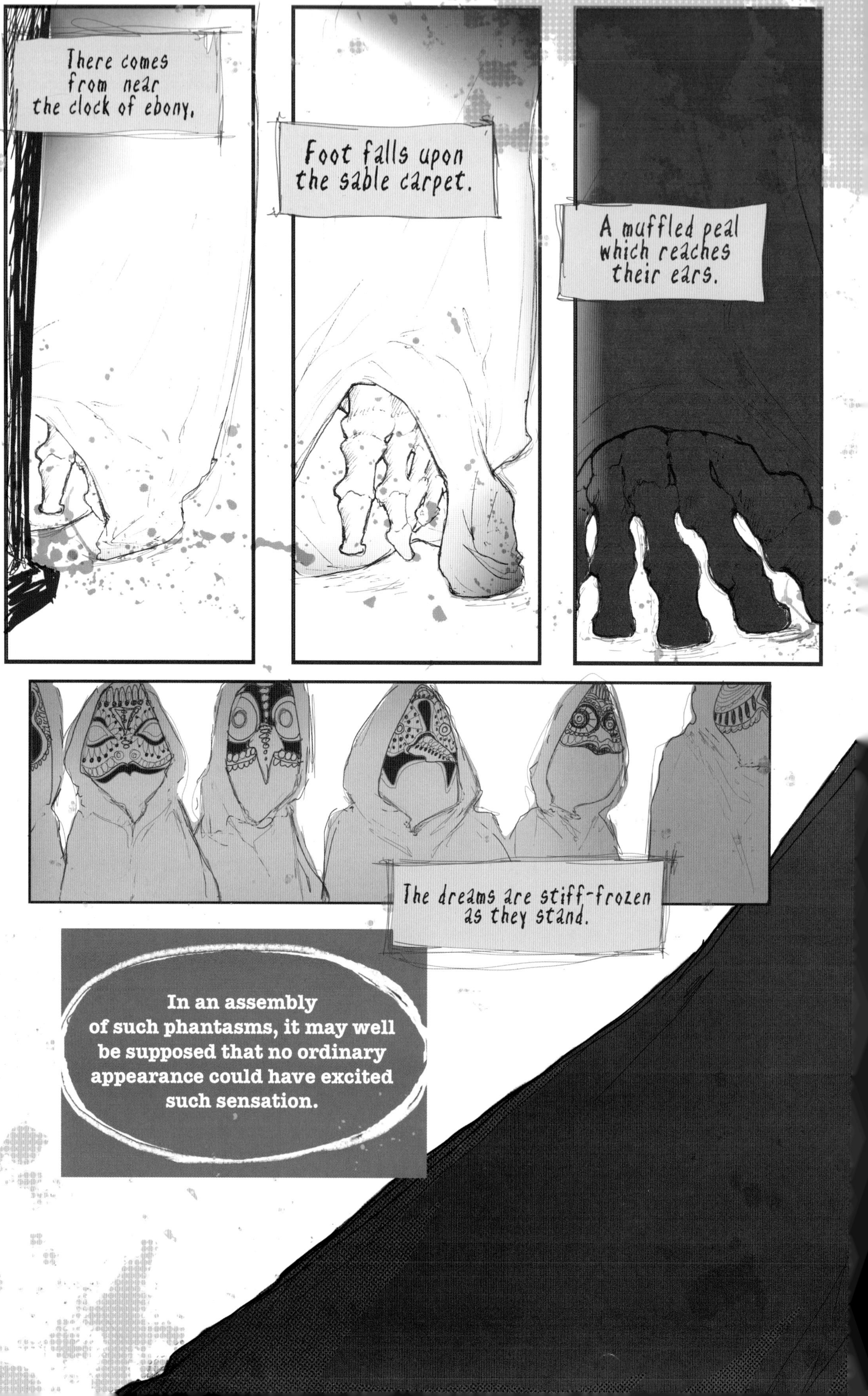
There comes from near the clock of ebony.
Foot falls upon the sable carpet.
A muffled peal which reaches their ears.
The dreams are stiff-frozen as they stand.
In an assembly of such phantasms, it may well be supposed that no ordinary appearance could have excited such sensation.

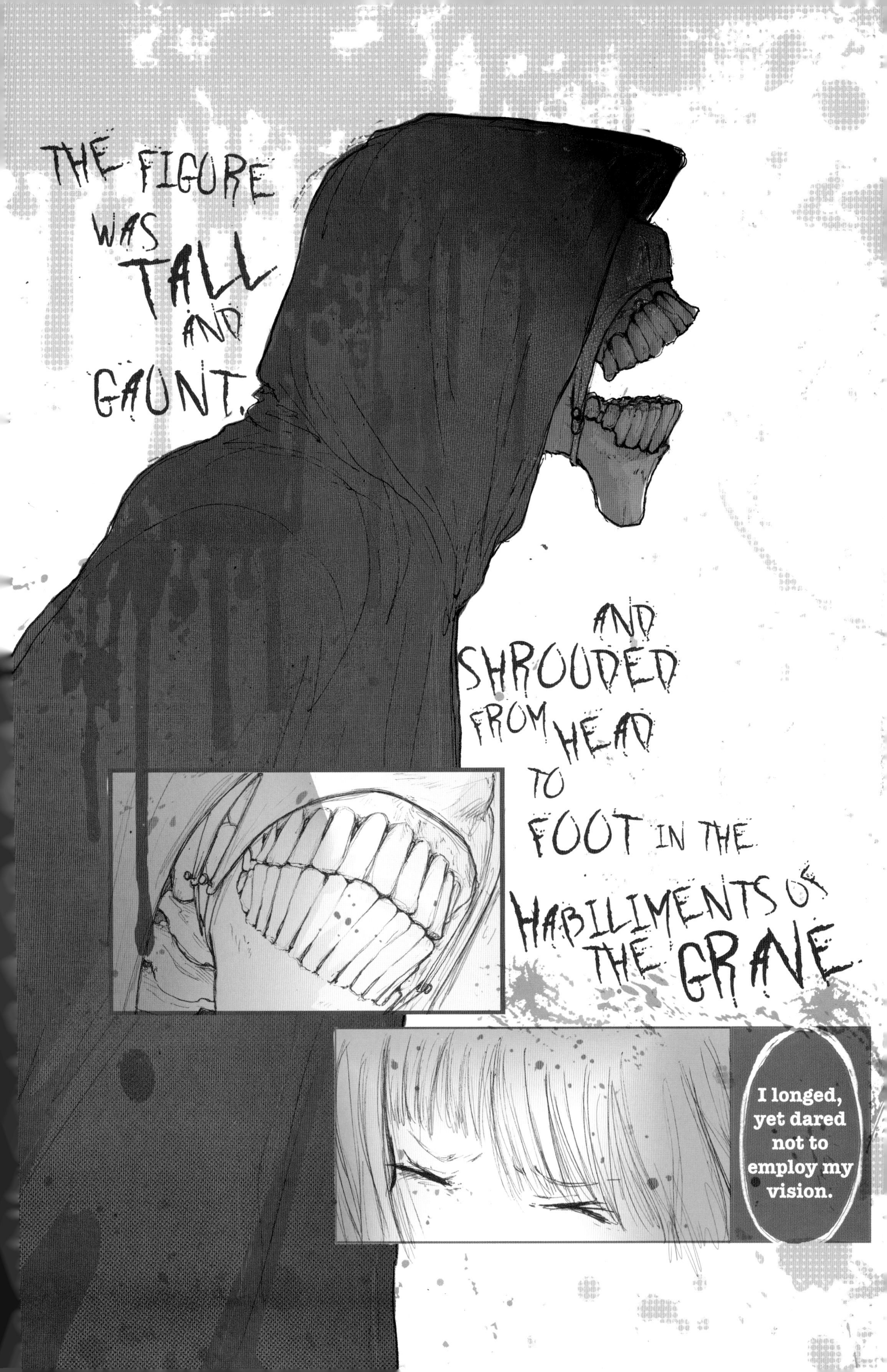
THE FIGURE WAS TALL AND GAUNT,
AND SHROUDED FROM HEAD TO FOOT IN THE HABILIMENTS OF THE GRAVE
I longed, yet dared not to employ my vision.

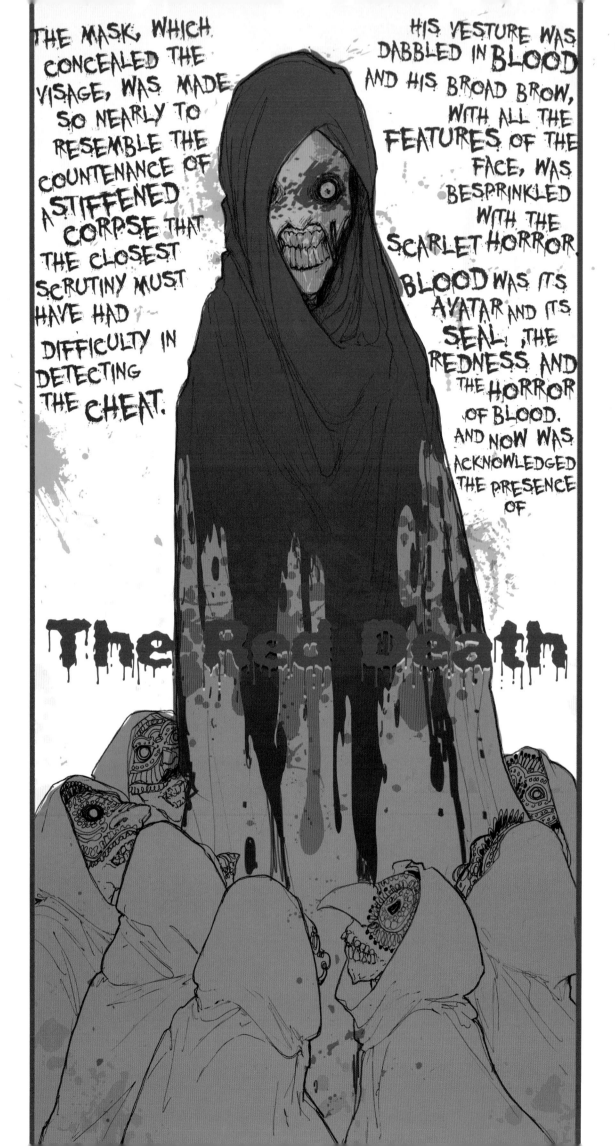

THE MASK, WHICH CONCEALED THE VISAGE, WAS MADE SO NEARLY TO RESEMBLE THE COUNTENANCE OF A STIFFENED CORPSE THAT THE CLOSEST SCRUTINY MUST HAVE HAD DIFFICULTY IN DETECTING THE CHEAT.

HIS VESTURE WAS DABBLED IN BLOOD AND HIS BROAD BROW, WITH ALL THE FEATURES OF THE FACE, WAS BESPRINKLED WITH THE SCARLET HORROR. BLOOD WAS ITS AVATAR AND ITS SEAL, THE REDNESS AND THE HORROR OF BLOOD. AND NOW WAS ACKNOWLEDGED THE PRESENCE OF

The Red Death

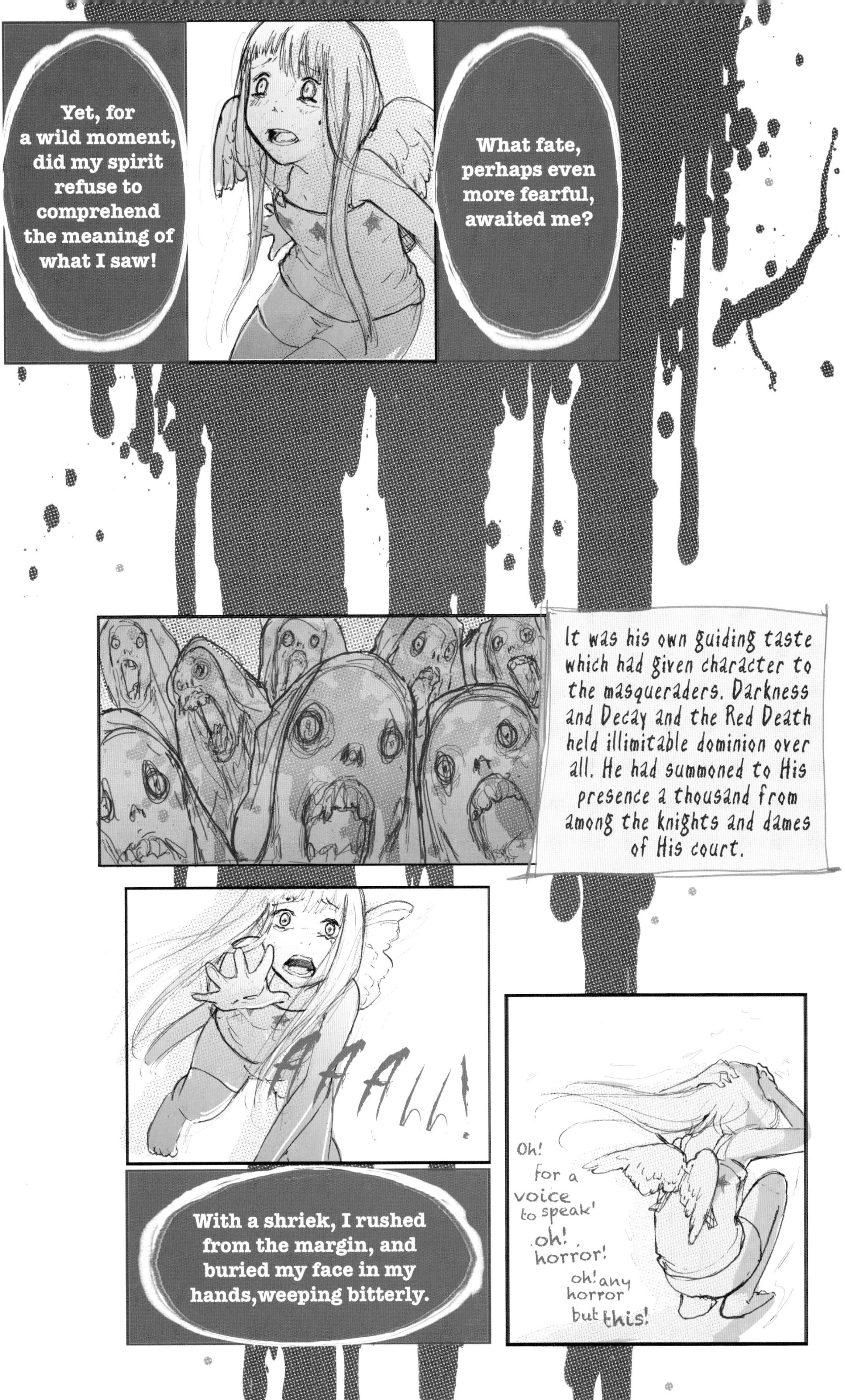
Yet, for a wild moment, did my spirit refuse to comprehend the meaning of what I saw!
What fate, perhaps even more fearful, awaited me?
It was his own guiding taste which had given character to the masqueraders. Darkness and Decay and the Red Death held illimitable dominion over all. He had summoned to His presence a thousand from among the knights and dames of His court.
AAAhh!
With a shriek, I rushed from the margin, and buried my face in my hands,weeping bitterly.
Oh! for a voice to speak! oh! horror! oh! any horror but this!

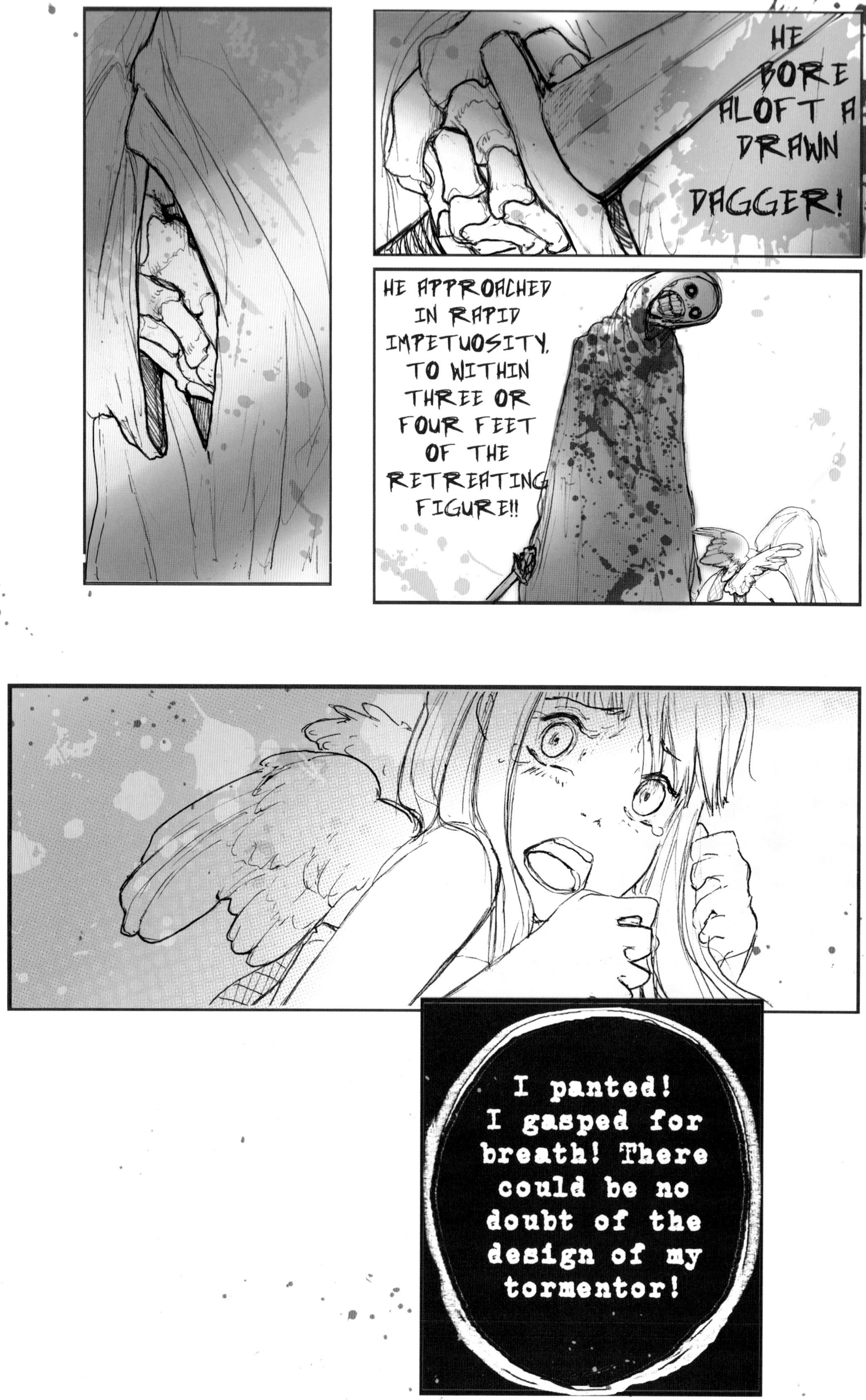
HE BORE ALOFT A DRAWN DAGGER!
HE APPROACHED IN RAPID IMPETUOSITY, TO WITHIN THREE OR FOUR FEET OF THE RETREATING FIGURE!!
I panted! I gasped for breath! There could be no doubt of the design of my tormentor!

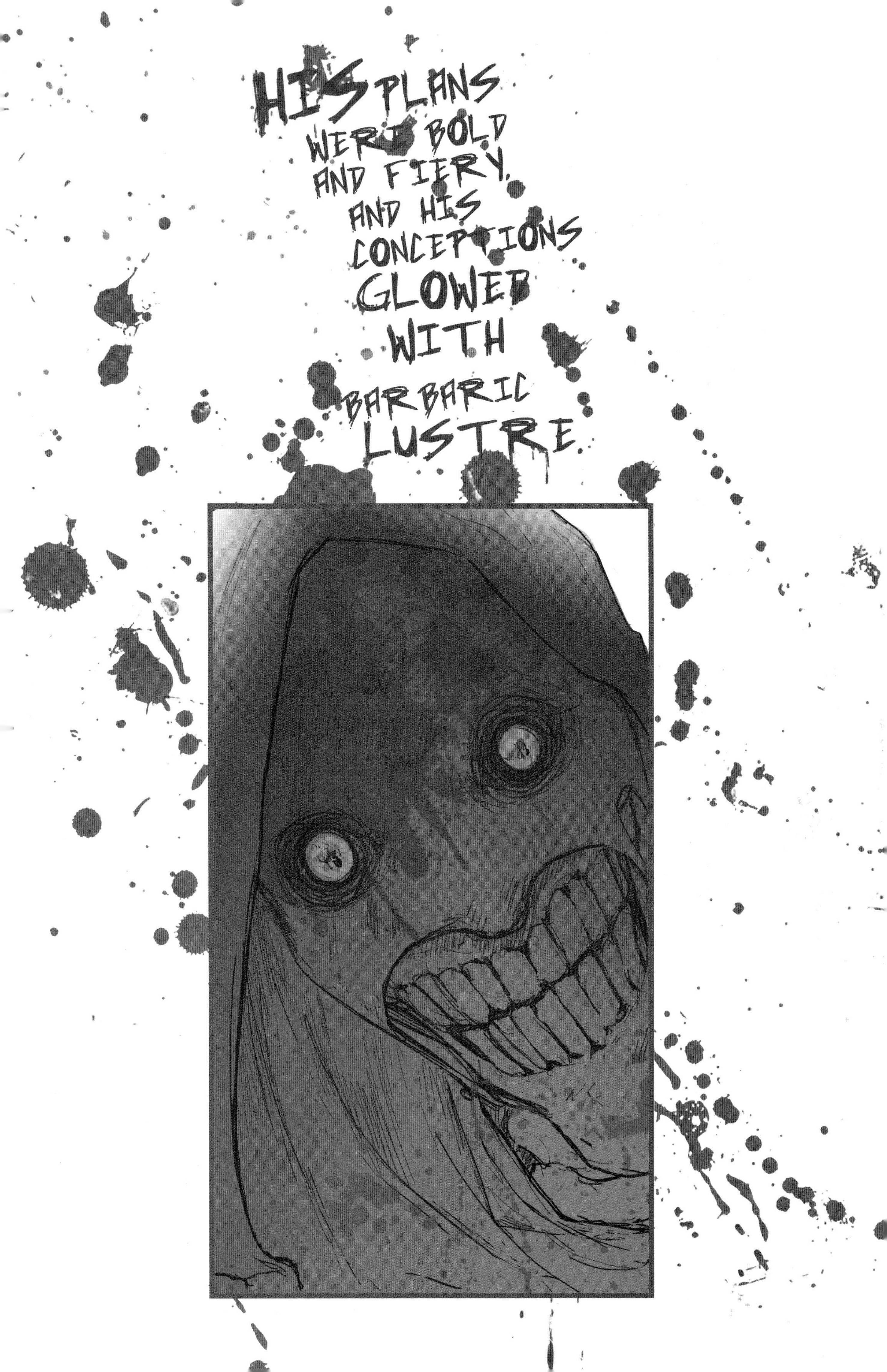
HIS PLANS WERE BOLD AND FIERY, AND HIS CONCEPTIONS GLOWED WITH BARBARIC LUSTRE.

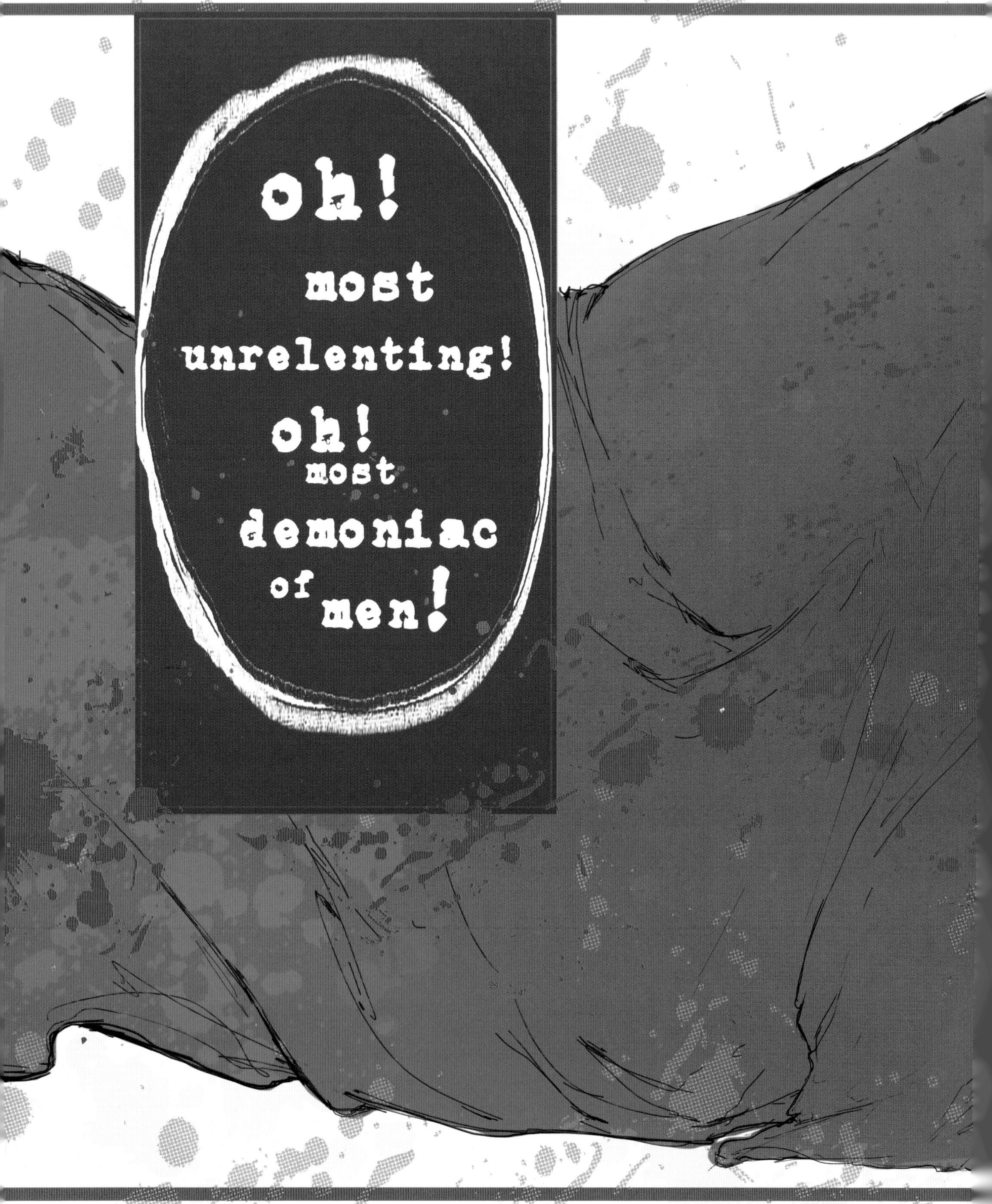
oh! most unrelenting! oh! most demoniac of men!

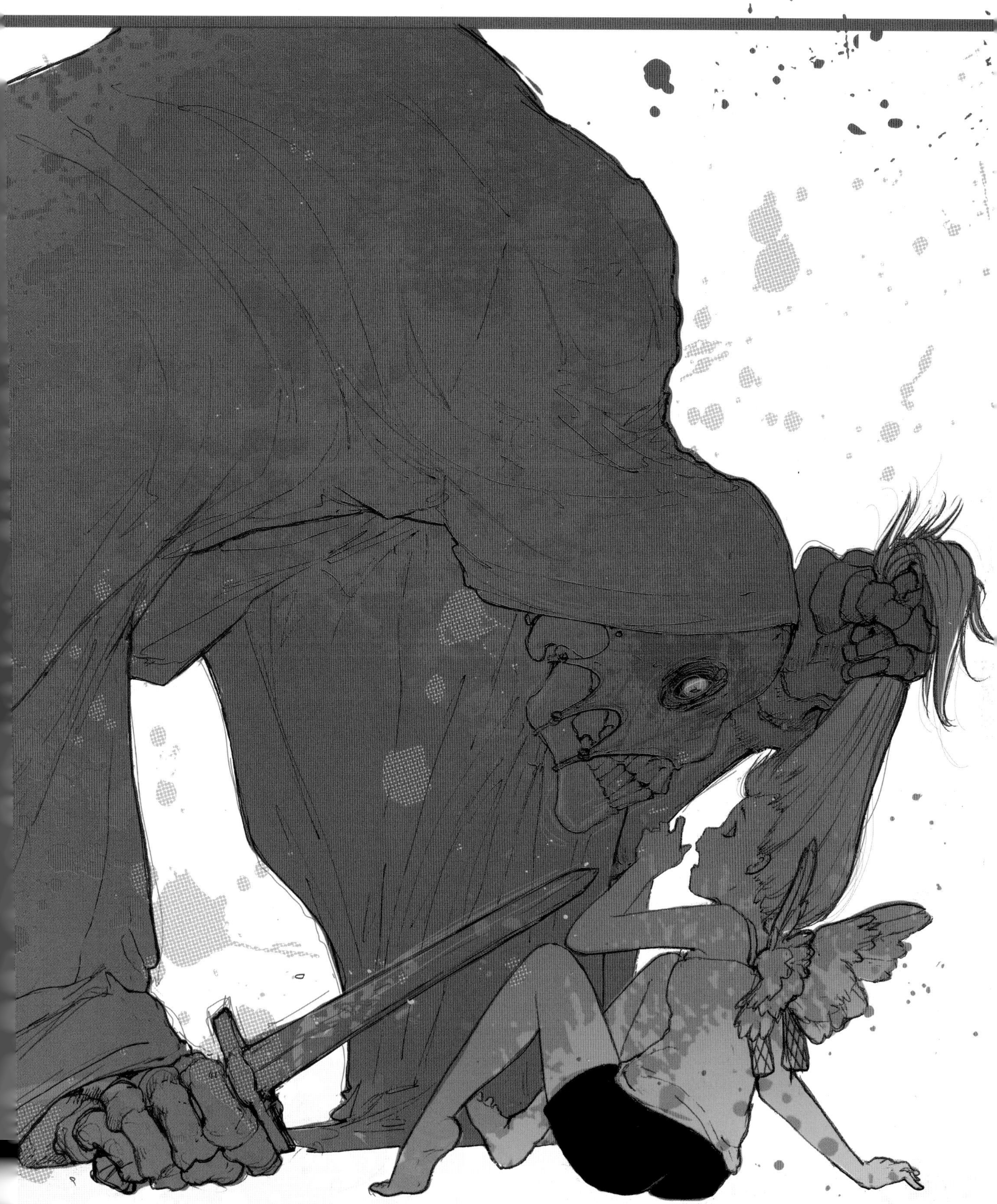

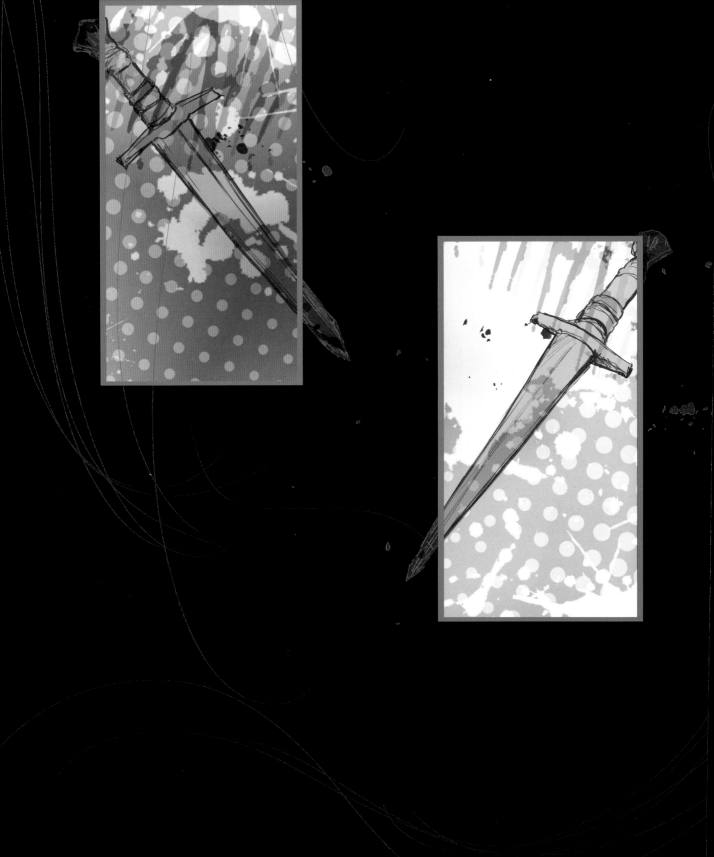

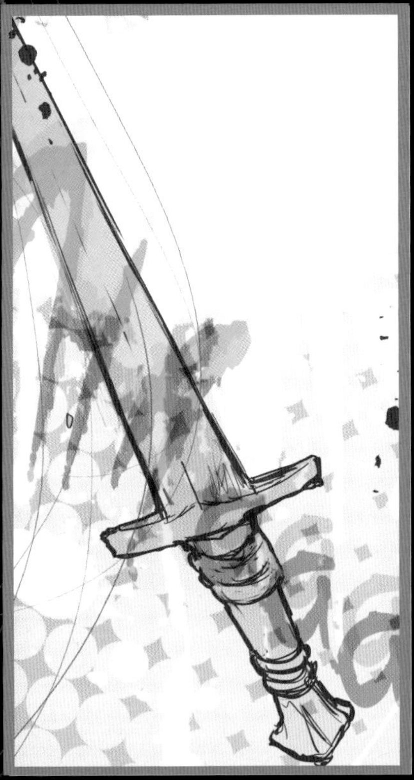

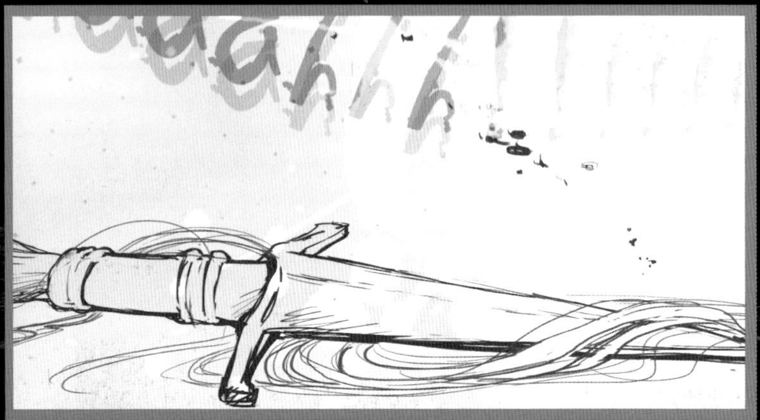

AND, ANON
THERE STRIKES
THE EBONY
CLOCK, WHICH
STANDS IN THE
HALL OF THE
VELVET.

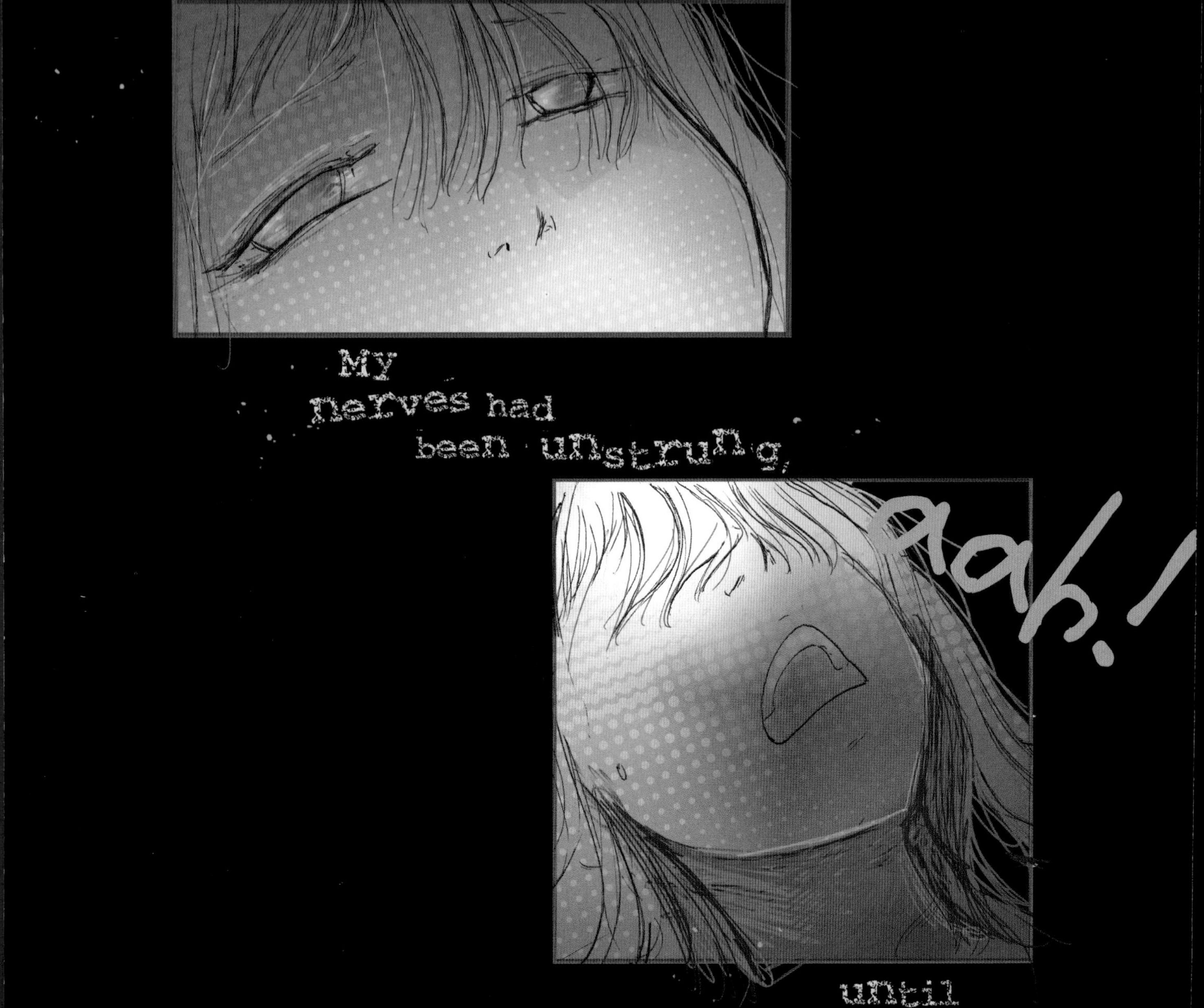
My nerves had been unstrung,
aah!
until

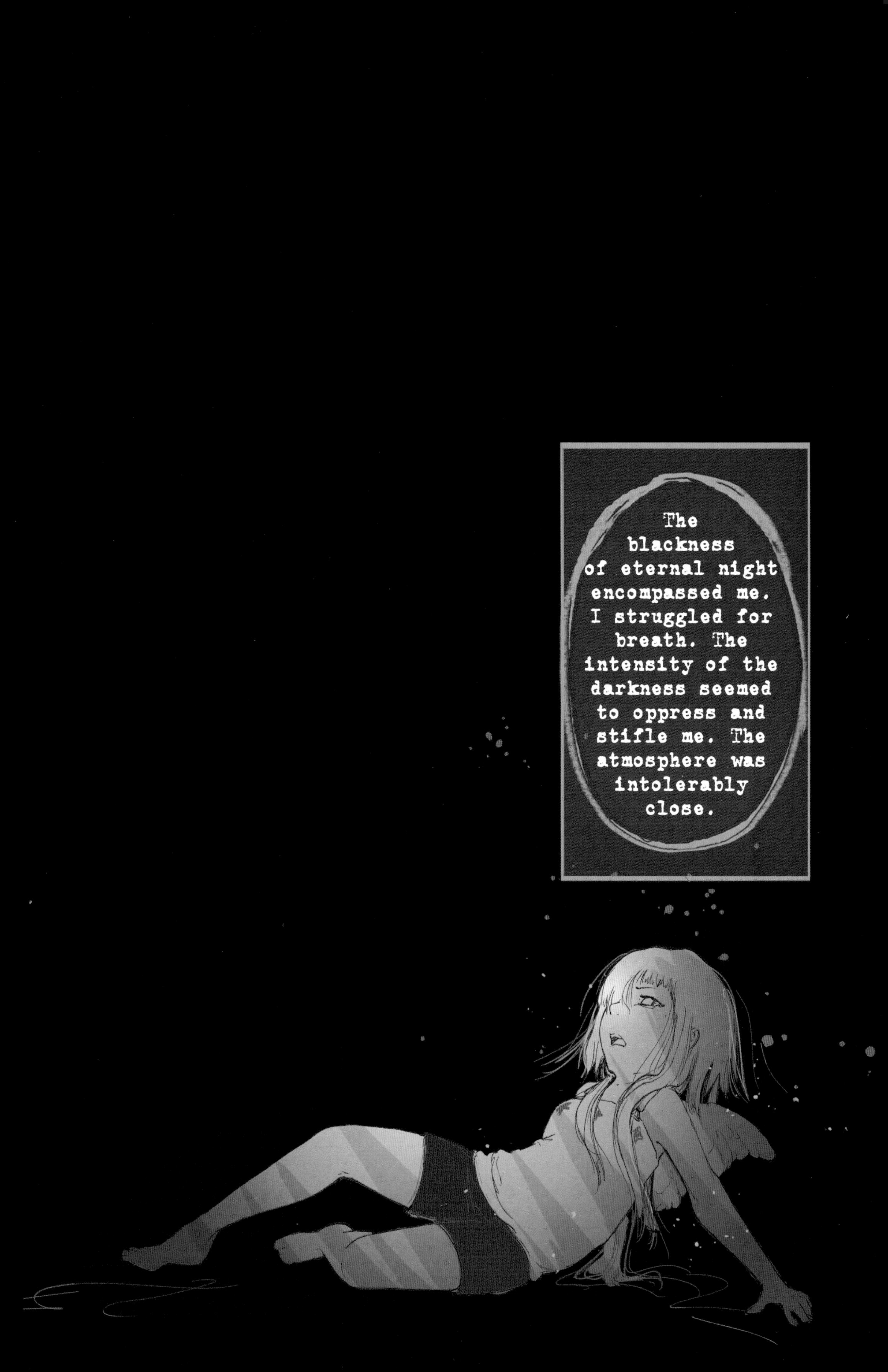
The blackness of eternal night encompassed me. I struggled for breath. The intensity of the darkness seemed to oppress and stifle me. The atmosphere was intolerably close.

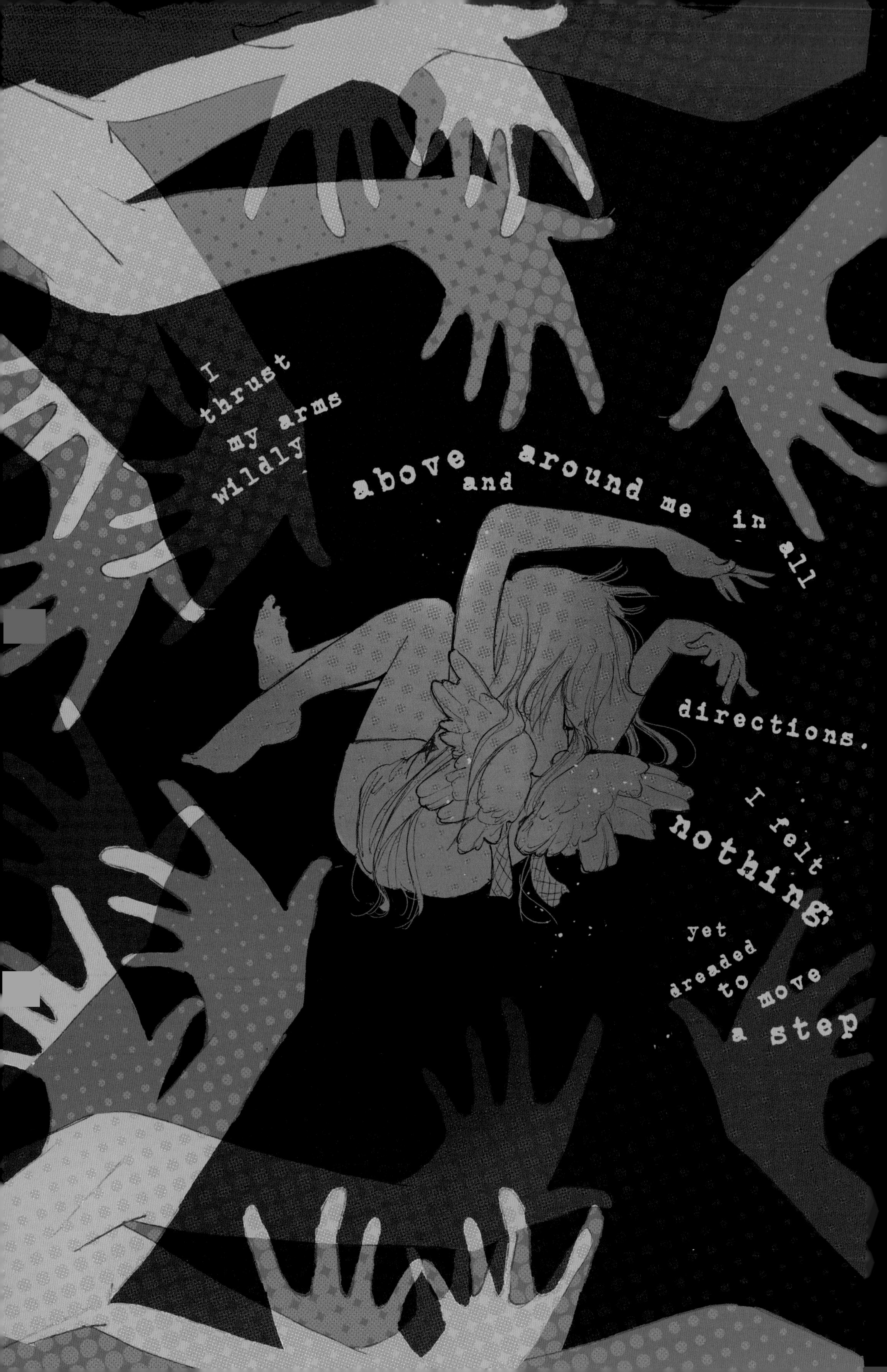
I thrust my arms wildly
above and around me in all directions.
I felt nothing,
yet dreaded to move a step

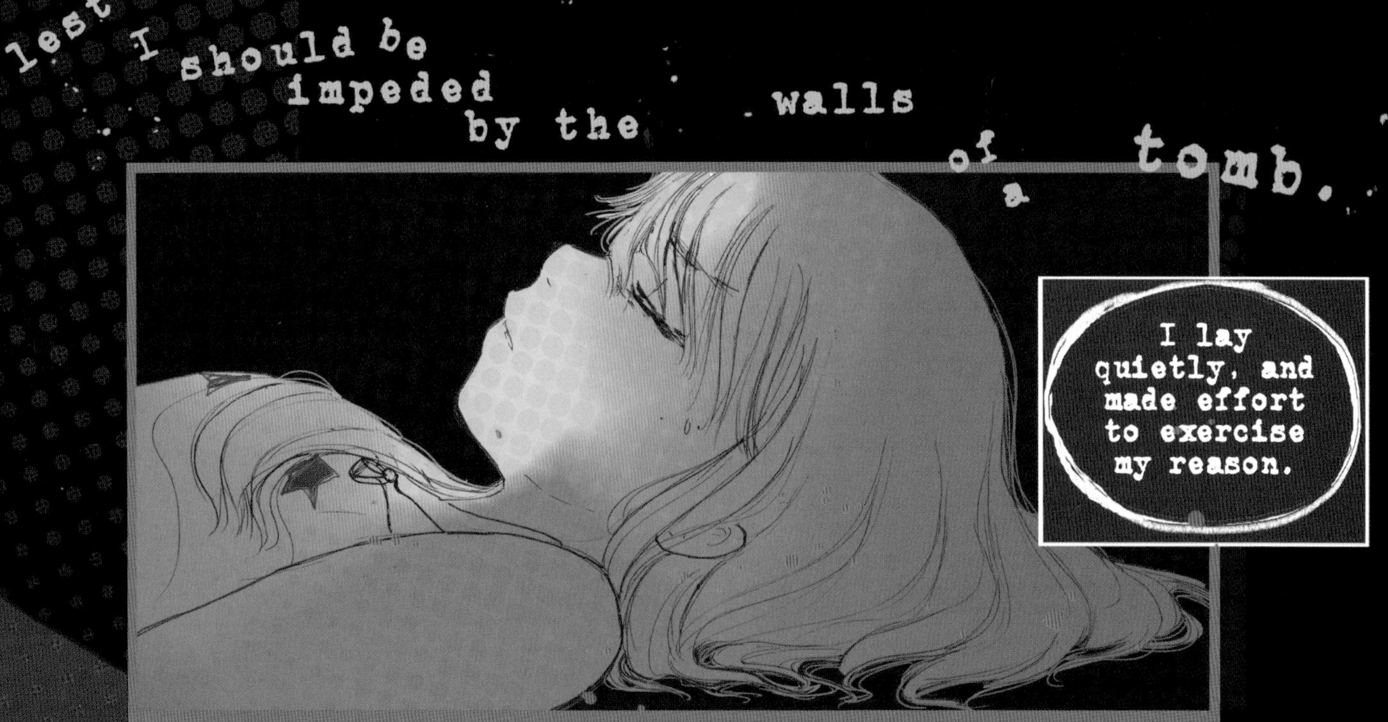
lest I should be impeded by the walls of a tomb.
I lay quietly, and made effort to exercise my reason.

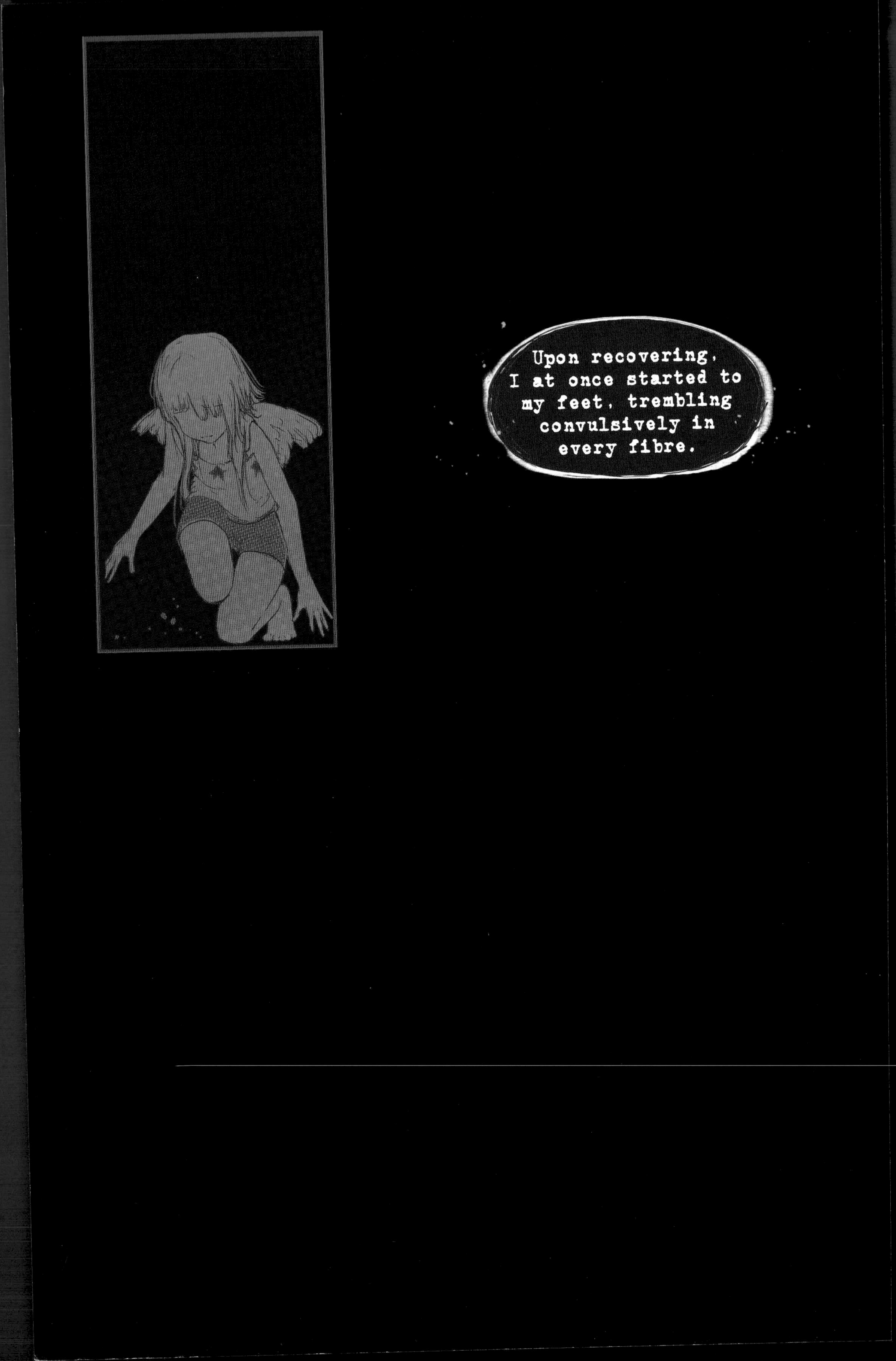
Upon recovering, I at once started to my feet, trembling convulsively in every fibre.

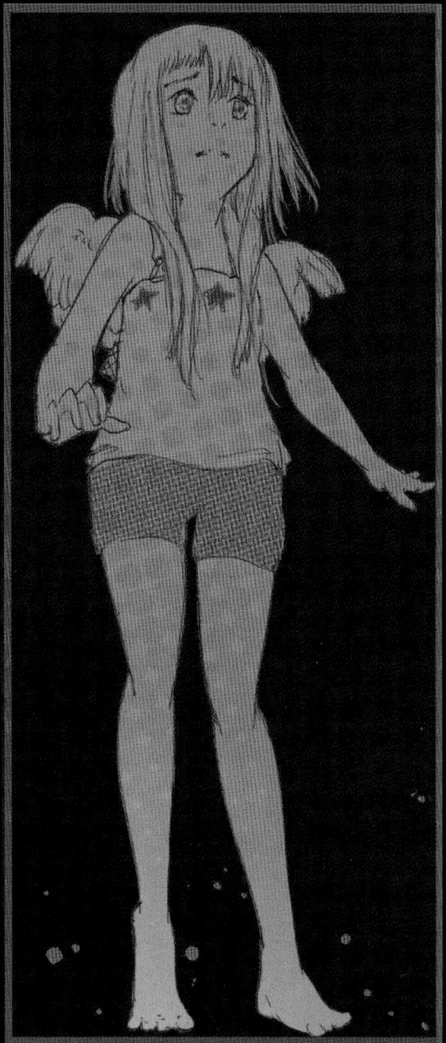
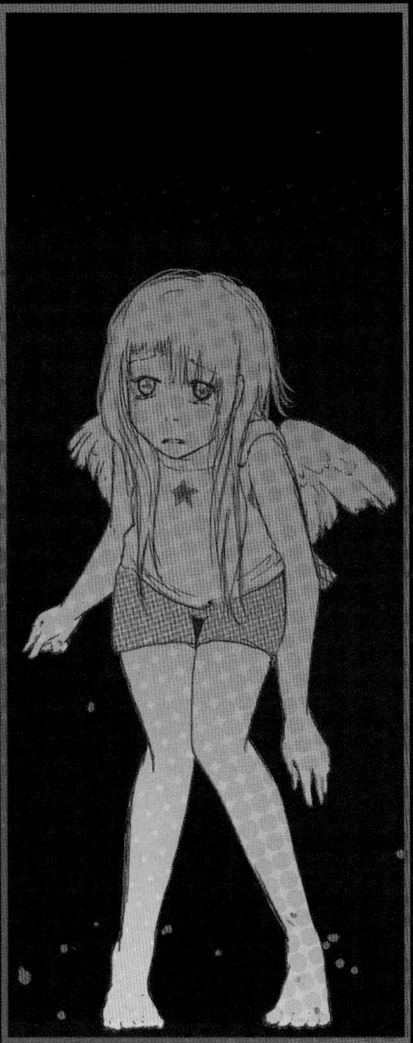

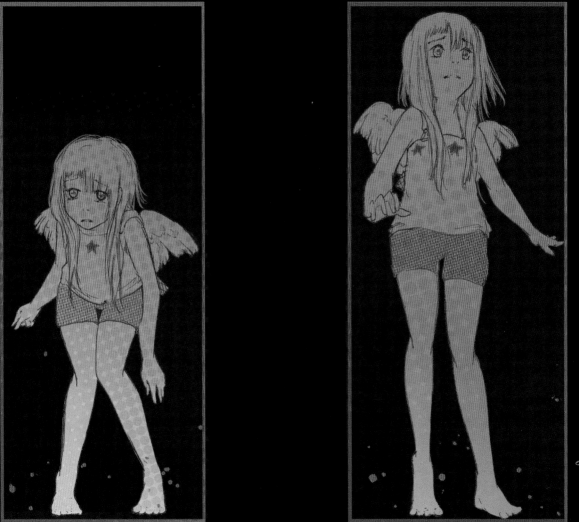

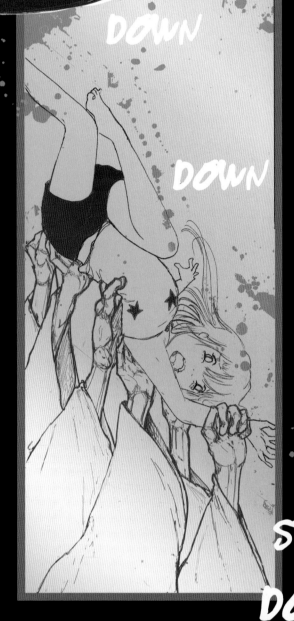

Shadows of memory tell, indistinctly, of tall figures that lifted and bore me in silence...

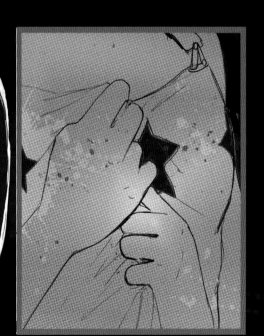

They tell also of a vague horror at my heart, on account of that heart's unnatural stillness.

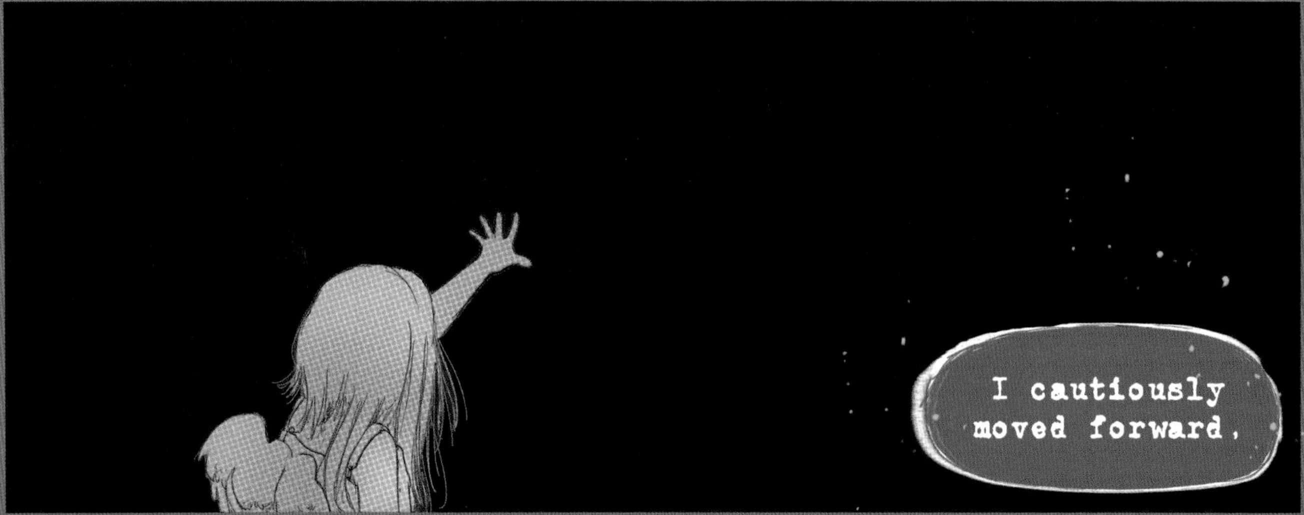
I cautiously moved forward,

with my
arms
extended

and
my
eyes
straining
from
their
sockets
in

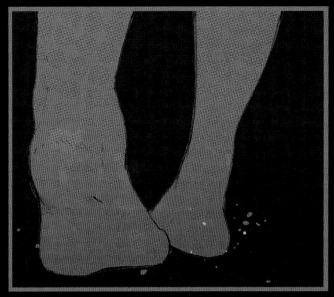

the

hope of

catching

some

faint

ray of

light.

I proceeded for many paces. But still all was blackness and vacancy. A hideous dizziness oppressed me at the mere idea of the interminableness of

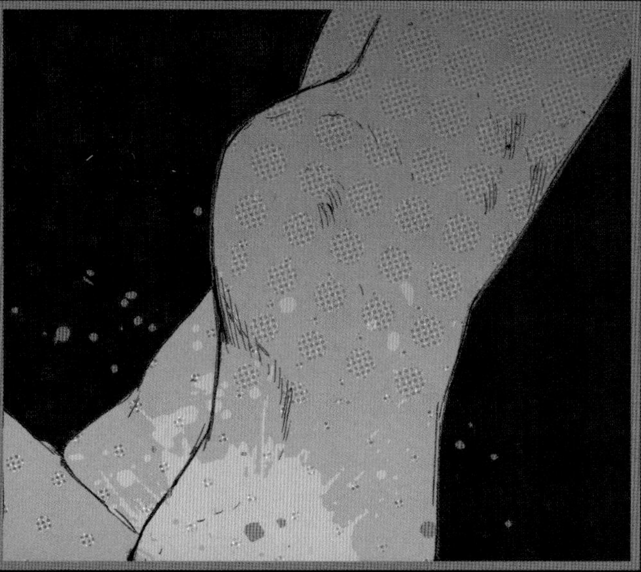

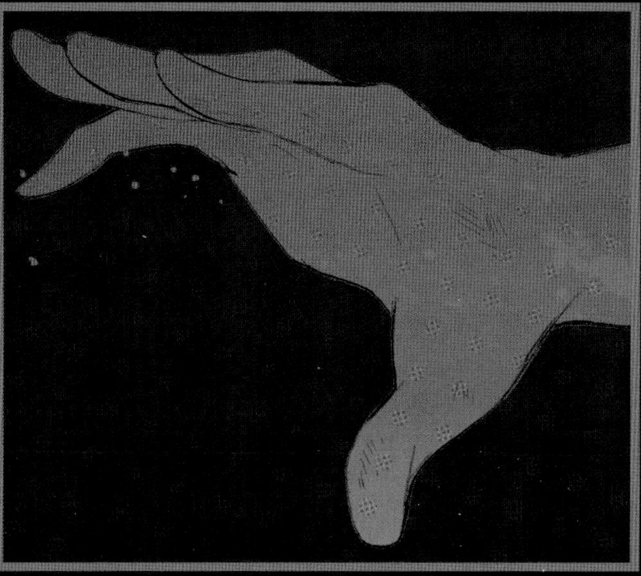

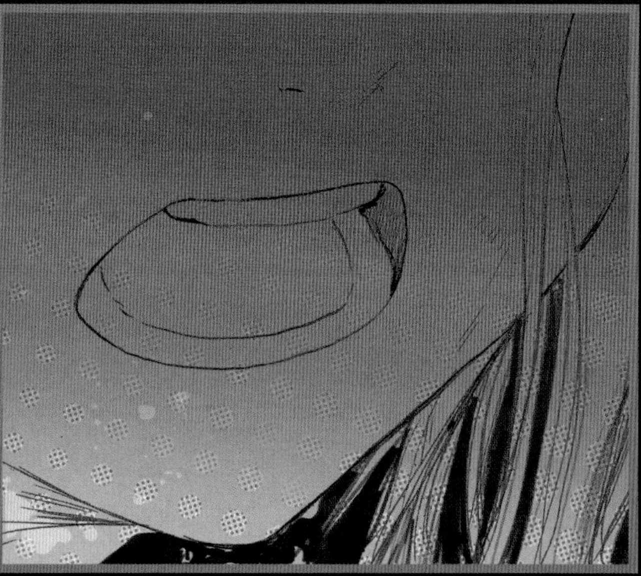

And now, as
I still continued
to step cautiously onward,
there came thronging upon
my recollection a
thousand vague rumors
of the horrors
of Toledo.

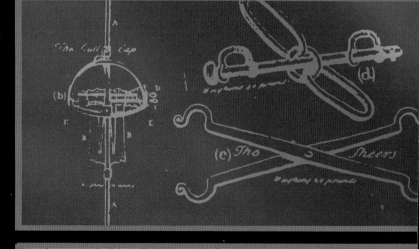

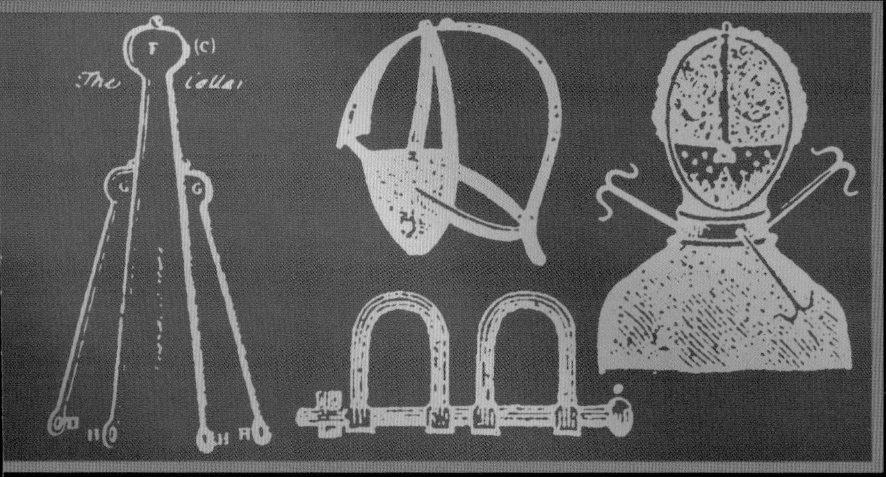
The collar

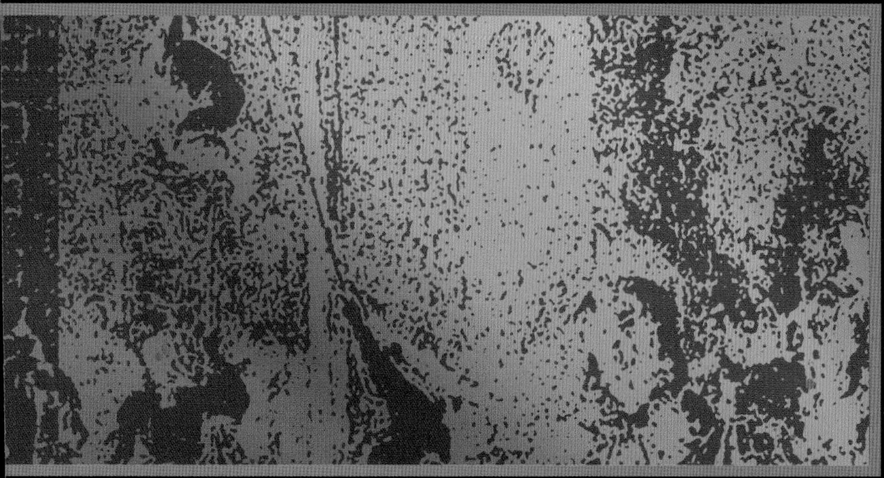

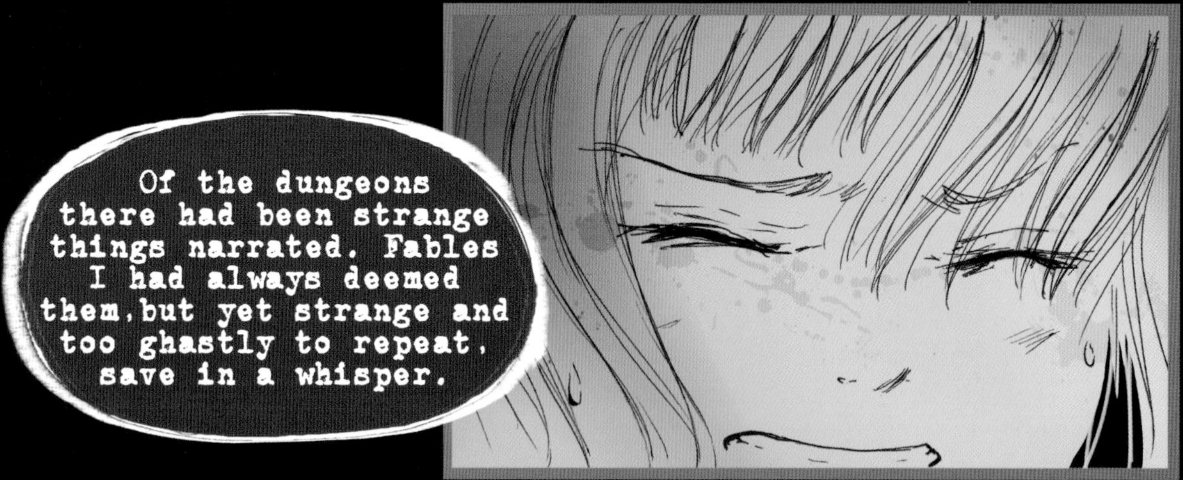
Of the dungeons there had been strange things narrated. Fables I had always deemed them,but yet strange and too ghastly to repeat, save in a whisper.

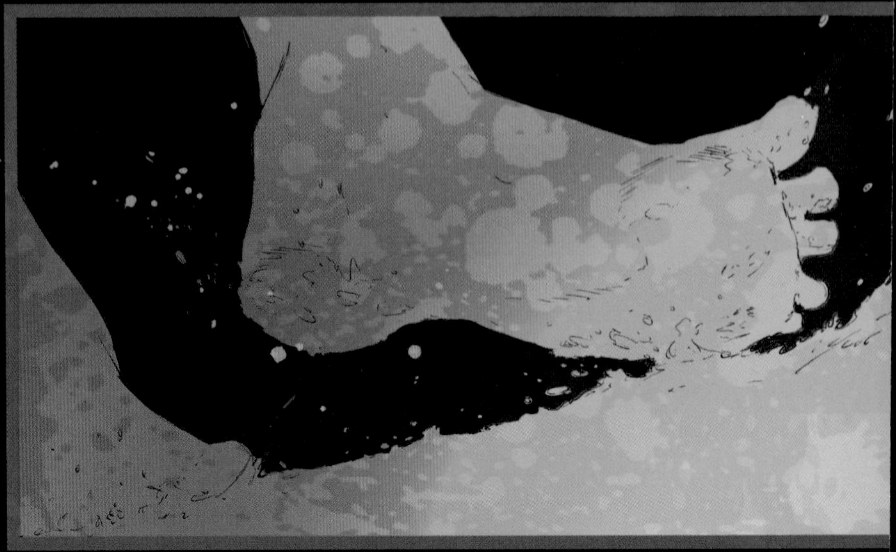

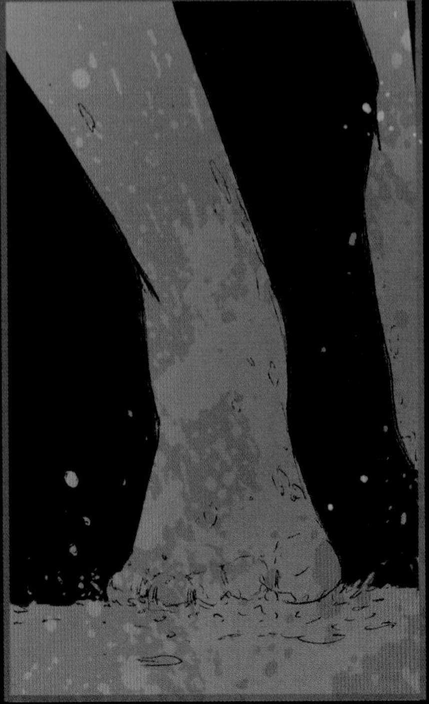

The ground was moist and slippery.

I staggered onward for some

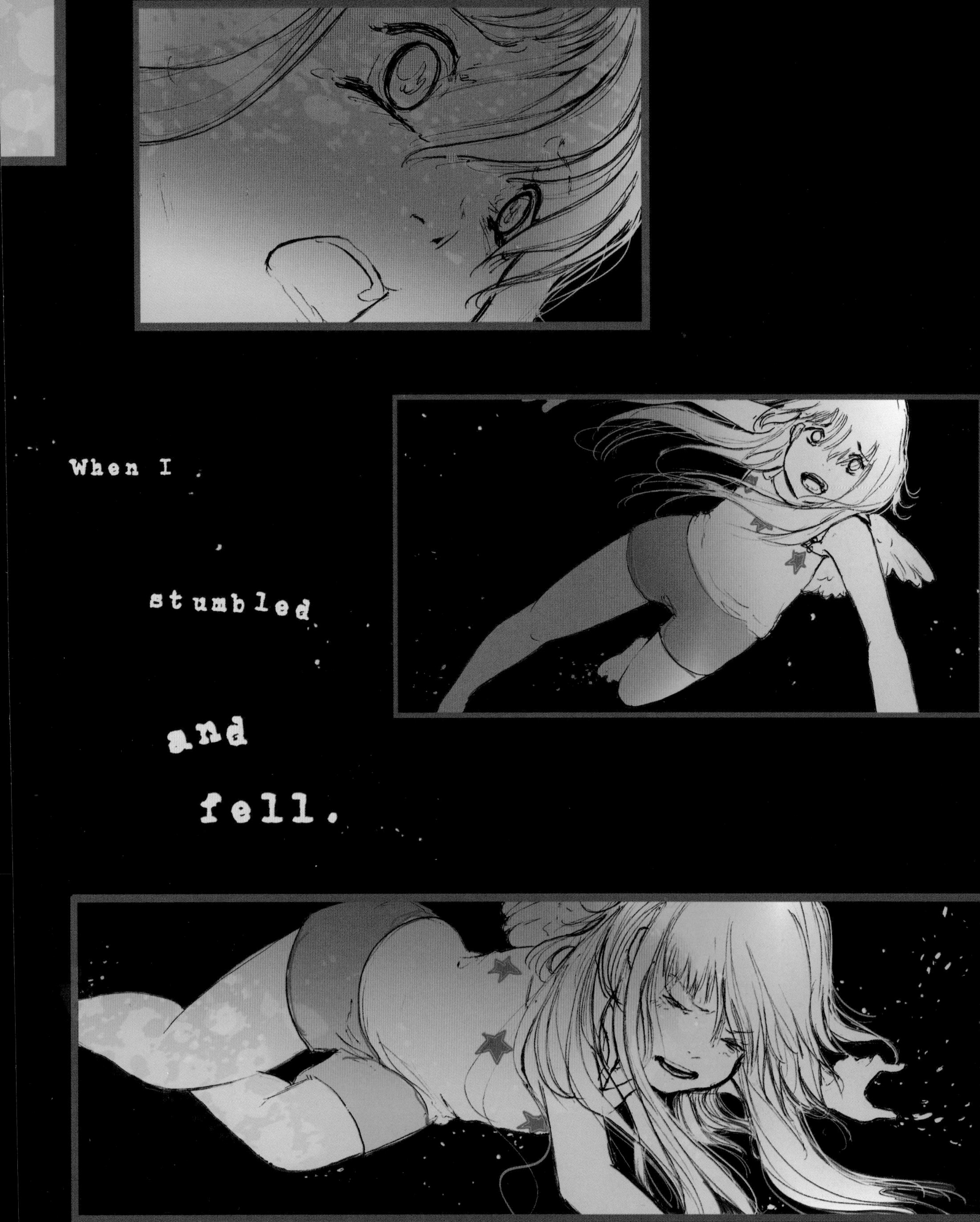
When I
stumbled
and
fell.

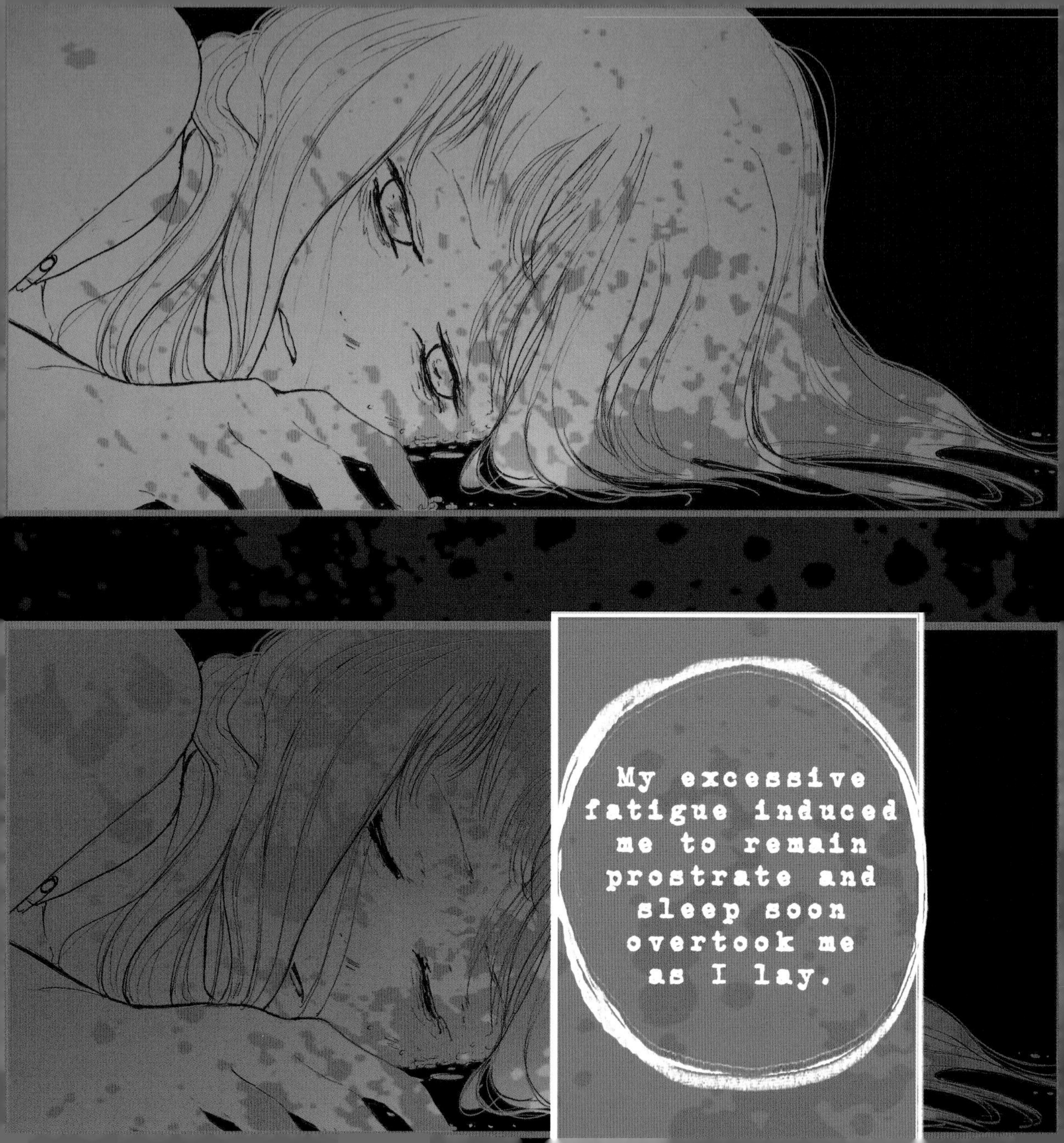
My excessive fatigue induced me to remain prostrate and sleep soon overtook me as I lay.

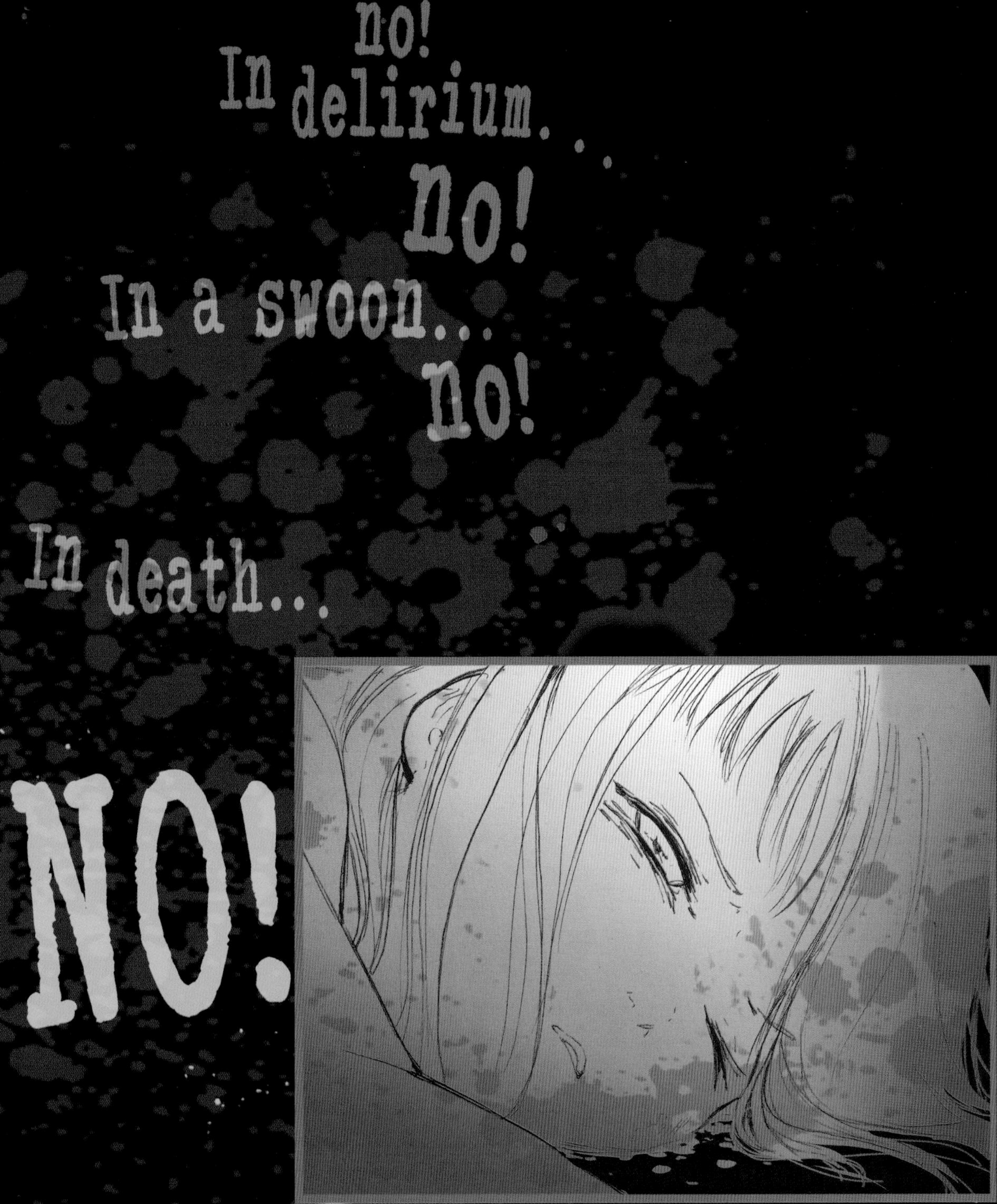
no!
In delirium...
No!
In a swoon...
No!
In death...
NO!

In the confusion attending my fall, I did not immediately apprehend a somewhat startling circumstance. By a wild sulphurous lustre, I was enabled to see the extent and aspect of the prison.

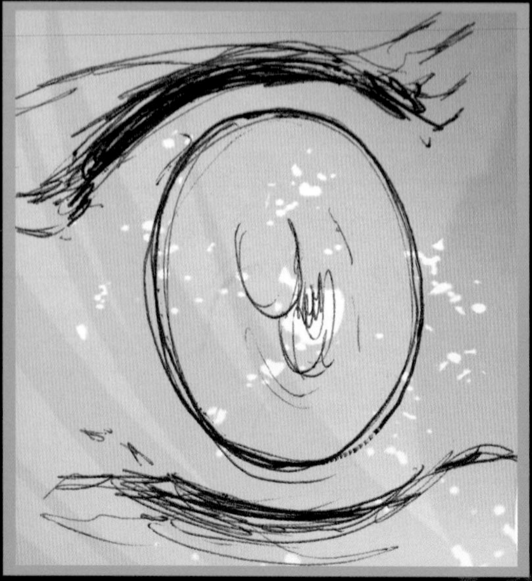

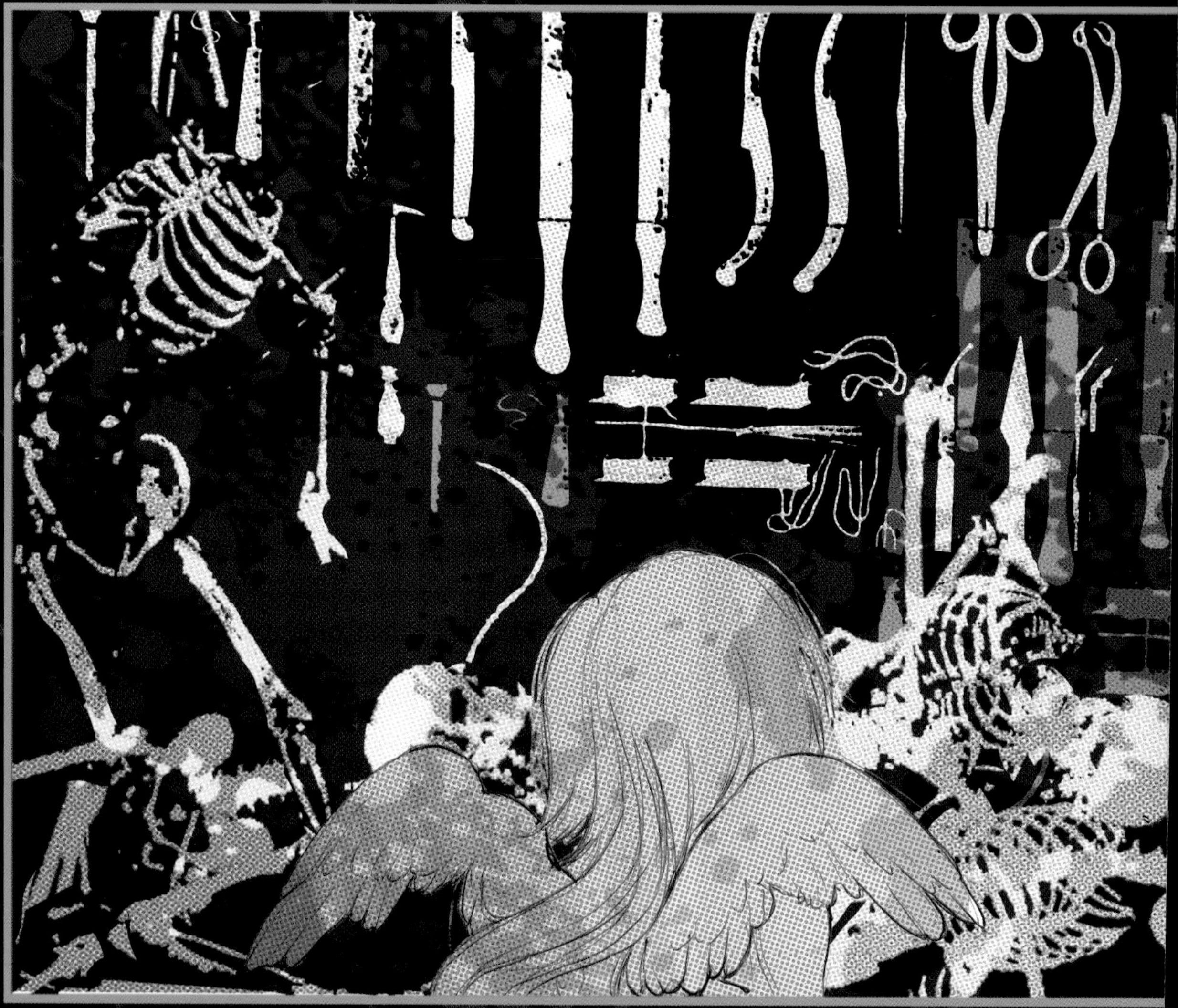

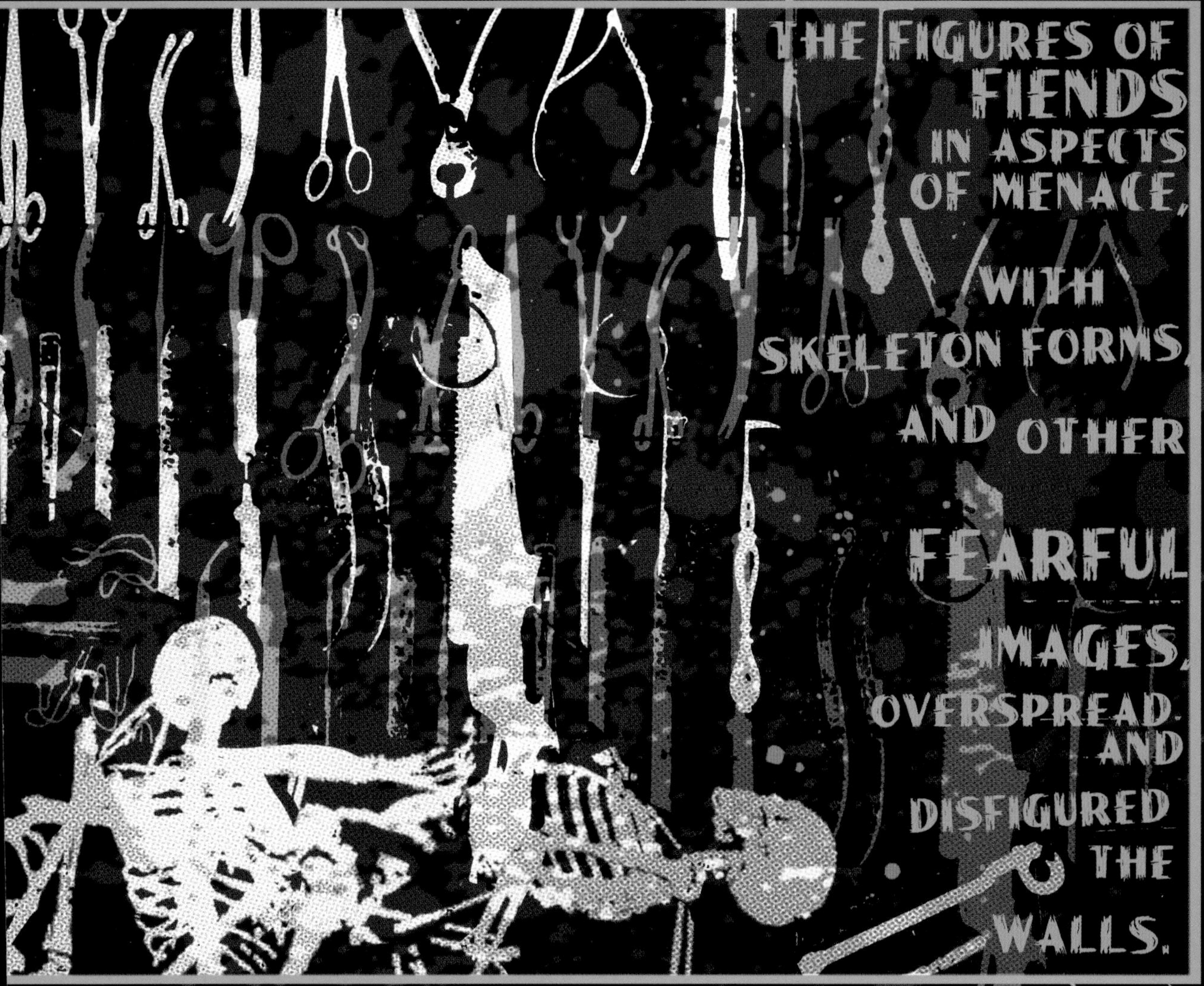
THE FIGURES OF FIENDS IN ASPECTS OF MENACE, WITH SKELETON FORMS, AND OTHER FEARFUL IMAGES, OVERSPREAD AND DISFIGURED THE WALLS.
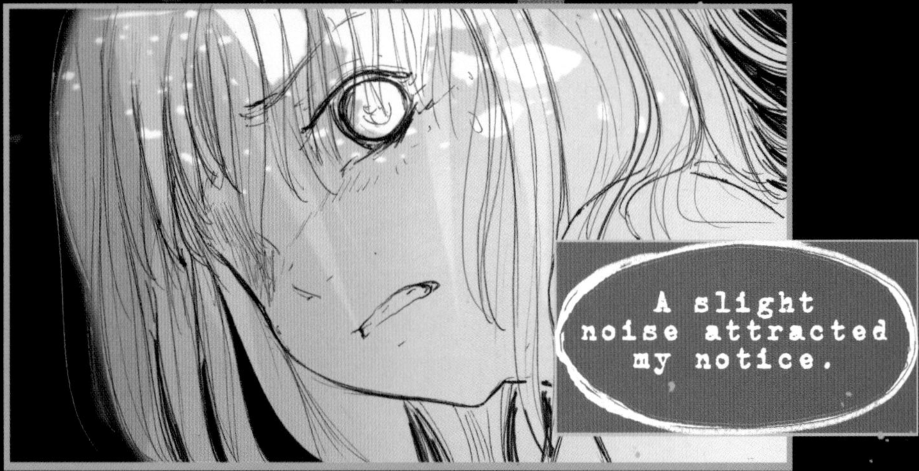
A slight noise attracted my notice.

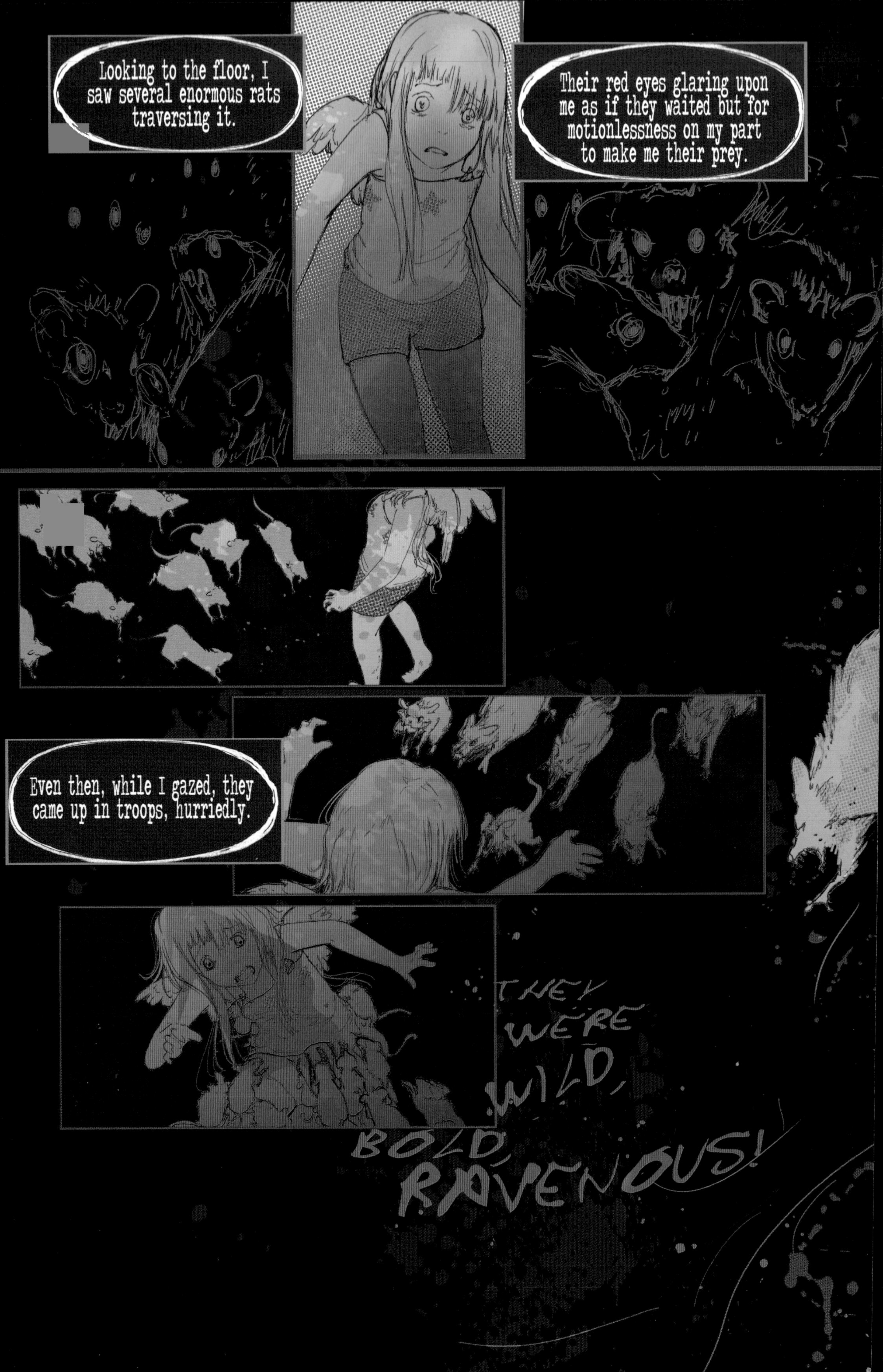
Looking to the floor, I saw several enormous rats traversing it.
Their red eyes glaring upon me as if they waited but for motionlessness on my part to make me their prey.
Even then, while I gazed, they came up in troops, hurriedly.
THEY WERE WILD, BOLD, RAVENOUS!

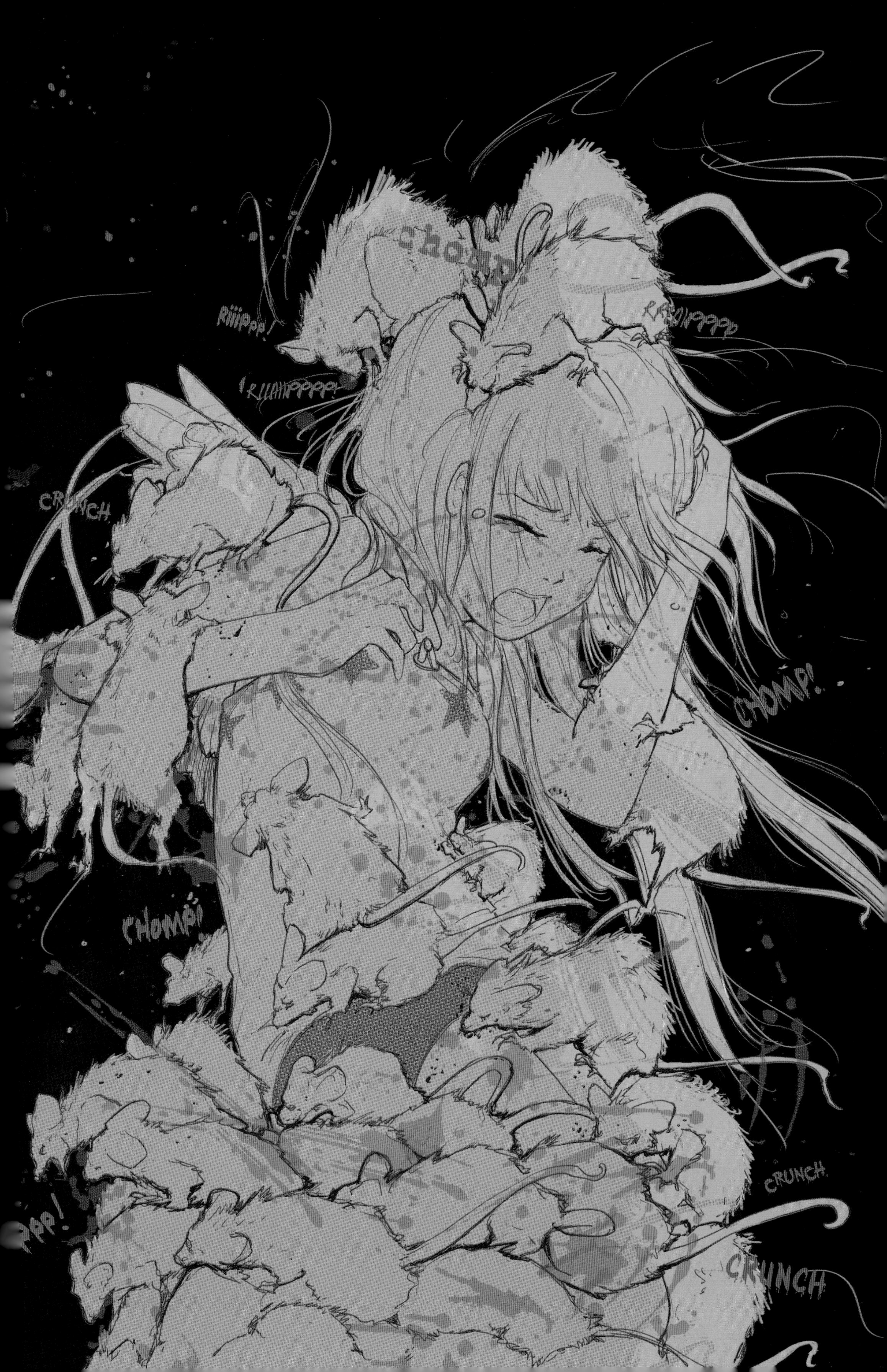
CHOMP
Riiippp!
RIIIIPPPPP!
CHOMP!
CRUNCH
CHOMP!
CRUNCH
CRUNCH

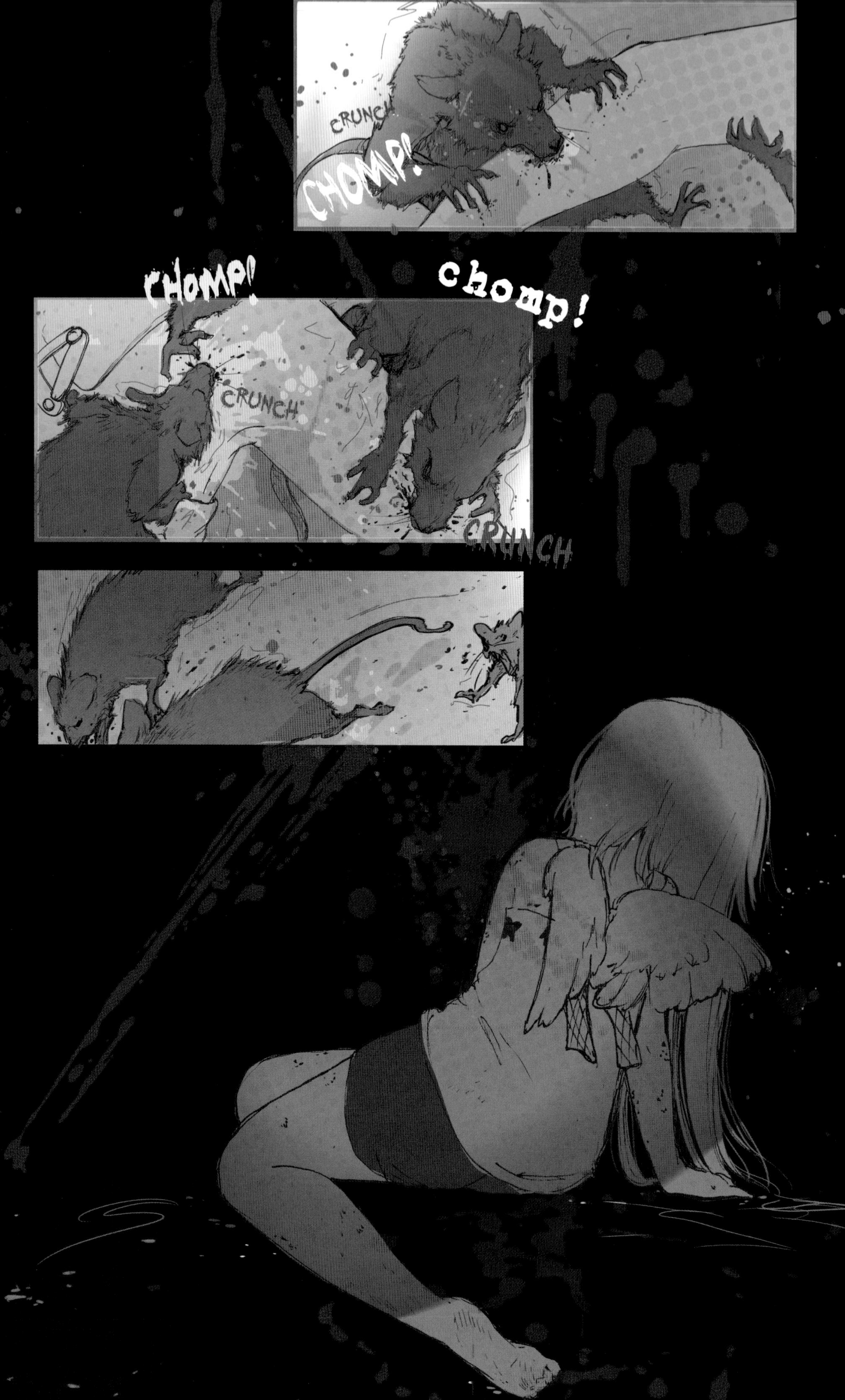
CRUNCH
CHOMP!
chomp!
CHOMP!
CRUNCH
CRUNCH

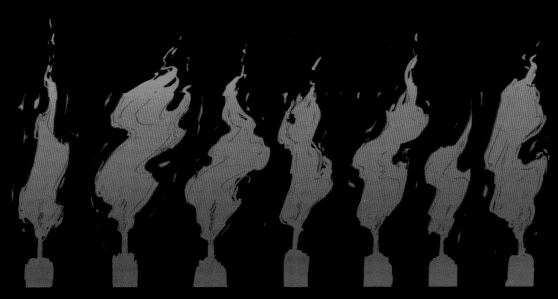

And then my
vision fell upon the
seven tall candles,
the colors seemed
faded and blurred, as
if from the effects
of a damp
atmosphere.

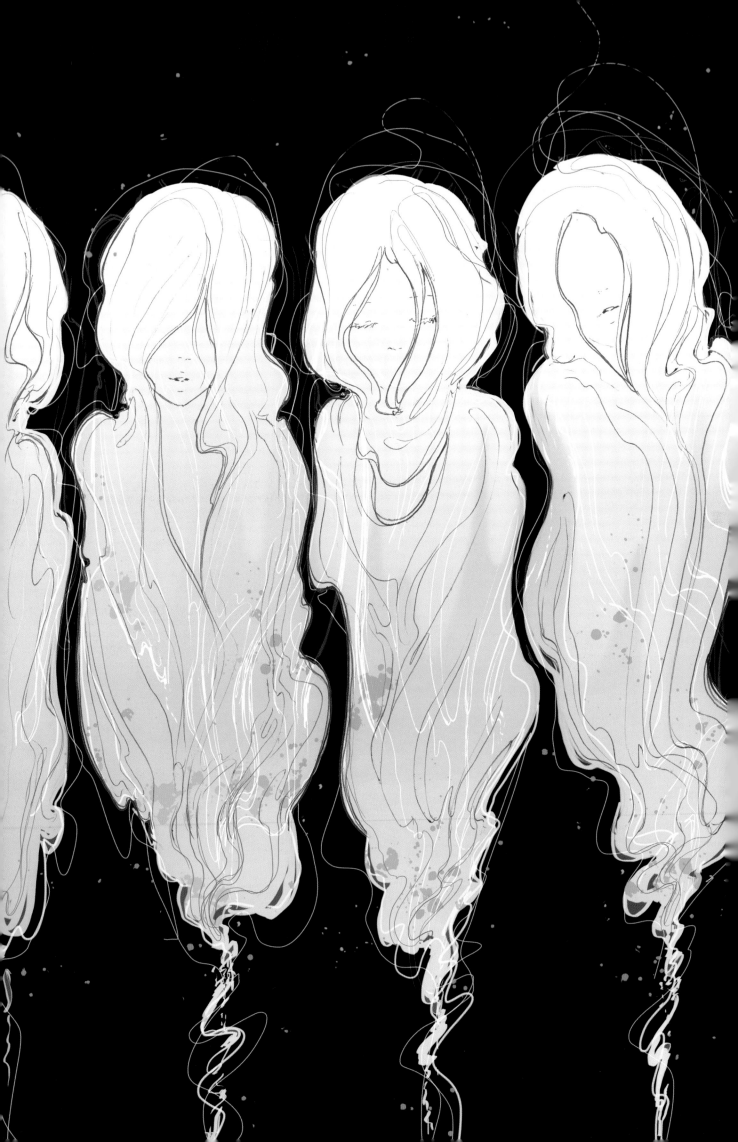

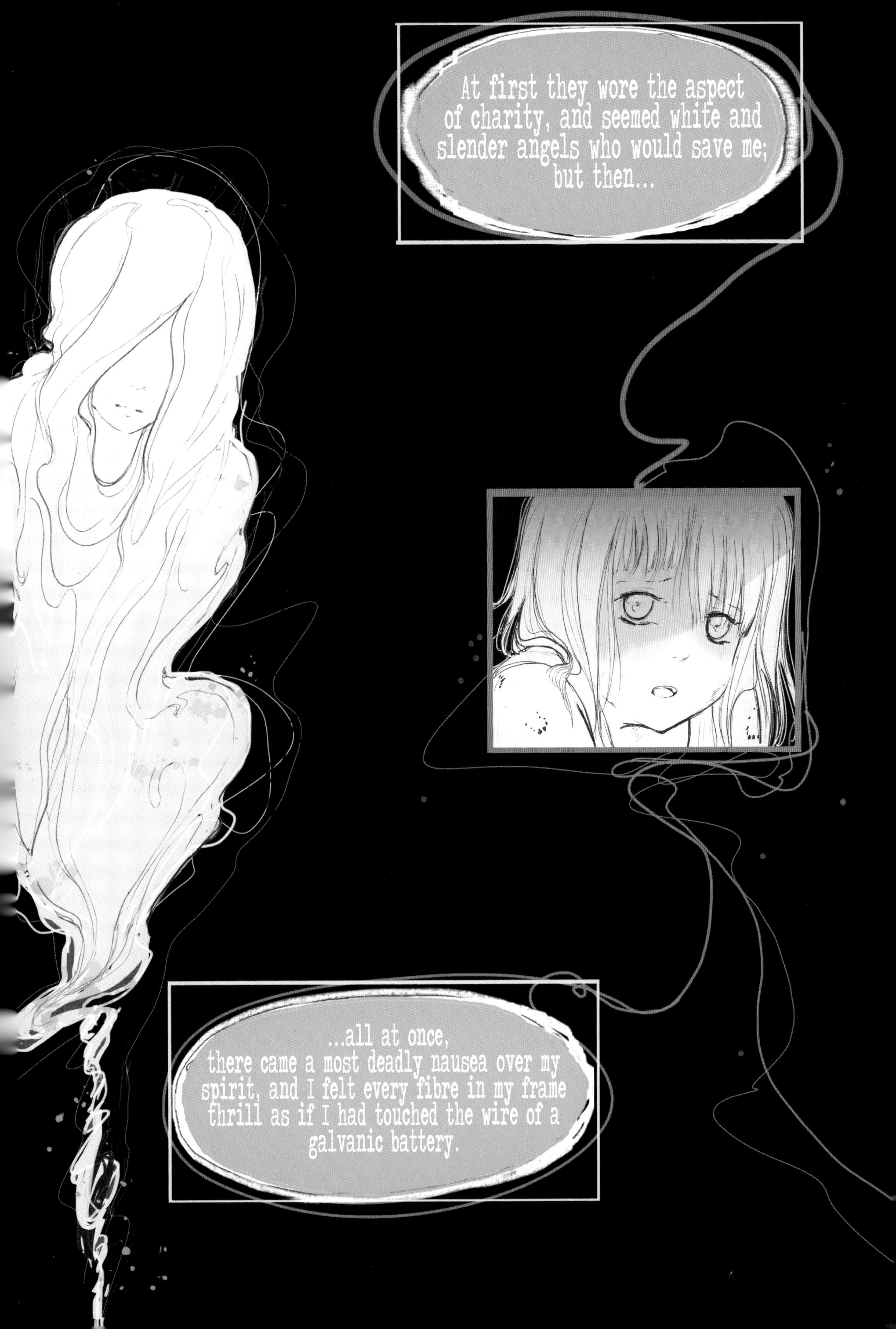
At first they wore the aspect of charity, and seemed white and slender angels who would save me; but then...
...all at once, there came a most deadly nausea over my spirit, and I felt every fibre in my frame thrill as if I had touched the wire of a galvanic battery.

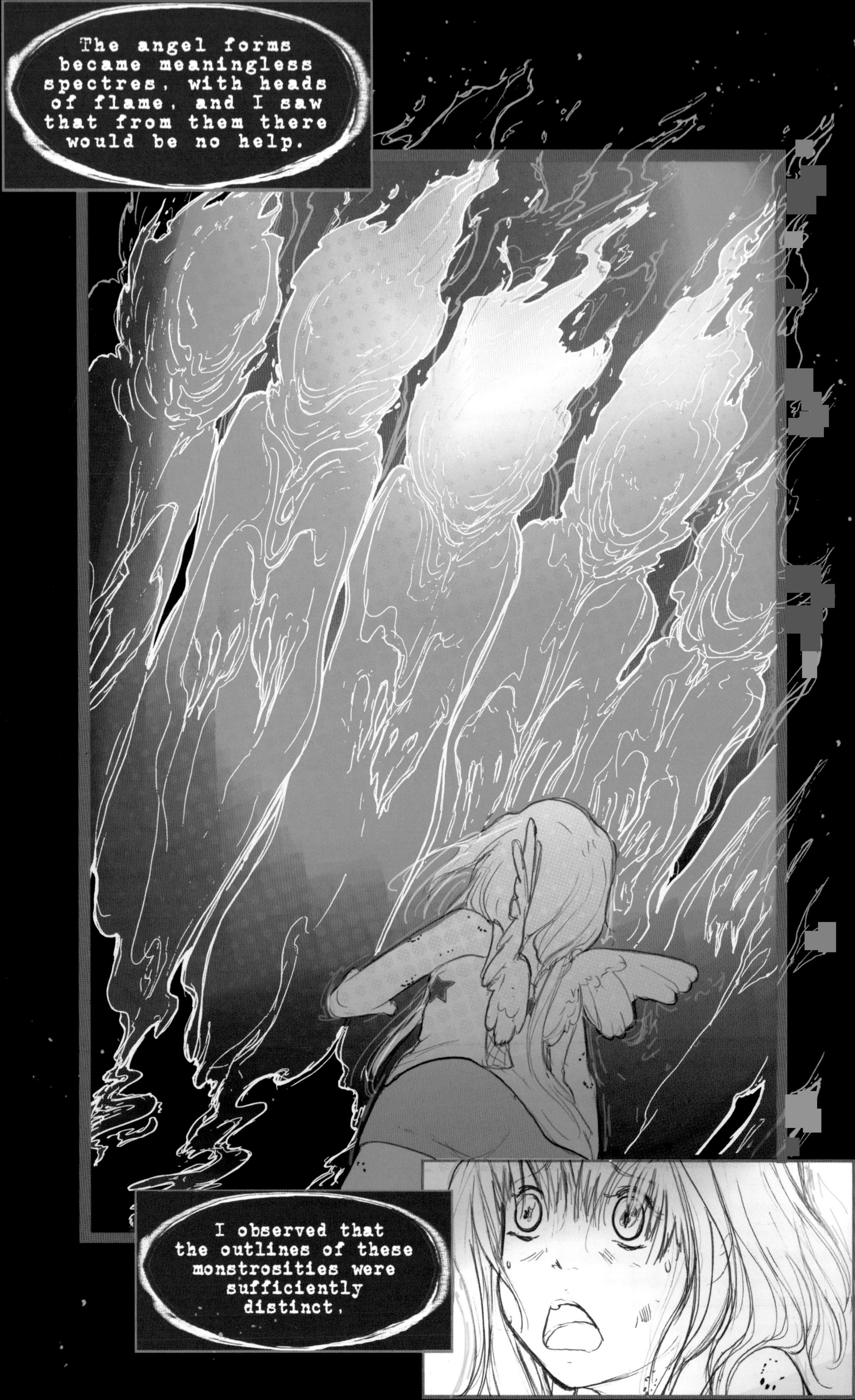
The angel forms became meaningless spectres, with heads of flame, and I saw that from them there would be no help.
I observed that the outlines of these monstrosities were sufficiently distinct.

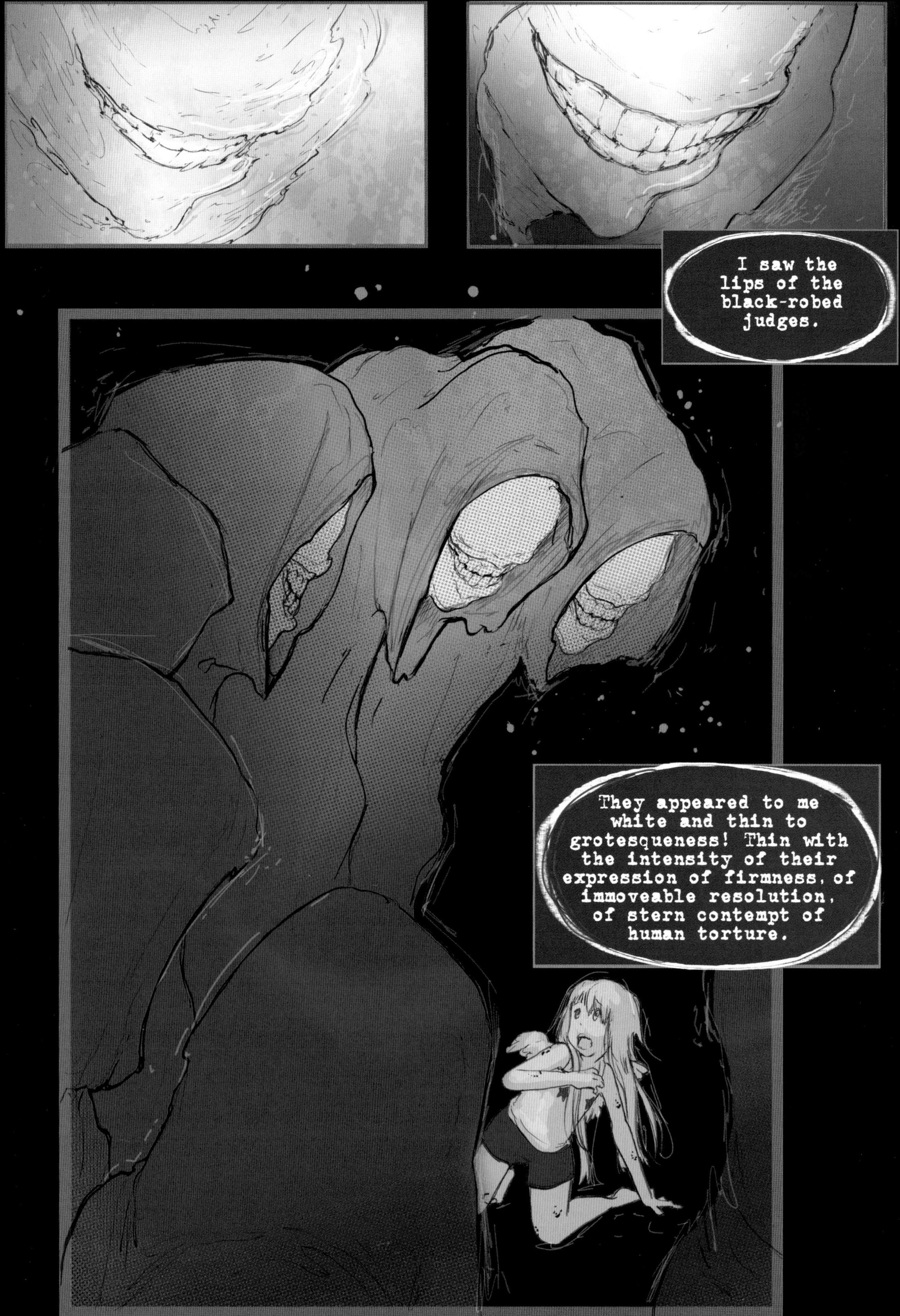
I saw the lips of the black-robed judges.
They appeared to me white and thin to grotesqueness! Thin with the intensity of their expression of firmness, of immoveable resolution, of stern contempt of human torture.

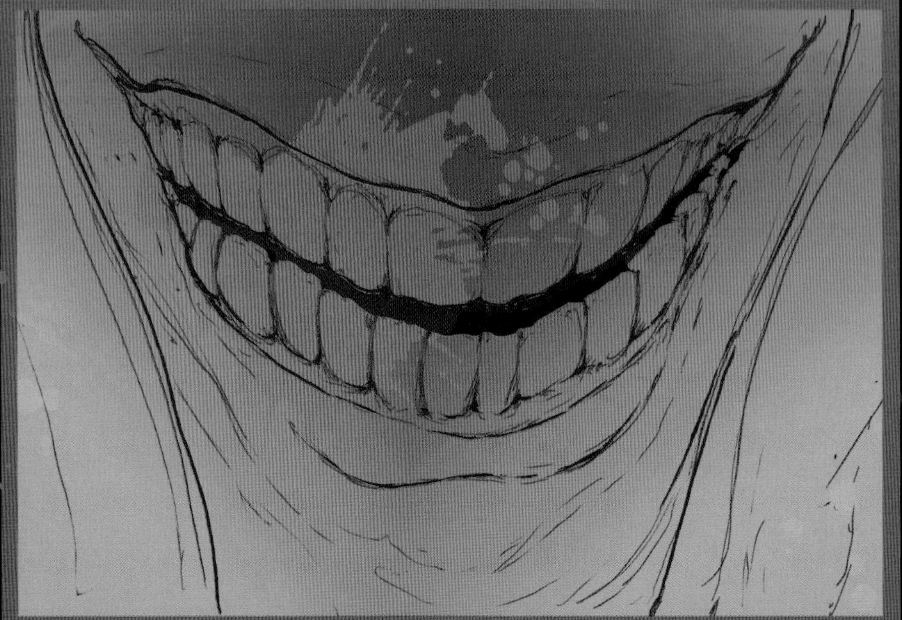

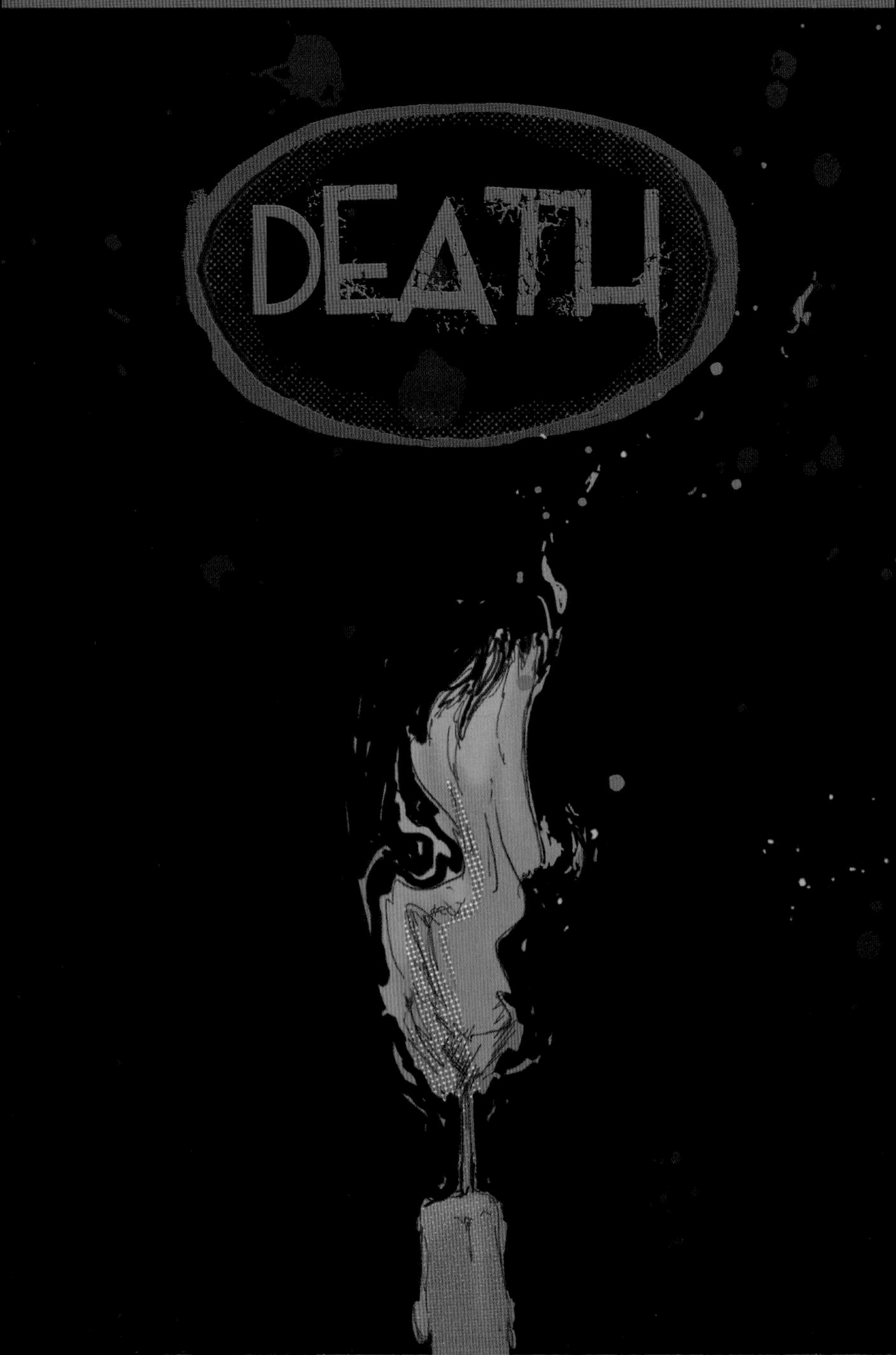
DEATH

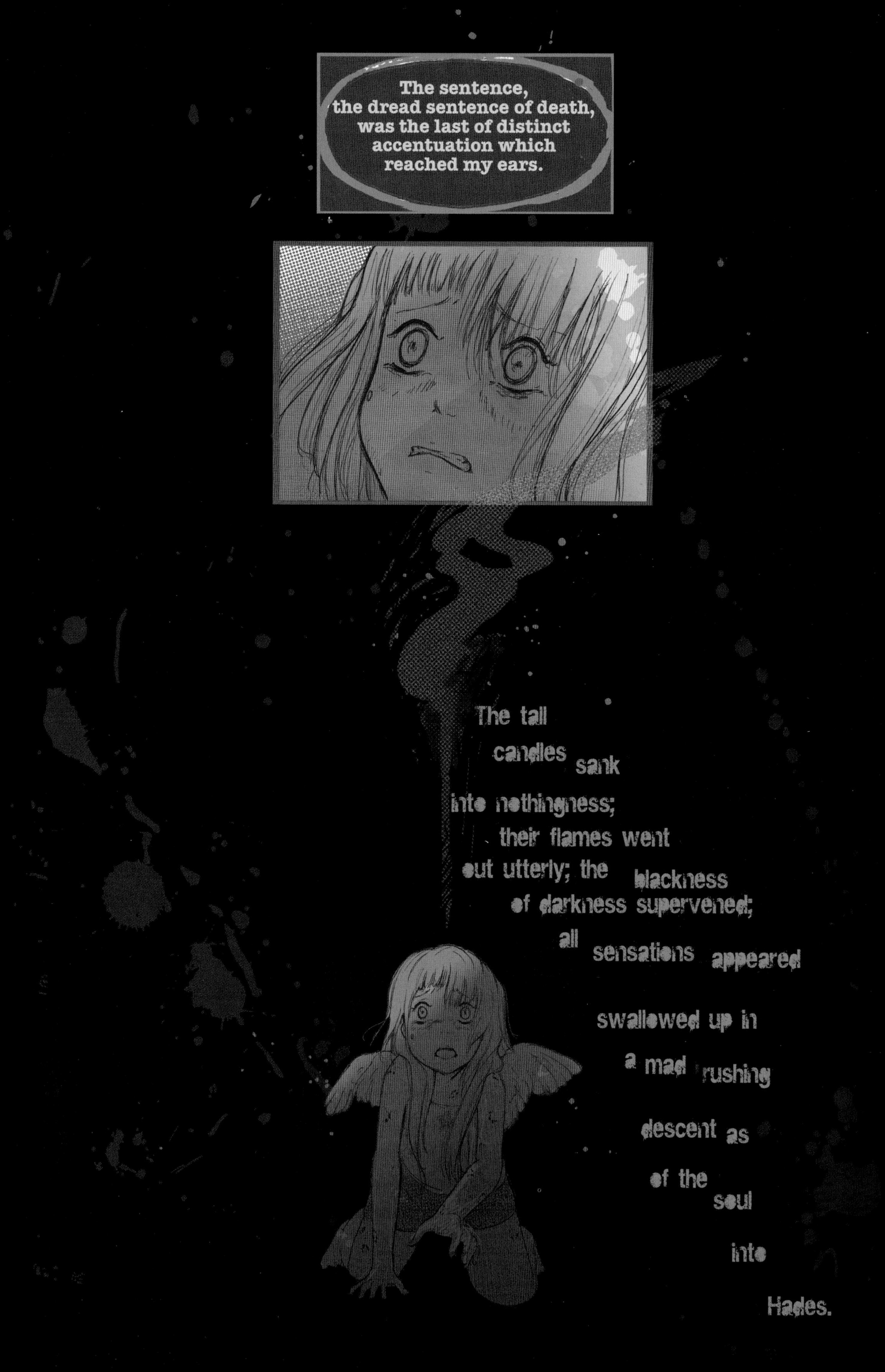
The sentence, the dread sentence of death, was the last of distinct accentuation which reached my ears.
The tall candles sank into nothingness; their flames went out utterly; the blackness of darkness supervened; all sensations appeared swallowed up in a mad rushing descent as of the soul into Hades.

THEN SILENCE, AND STILLNESS, NIGHT WERE THE UNIVERSE.

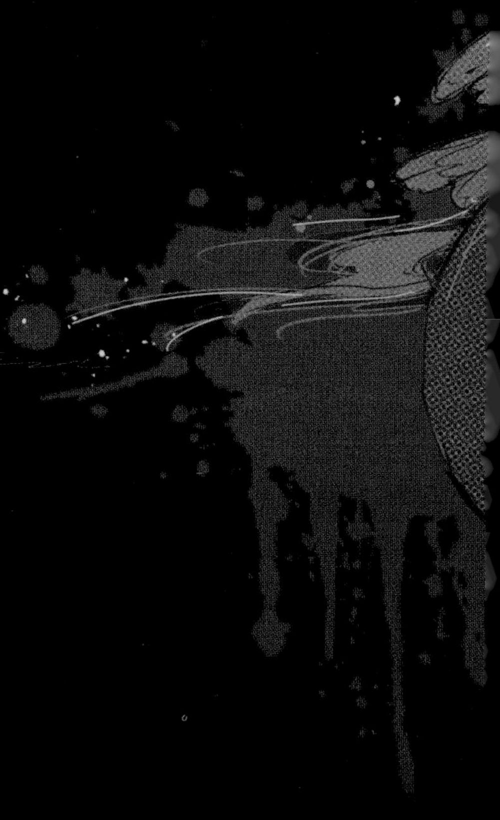

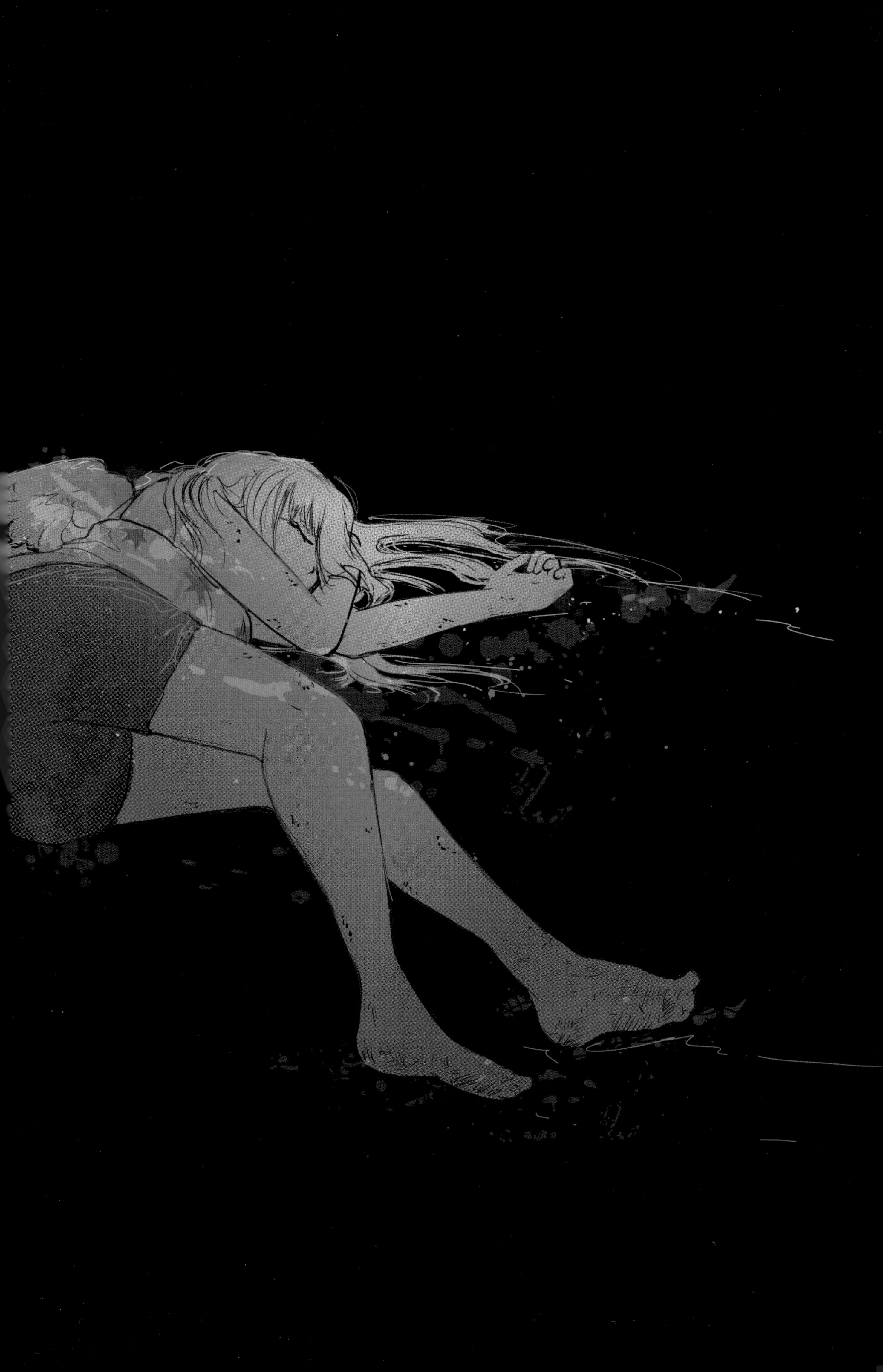

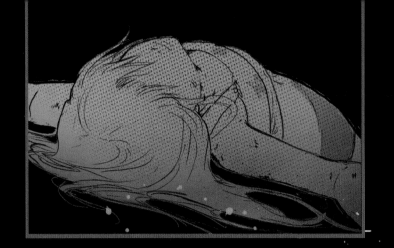

Plainly I perceived the bandages. They writhed upon my throat; I was half stifled by their thronging pressure; disgust, for which the world has no name, swelled my bosom, and chilled, with a heavy clamminess, my heart.

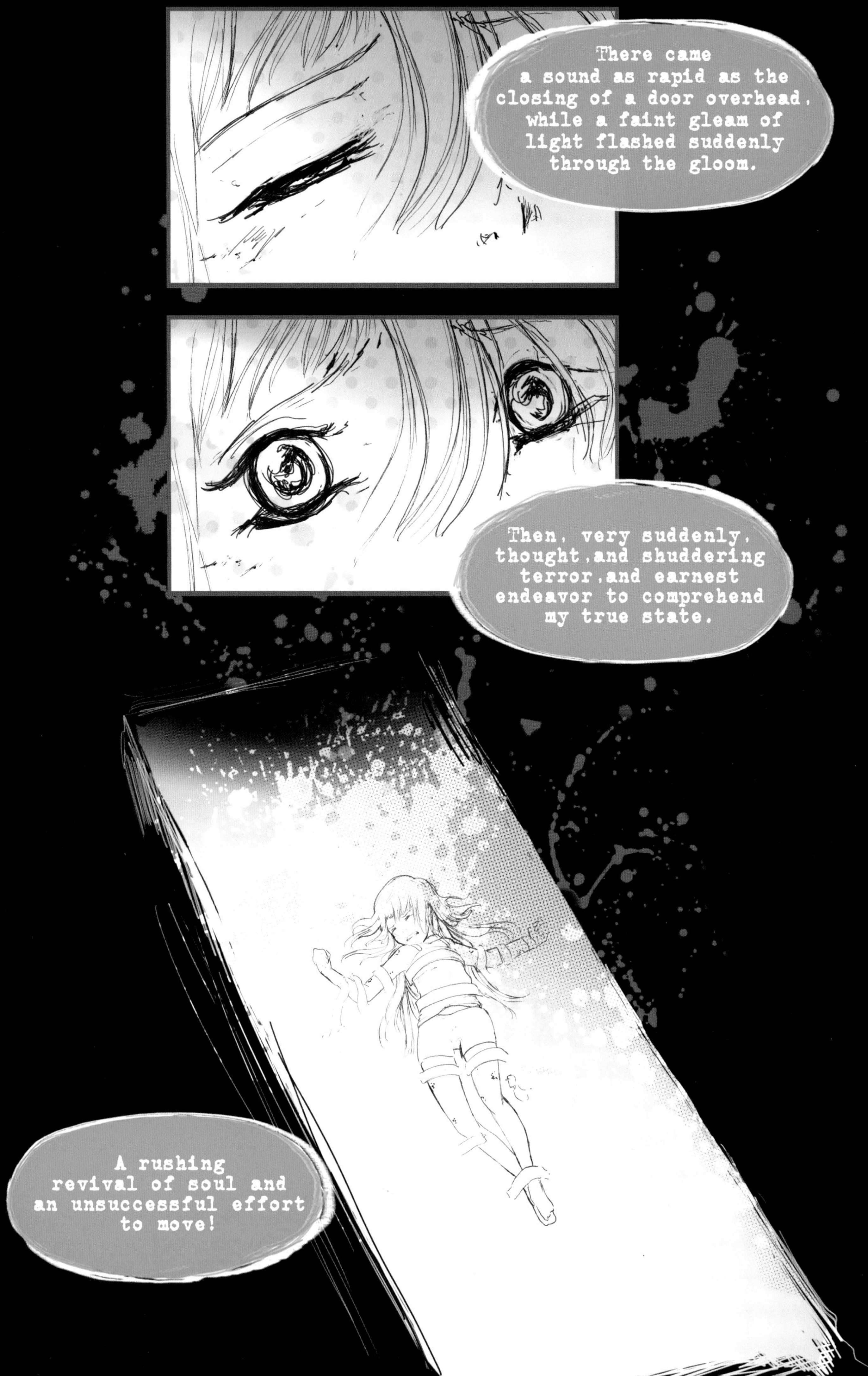
There came a sound as rapid as the closing of a door overhead, while a faint gleam of light flashed suddenly through the gloom.
Then, very suddenly, thought,and shuddering terror,and earnest endeavor to comprehend my true state.
A rushing revival of soul and an unsuccessful effort to move!

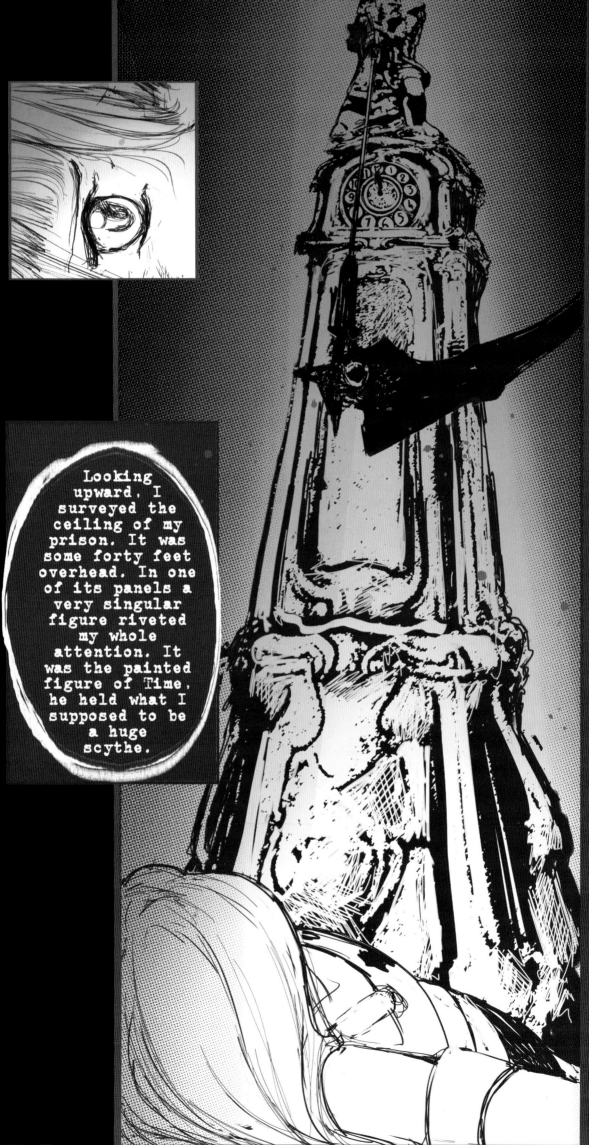

Looking upward, I surveyed the ceiling of my prison. It was some forty feet overhead. In one of its panels a very singular figure riveted my whole attention. It was the painted figure of Time, he held what I supposed to be a huge scythe.

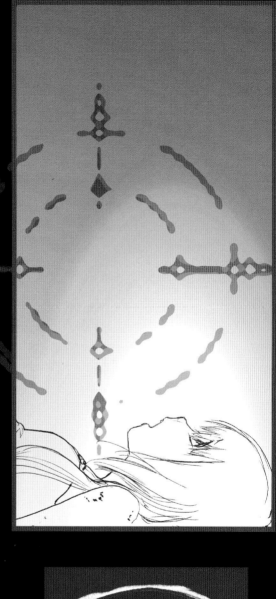

I saw
that the
crescent was
designed to
cross the region
of the heart.

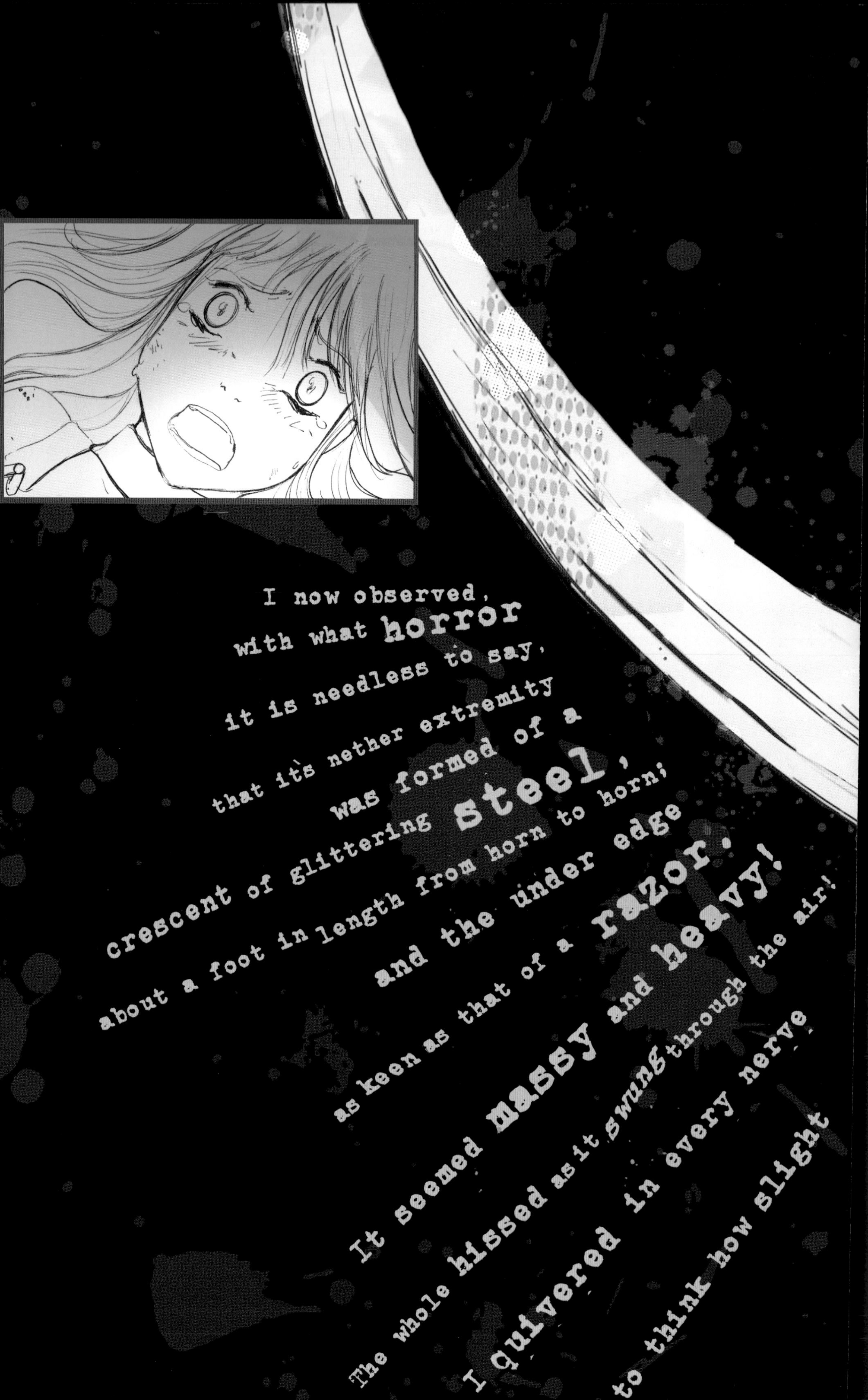
I now observed,
with what horror
it is needless to say,
that it's nether extremity
was formed of a
crescent of glittering steel,
about a foot in length from horn to horn;
and the under edge
as keen as that of a razor.
It seemed massy and heavy!
The whole hissed as it swung through the air!
I quivered in every nerve
to think how slight

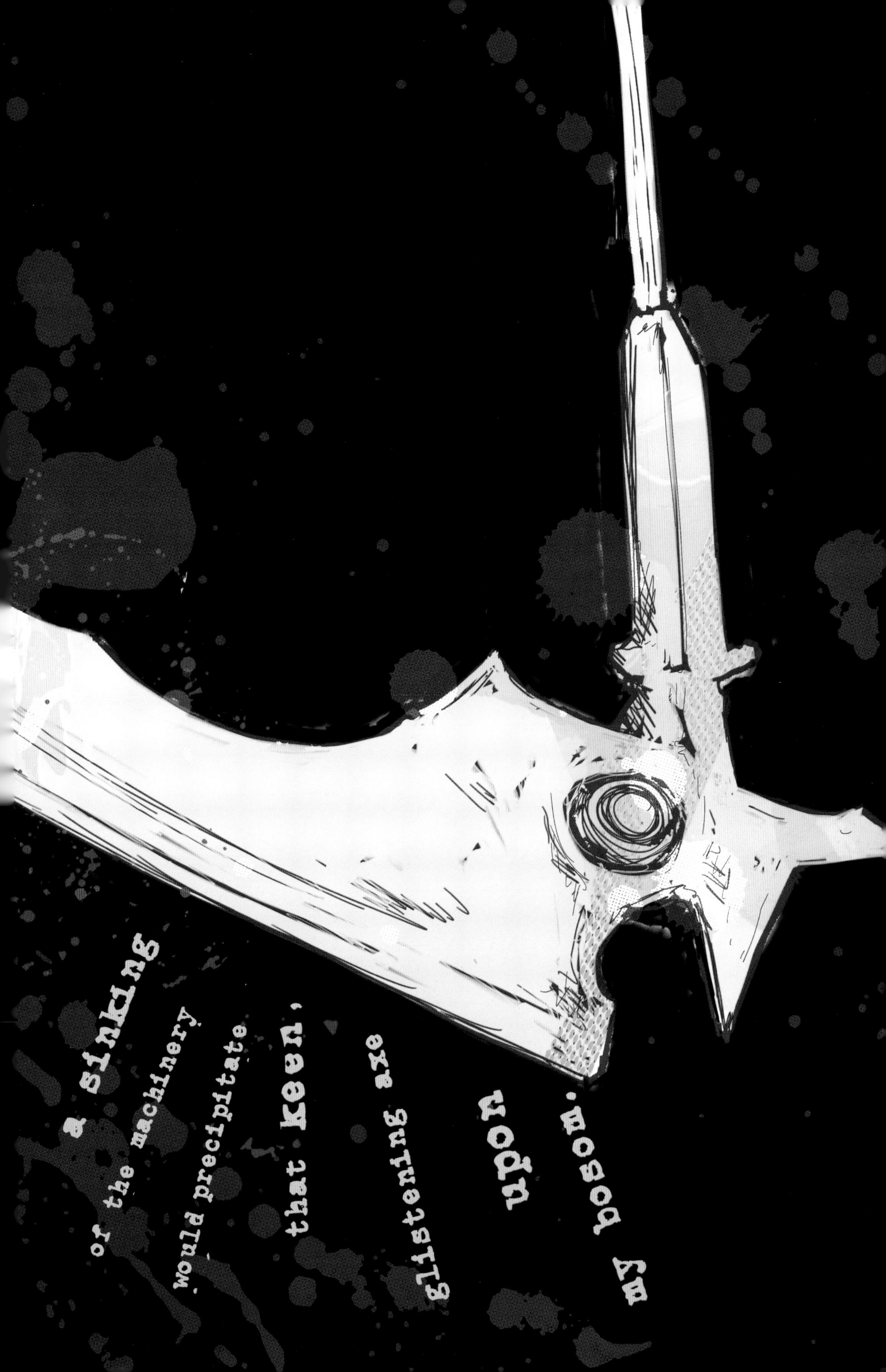
a sinking
of the machinery
would precipitate
that keen,
glistening axe
upon
my bosom.

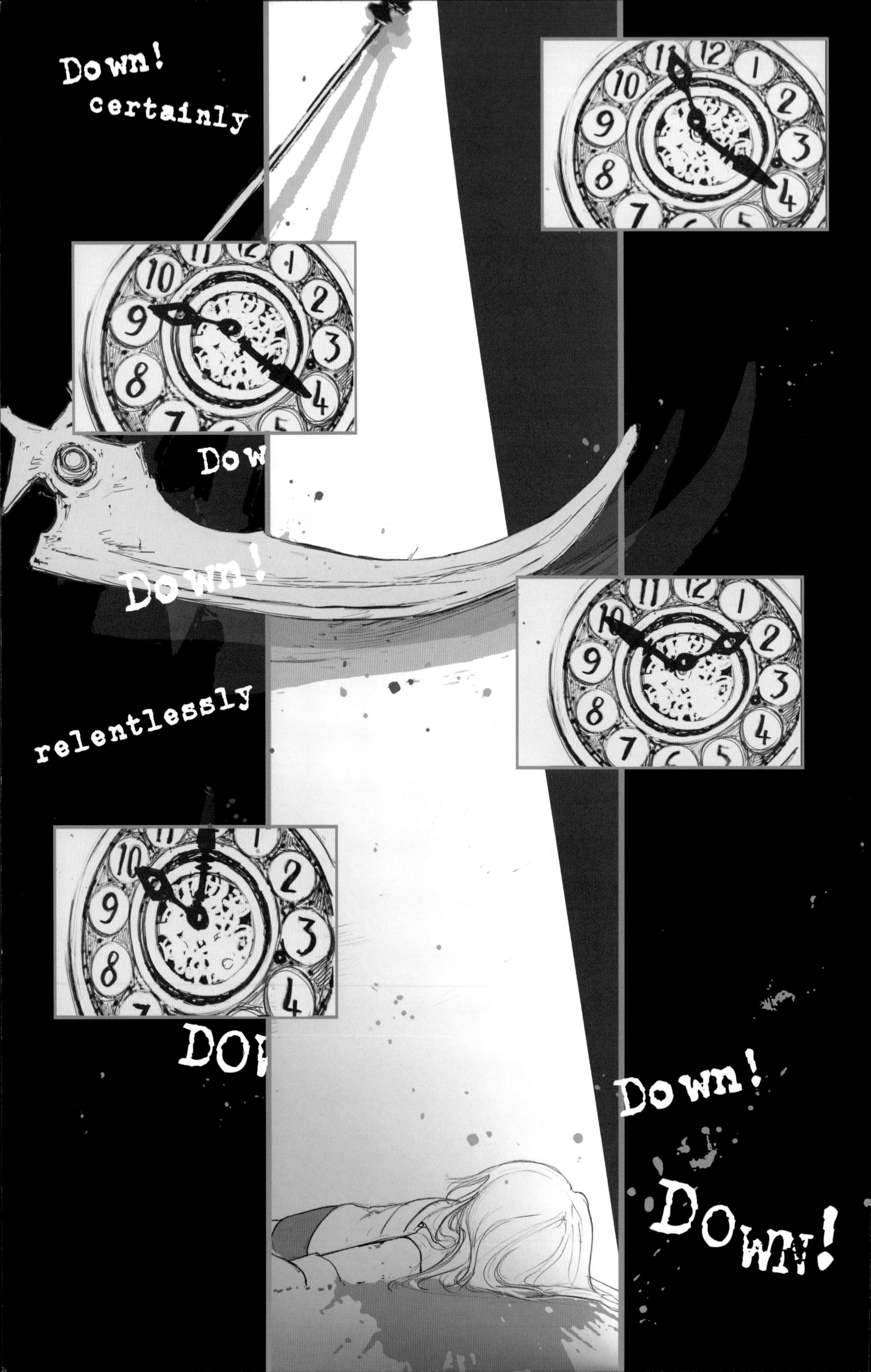
Down!
certainly
Dow
Down!
relentlessly
DOW
Down!
DOWN!

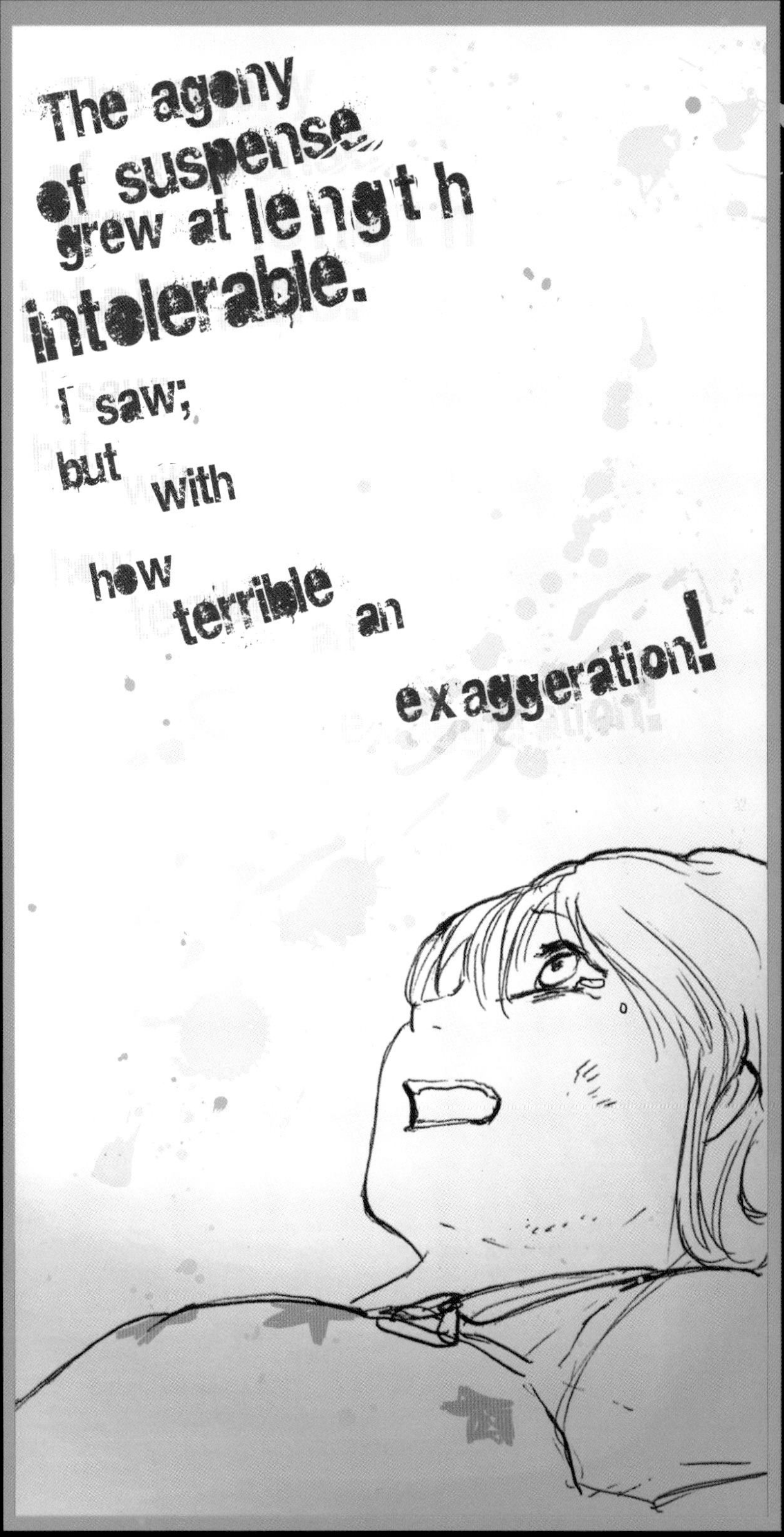
The agony of suspense grew at length intolerable.
I saw; but with how terrible an exaggeration!

What boots it to tell of the long, long hours of horror more than mortal, during which I counted the rushing vibrations of the steel!

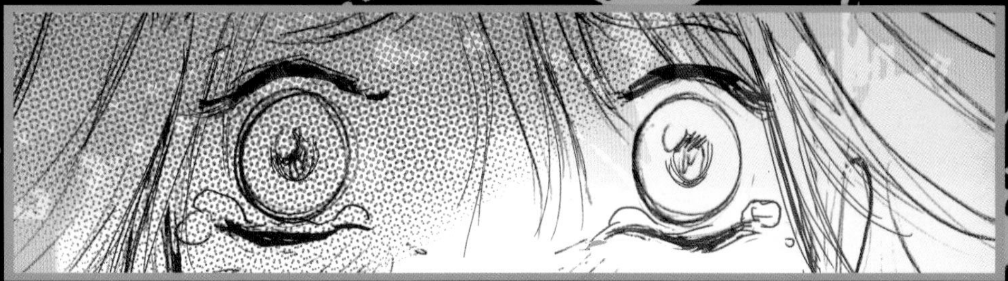

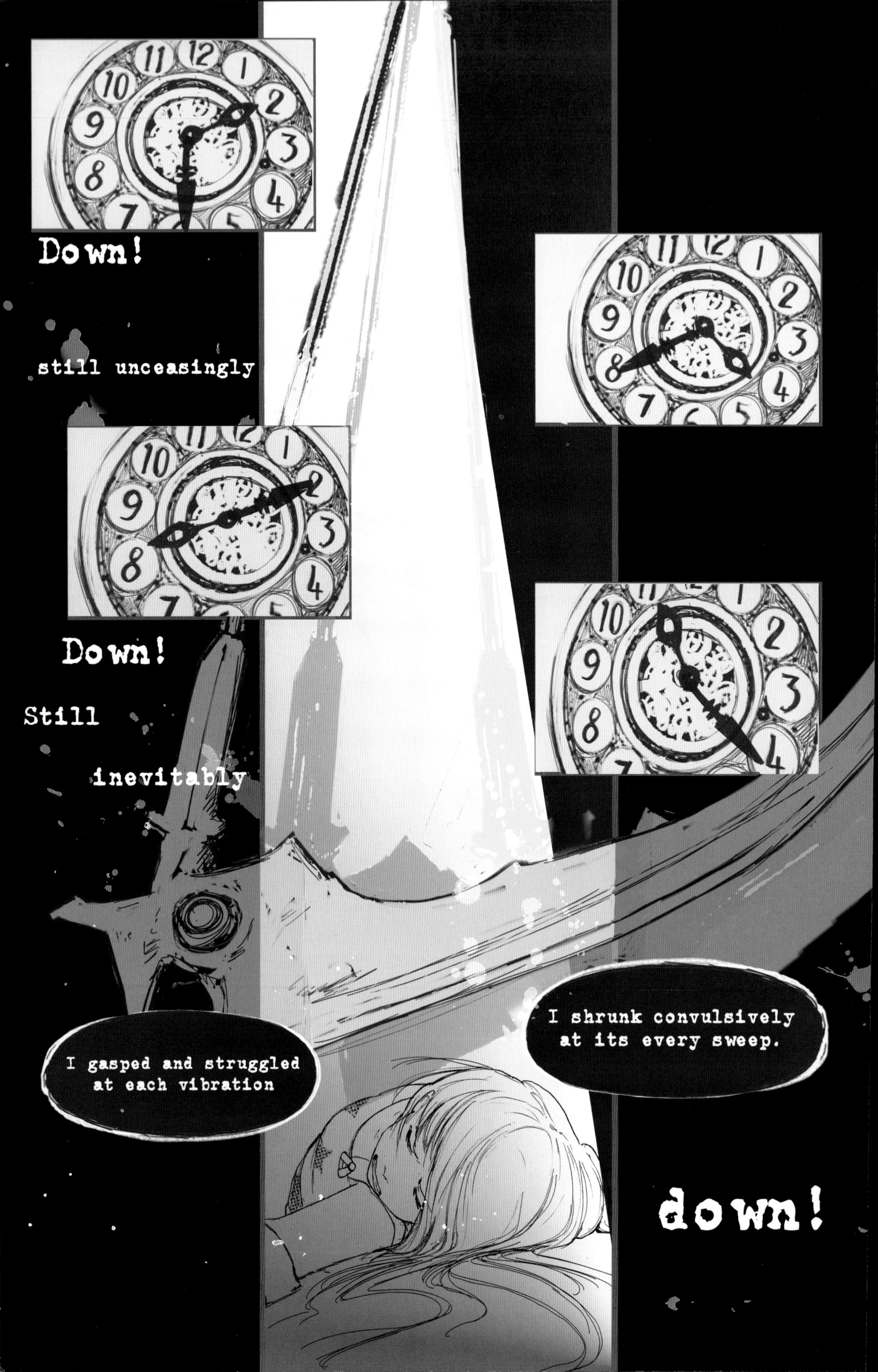
Down!
still unceasingly
Down!
Still
inevitably
down!
I gasped and struggled at each vibration
I shrunk convulsively at its every sweep.

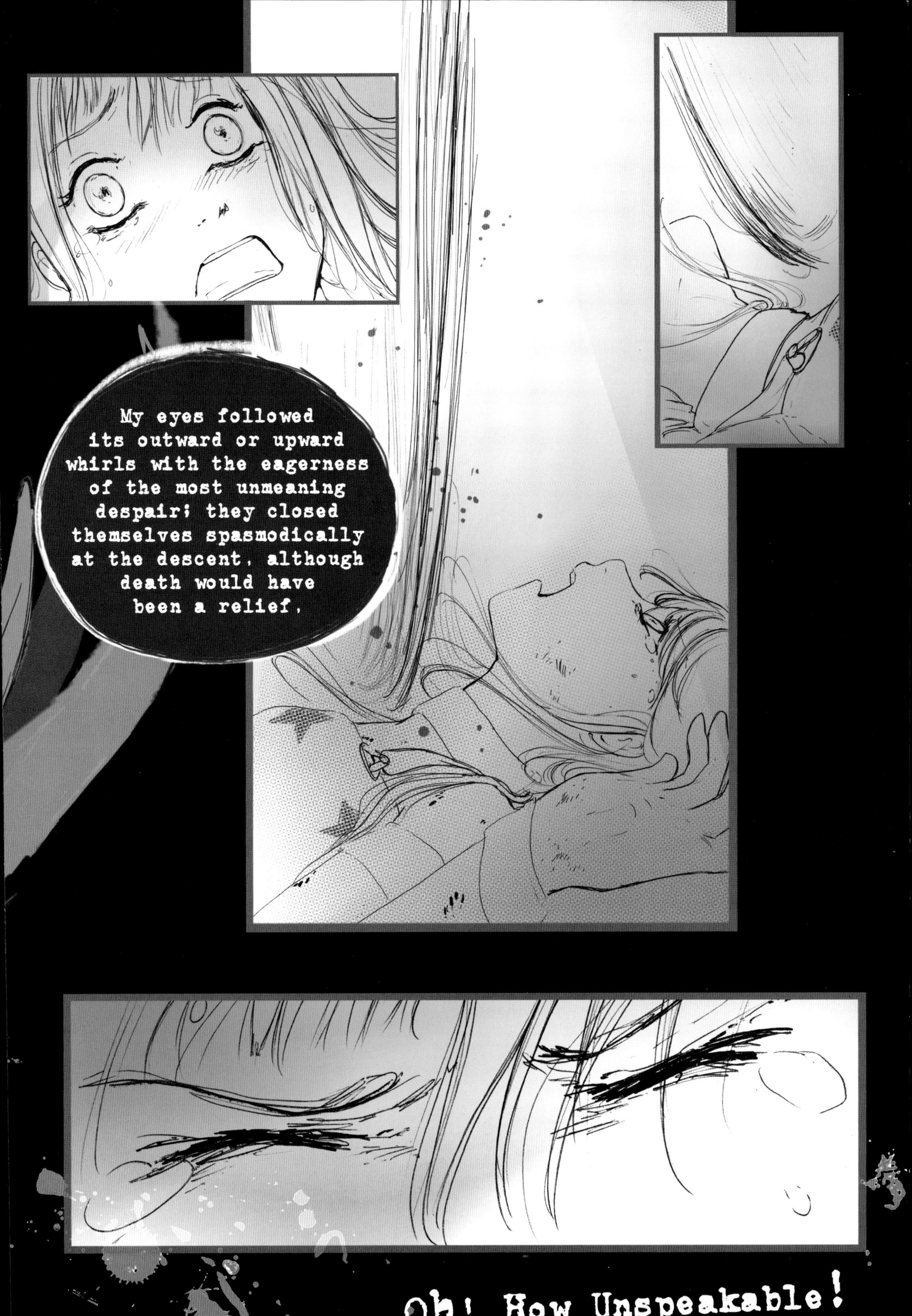
My eyes followed its outward or upward whirls with the eagerness of the most unmeaning despair; they closed themselves spasmodically at the descent, although death would have been a relief.
Oh! How Unspeakable!

To the
victims of its
tyranny, there was
the choice of death
with its direst
physical agonies,
or death with its
most hideous moral
horrors.

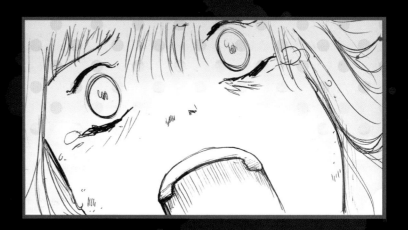

I panted!

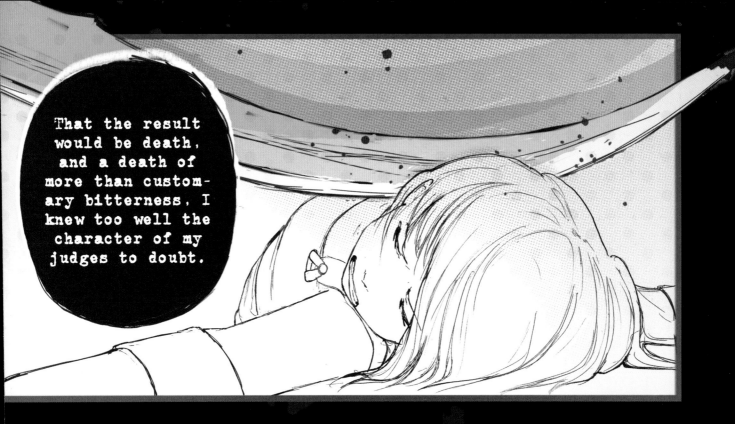

That the result would be death, and a death of more than customary bitterness, I knew too well the character of my judges to doubt.

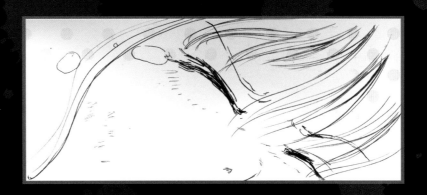

I gasped for breath!

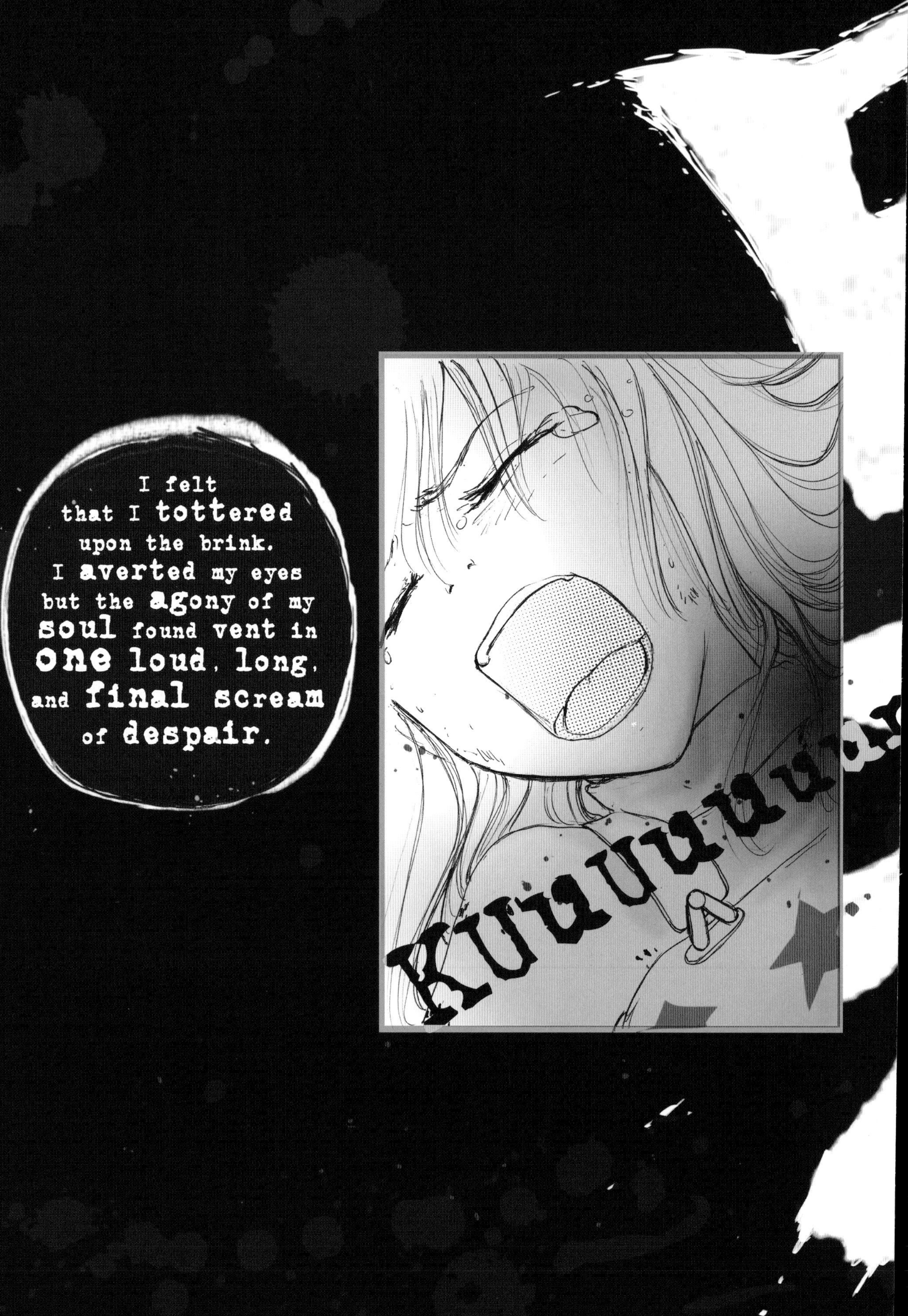
I felt that I tottered upon the brink. I averted my eyes but the agony of my soul found vent in one loud, long, and final scream of despair.

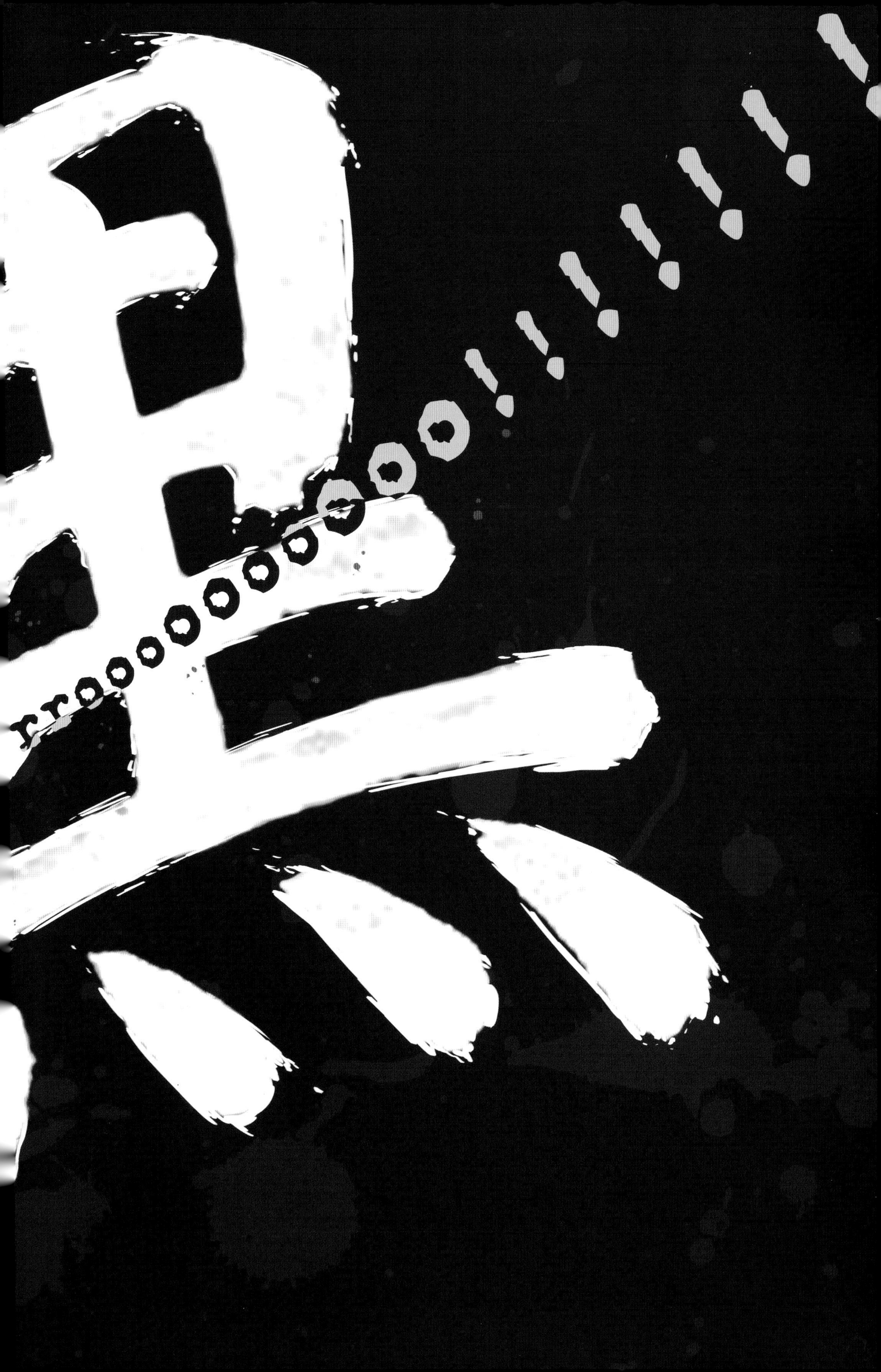
rroooooooooo!!!!!!!!

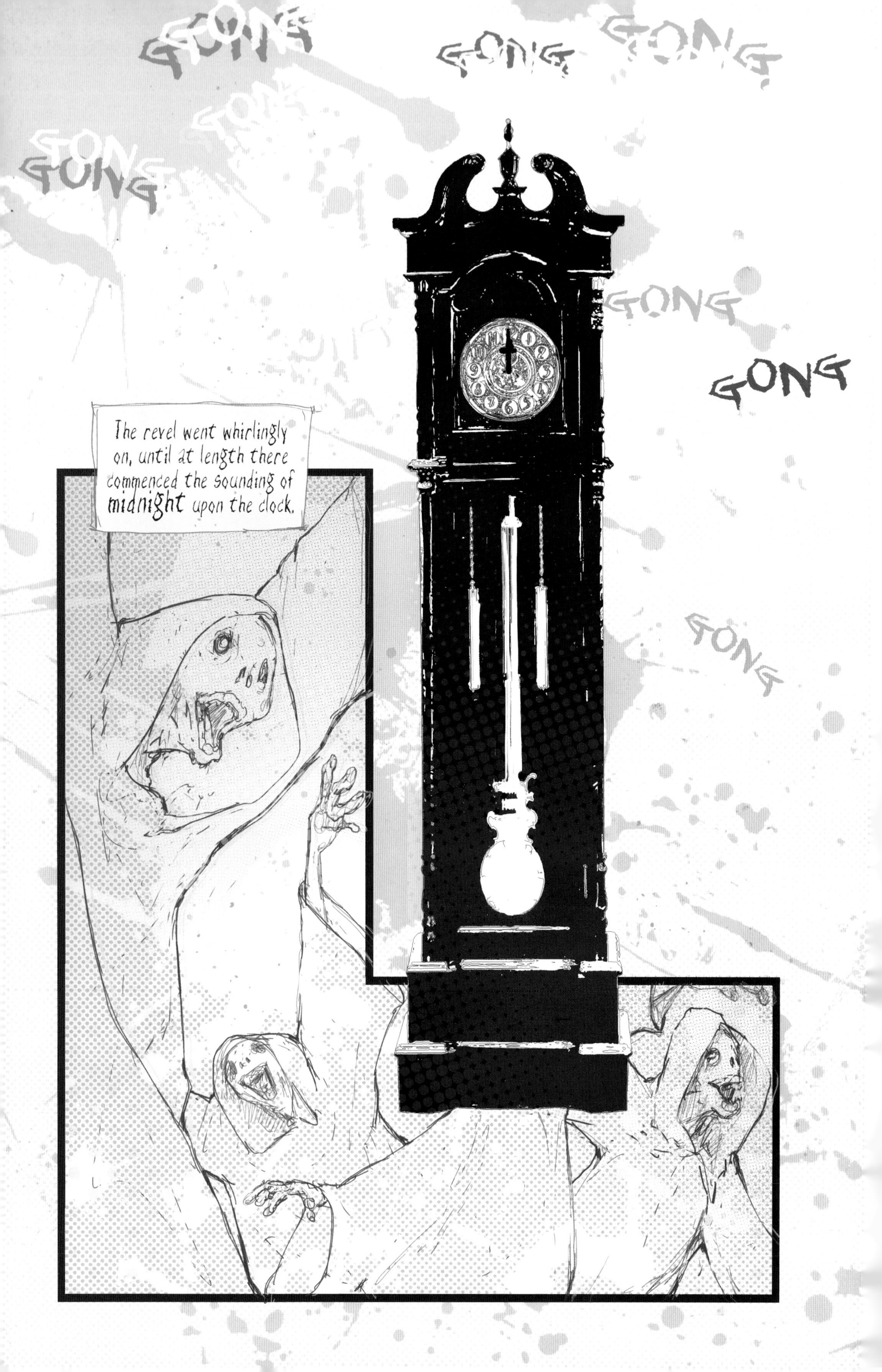

GONG
GONG
GONG
GONG
GONG
GONG
GONG
GONG
The revel went whirlingly on, until at length there commenced the sounding of midnight upon the clock.

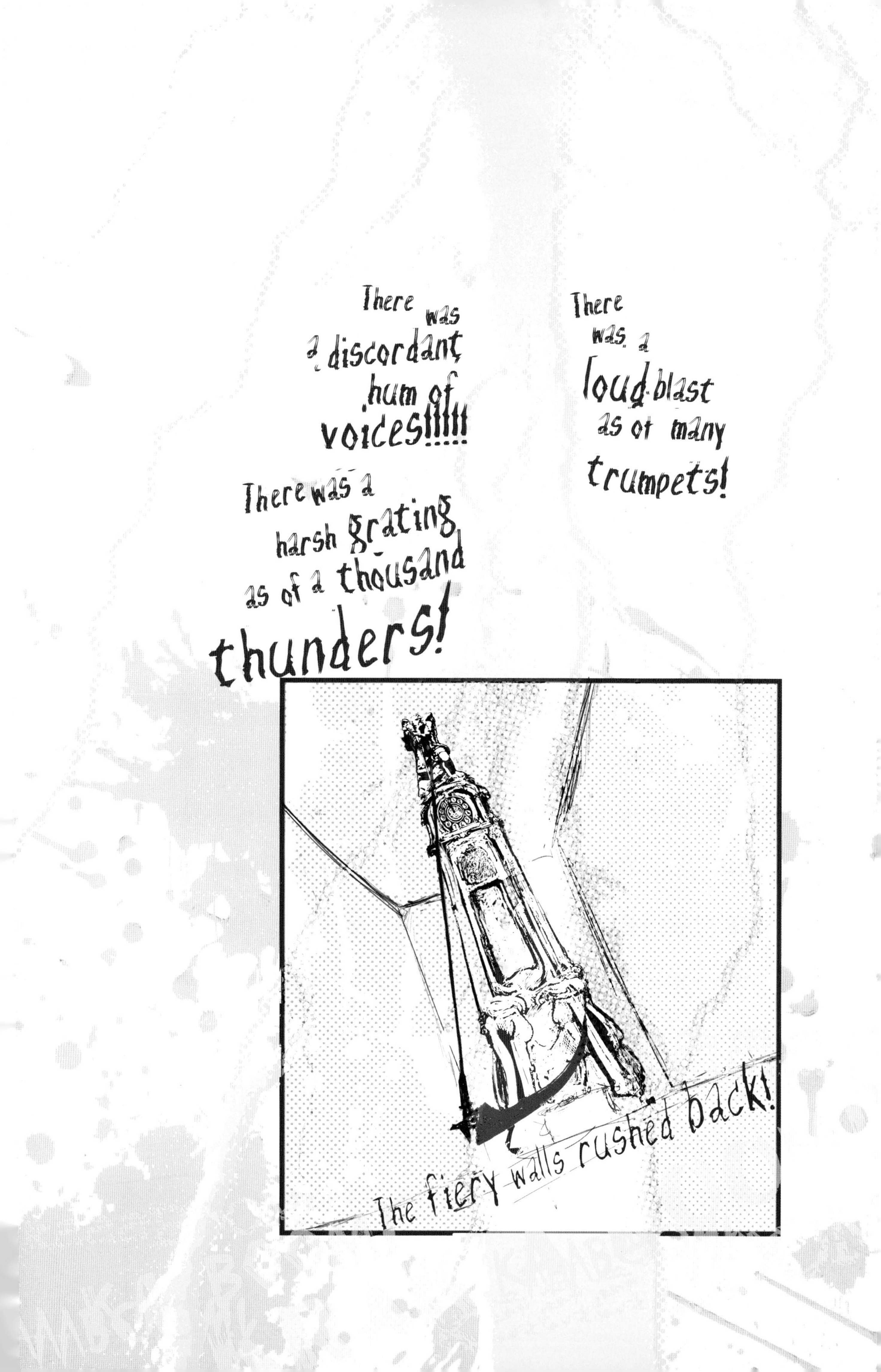
There was a loud blast as of many trumpets!
There was a discordant hum of voices!!!!!!
There was a harsh grating as of a thousand thunders!
The fiery walls rushed back!

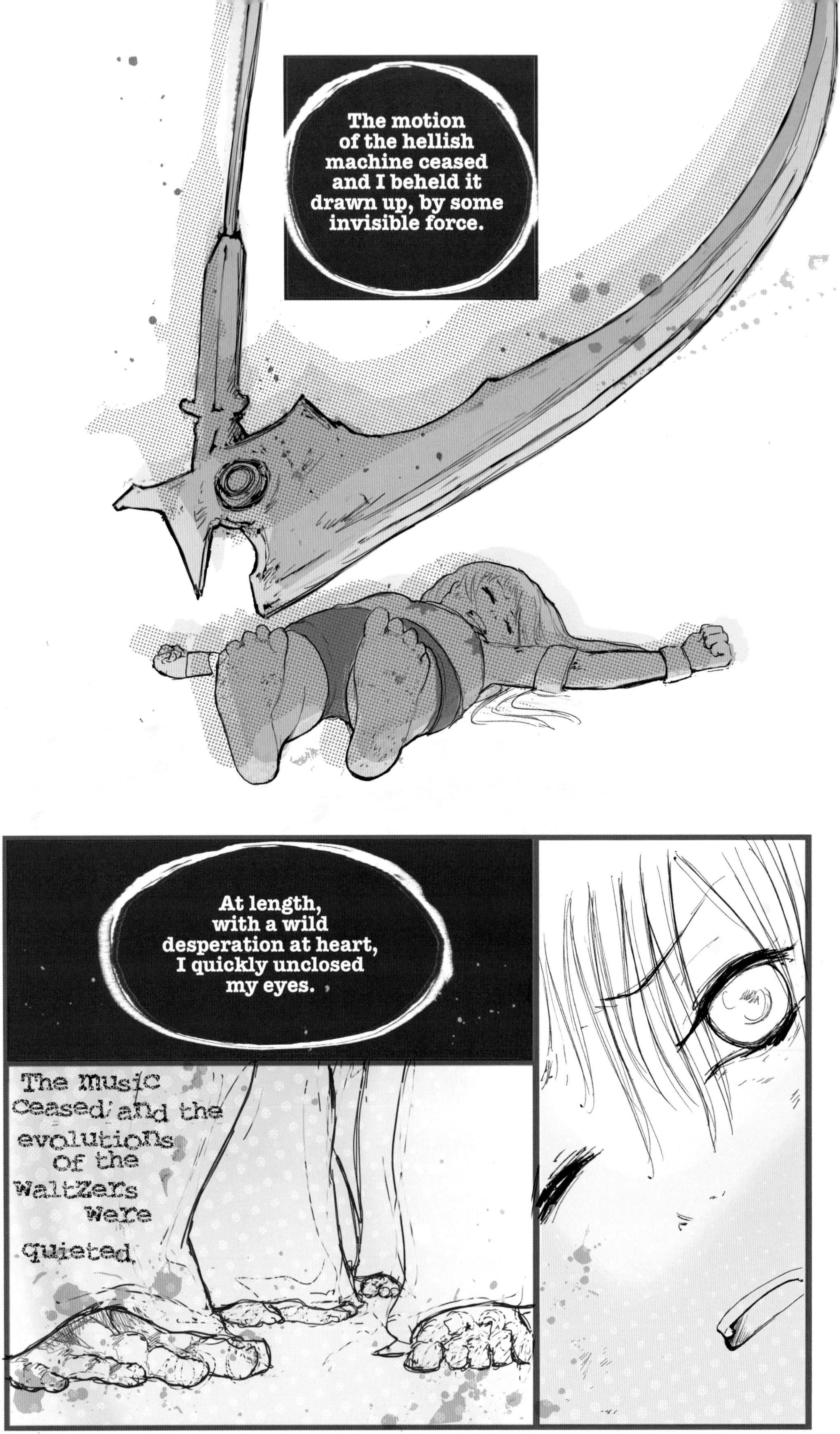
The motion of the hellish machine ceased and I beheld it drawn up, by some invisible force.
At length, with a wild desperation at heart, I quickly unclosed my eyes.
The music ceased, and the evolutions of the waltzers were quieted.

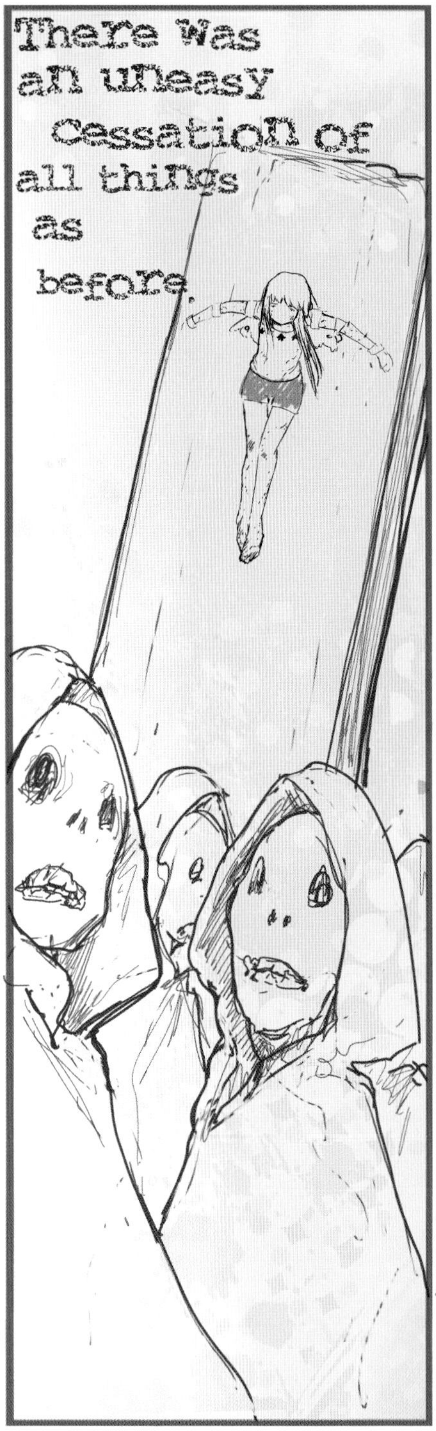
There was an uneasy cessation of all things as before.

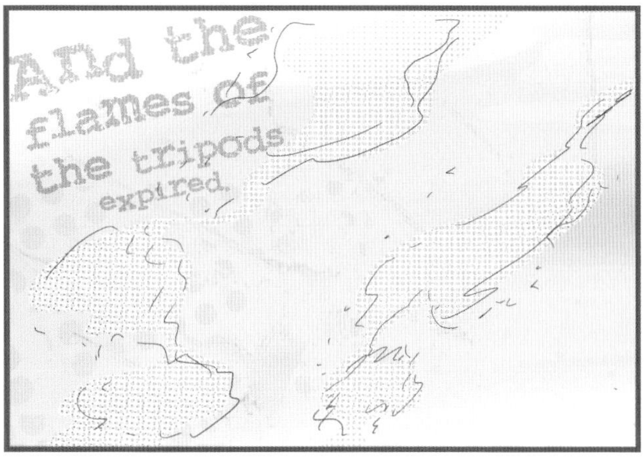
And the flames of the tripods expired

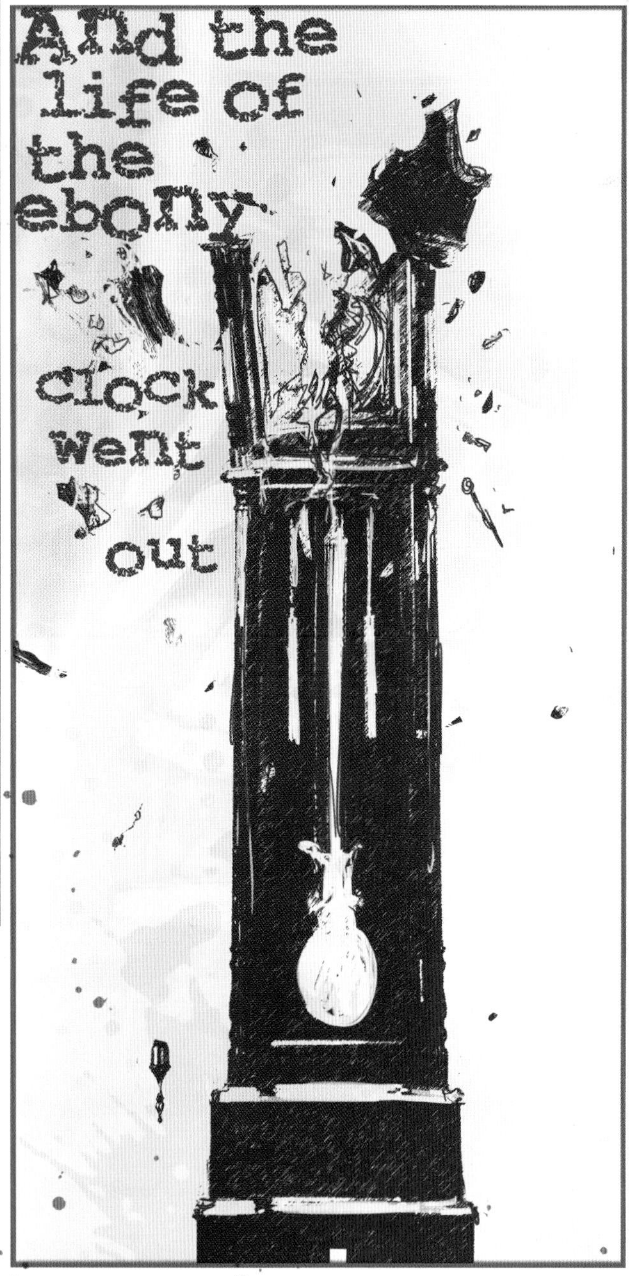
And the life of the ebony clock went out

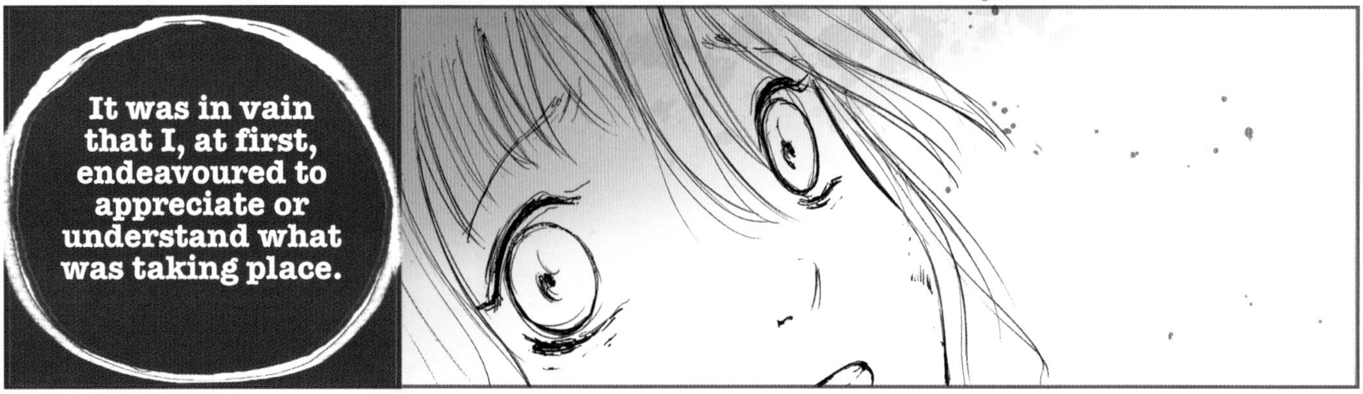
It was in vain that I, at first, endeavoured to appreciate or understand what was taking place.

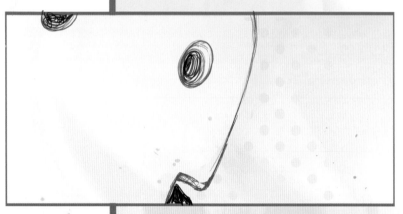

But not
long was I
left in
doubt.

HE HAD COME
LIKE A
THIEF IN THE NIGHT.

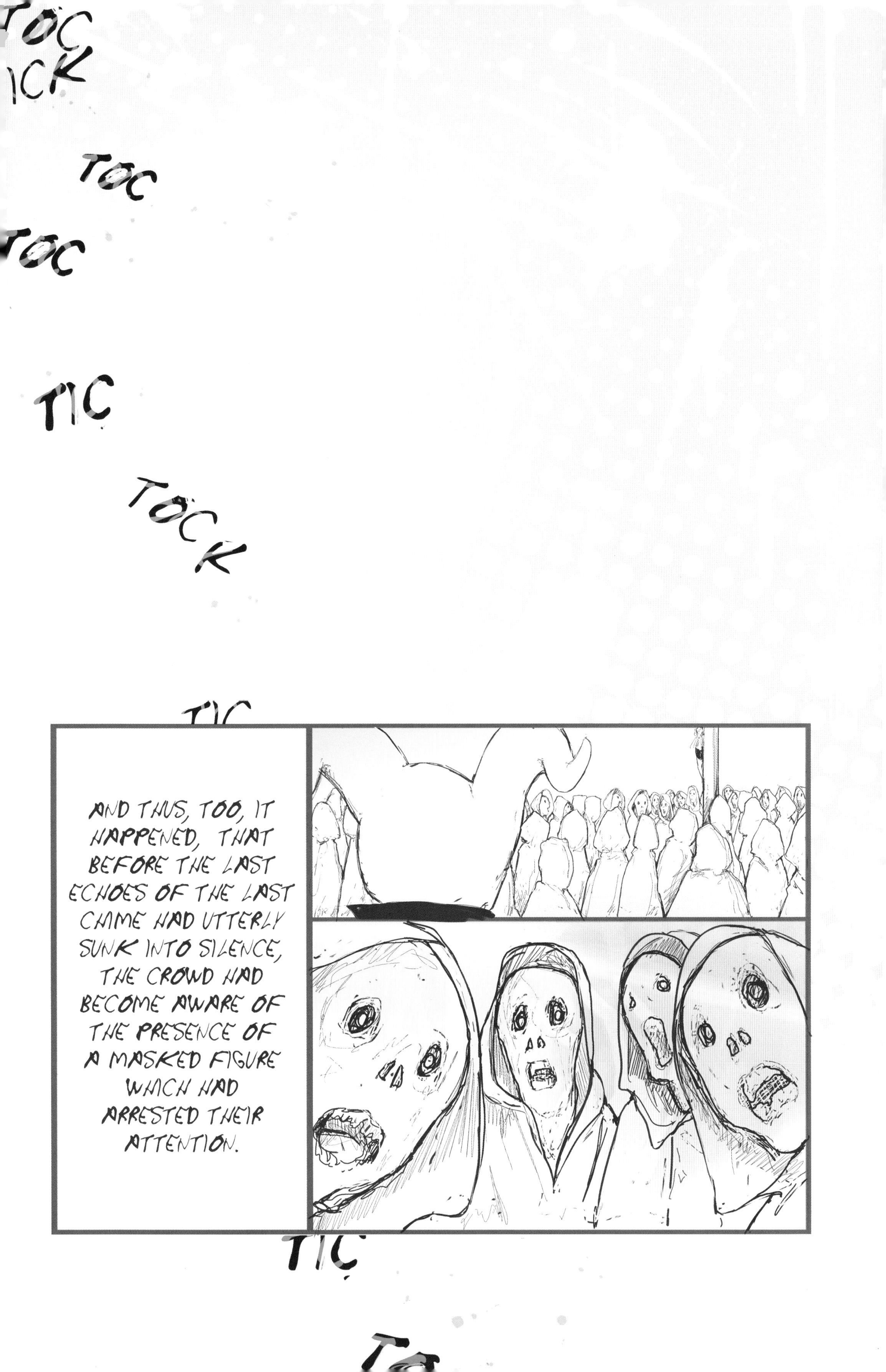
TOC
TOC
TOC
TIC
TOCK
TIC
AND THUS, TOO, IT HAPPENED, THAT BEFORE THE LAST ECHOES OF THE LAST CHIME HAD UTTERLY SUNK INTO SILENCE, THE CROWD HAD BECOME AWARE OF THE PRESENCE OF A MASKED FIGURE WHICH HAD ARRESTED THEIR ATTENTION.
TIC

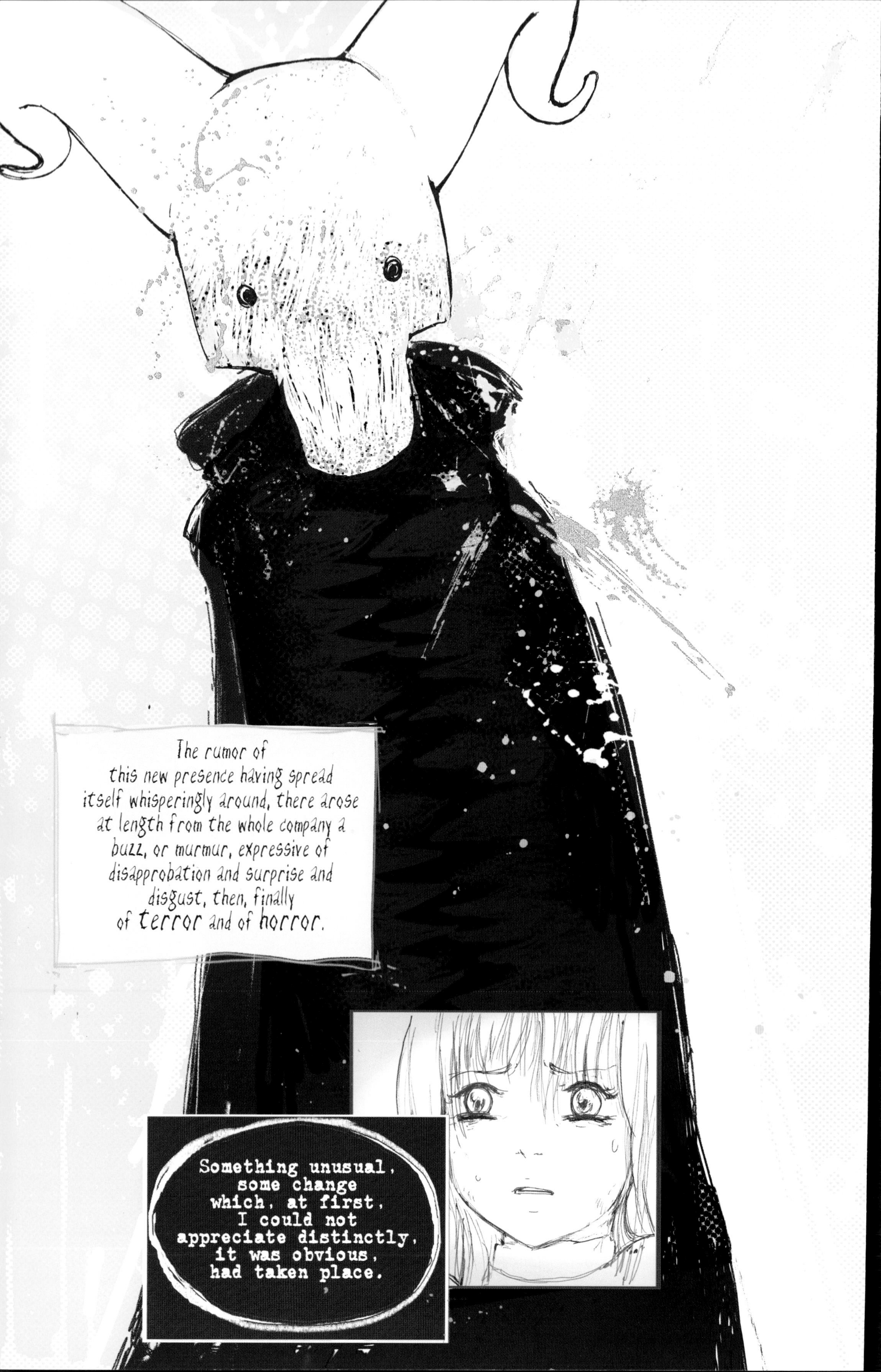
The rumor of this new presence having spread itself whisperingly around, there arose at length from the whole company a buzz, or murmur, expressive of disapprobation and surprise and disgust, then, finally of terror and of horror.
Something unusual, some change which, at first, I could not appreciate distinctly, it was obvious, had taken place.

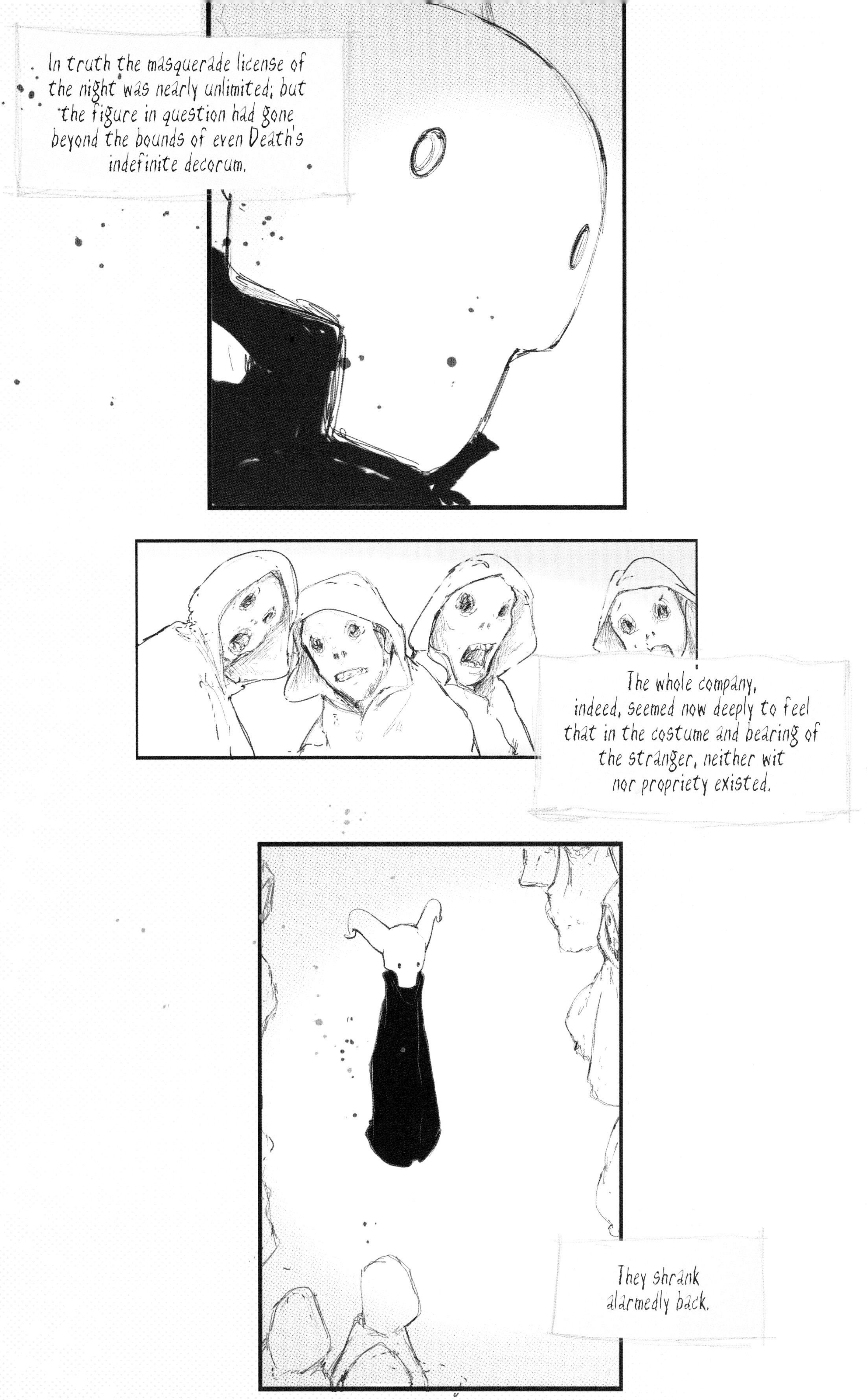
In truth the masquerade license of the night was nearly unlimited; but the figure in question had gone beyond the bounds of even Death's indefinite decorum.
The whole company, indeed, seemed now deeply to feel that in the costume and bearing of the stranger, neither wit nor propriety existed.
They shrank alarmedly back.

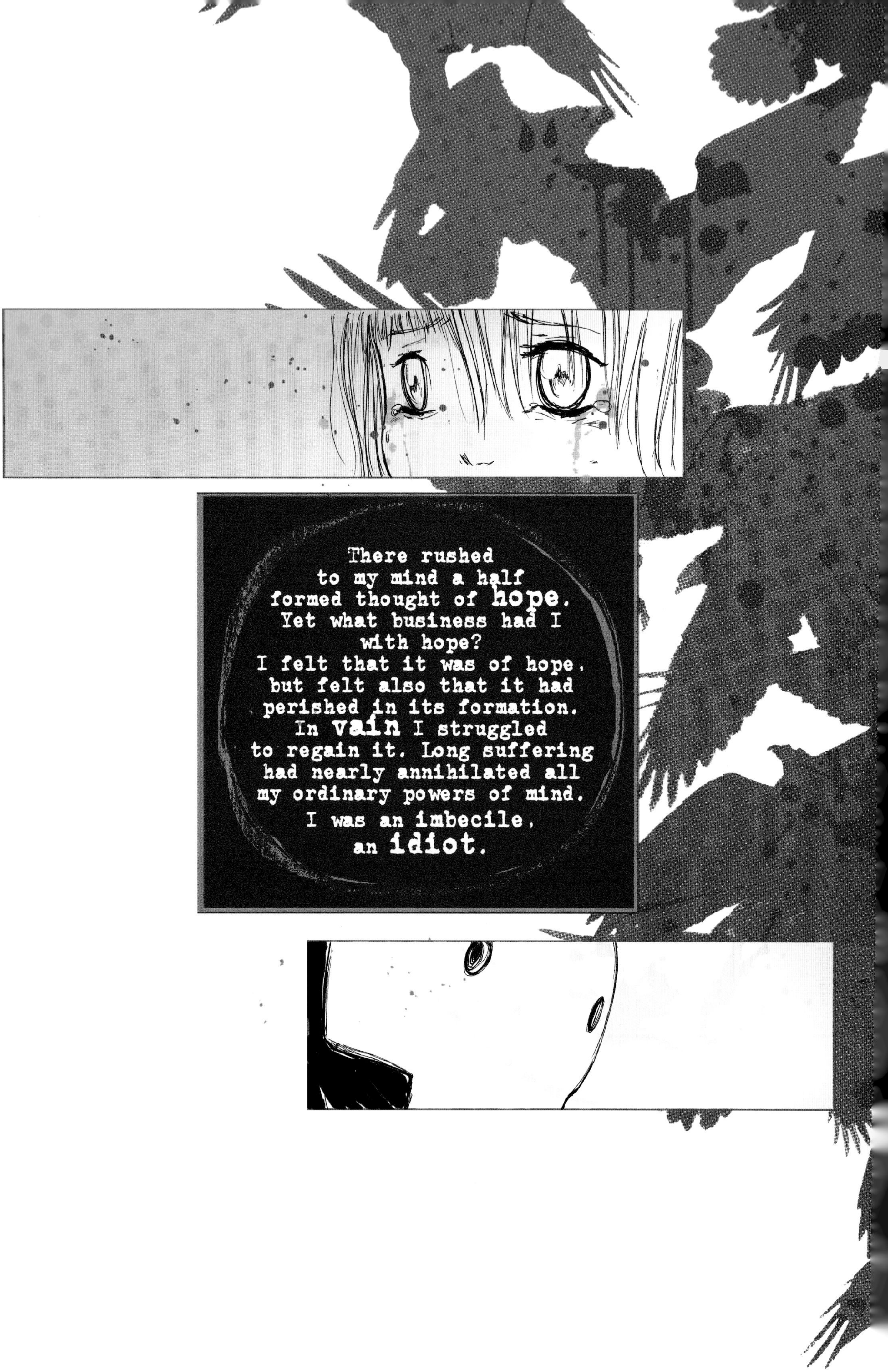
There rushed to my mind a half formed thought of hope. Yet what business had I with hope? I felt that it was of hope, but felt also that it had perished in its formation. In vain I struggled to regain it. Long suffering had nearly annihilated all my ordinary powers of mind. I was an imbecile, an idiot.

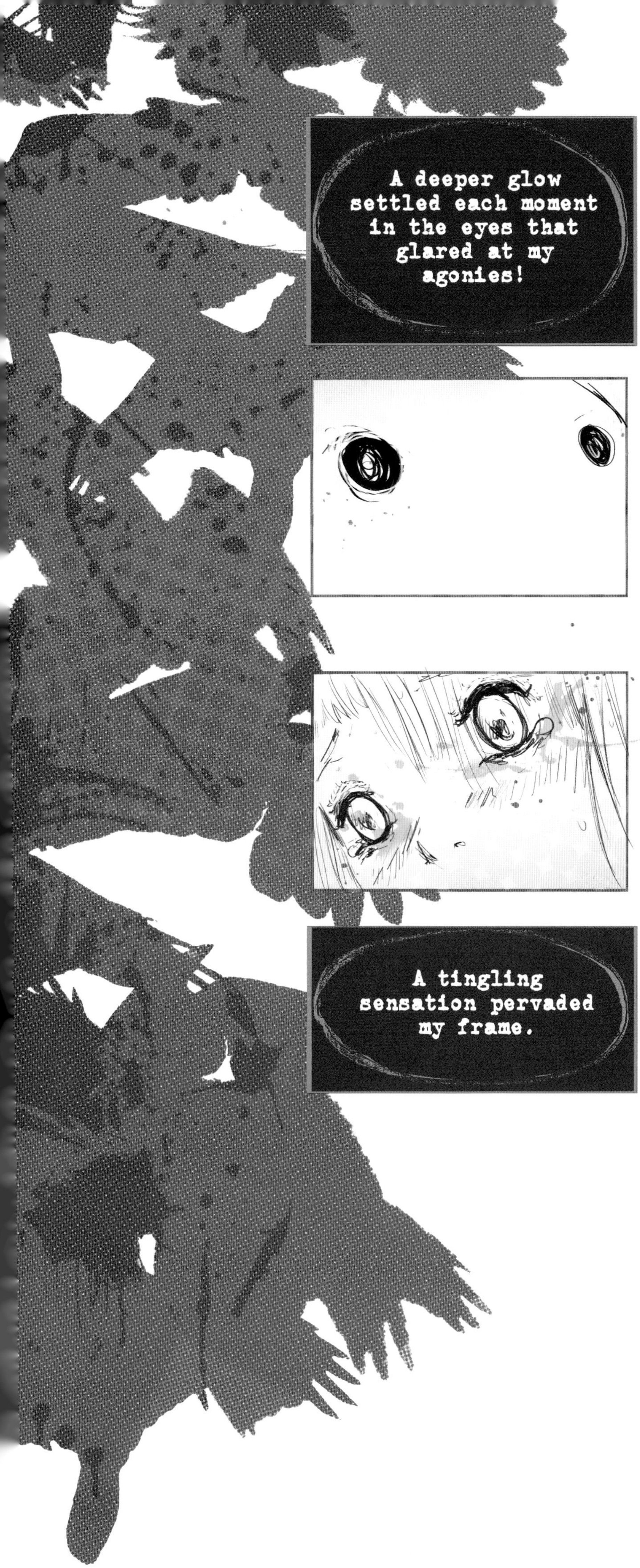
A deeper glow settled each moment in the eyes that glared at my agonies!
A tingling sensation pervaded my frame.

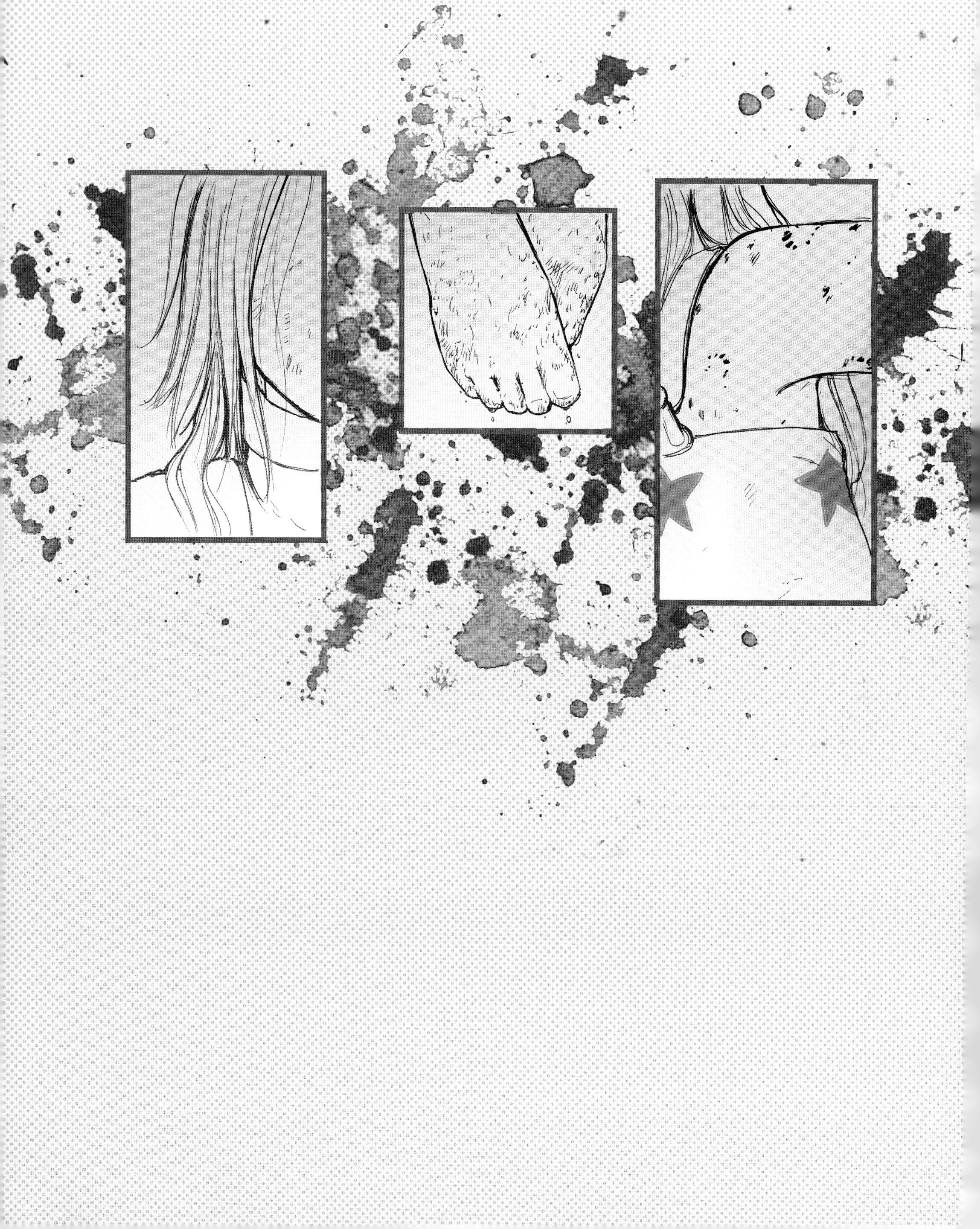

WHEN THE EYES OF THE PRINCE FELL UPON HER IMAGE, HE WAS SEEN TO BE CONVULSED,

IN THE FIRST MOMENT WITH A STRONG SHUDDER EITHER OF TERROR OR DISTASTE.

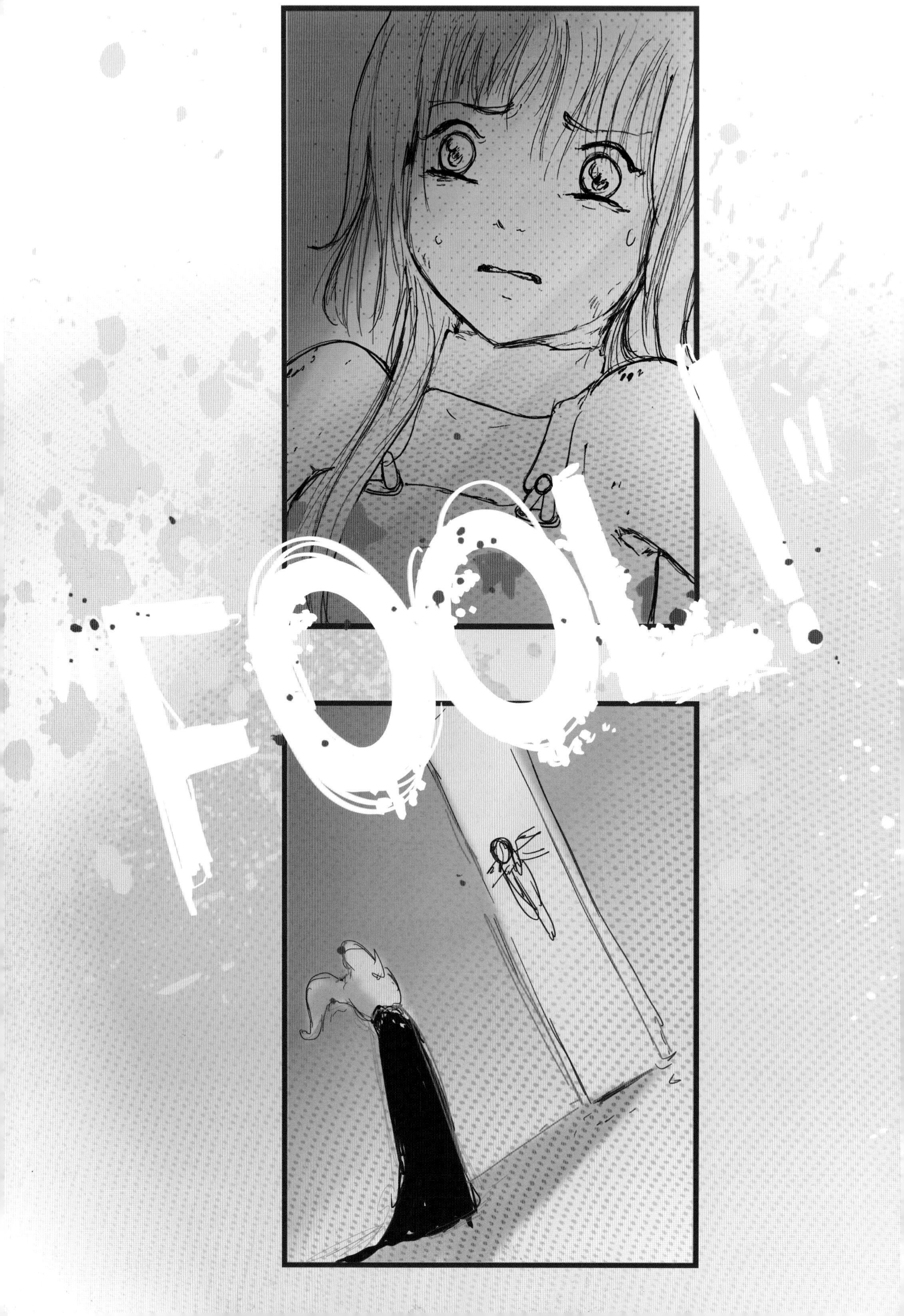
FOOL!!

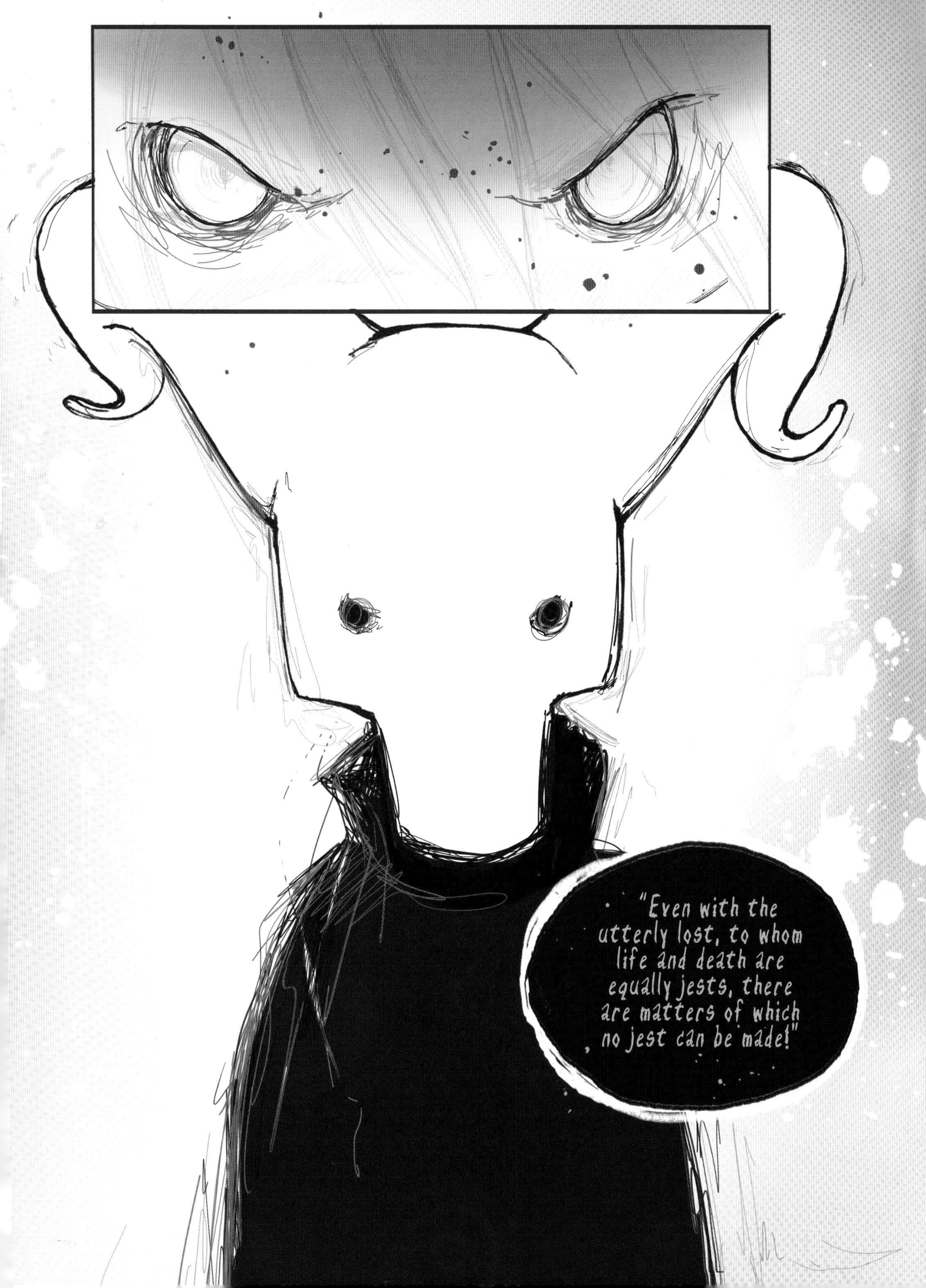
"Even with the utterly lost, to whom life and death are equally jests, there are matters of which no jest can be made!"

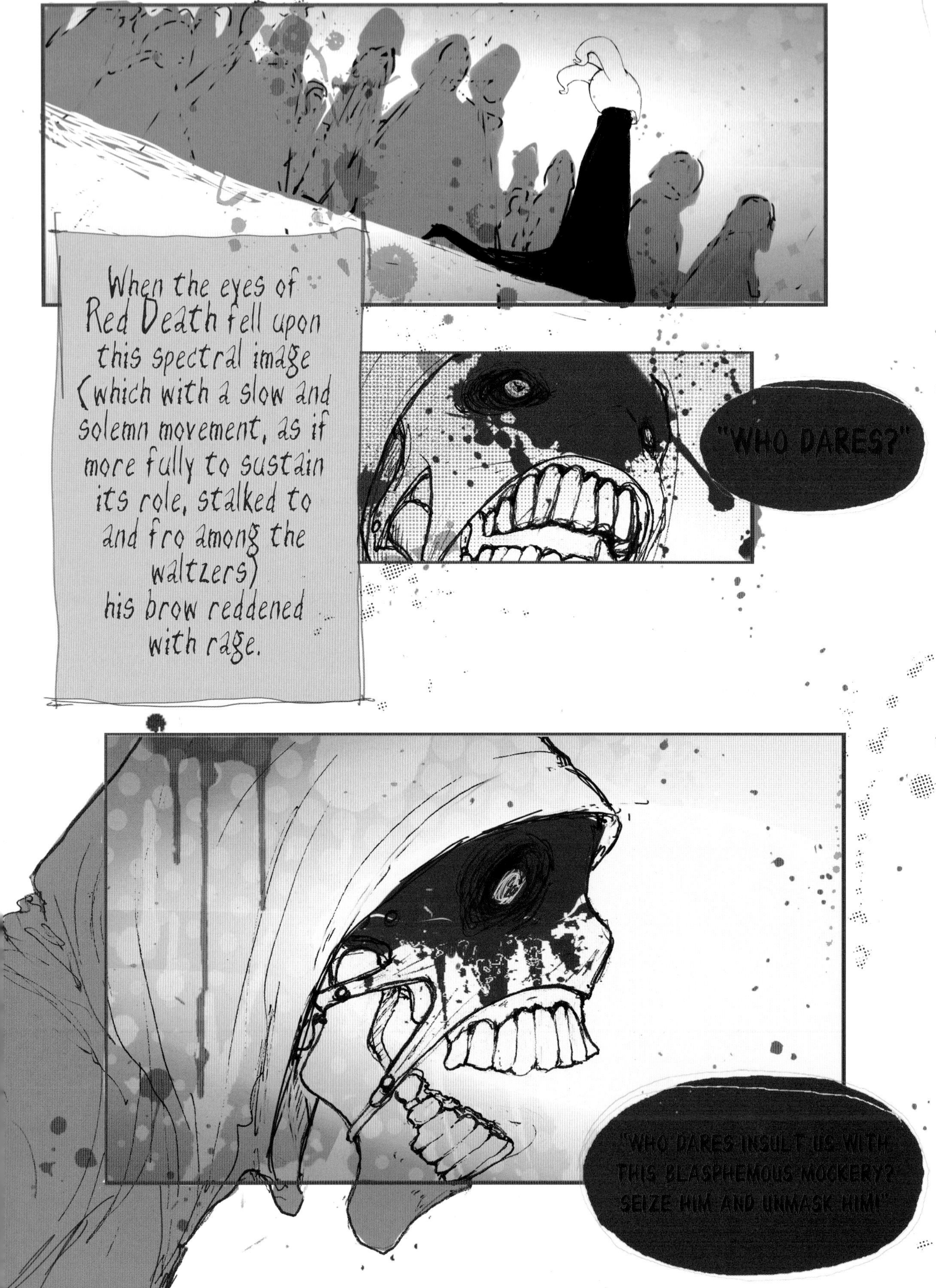
When the eyes of Red Death fell upon this spectral image (which with a slow and solemn movement, as if more fully to sustain its role, stalked to and fro among the waltzers) his brow reddened with rage.
"WHO DARES?"
"WHO DARES INSULT US WITH THIS BLASPHEMOUS MOCKERY? SEIZE HIM AND UNMASK HIM!"

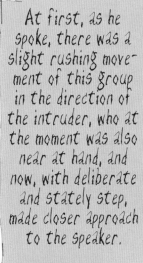

At first, as he spoke, there was a slight rushing movement of this group in the direction of the intruder, who at the moment was also near at hand, and now, with deliberate and stately step, made closer approach to the speaker.

A fearful idea now suddenly drove the blood in torrents upon my heart, and for a brief period, I once more relapsed into insensibility.

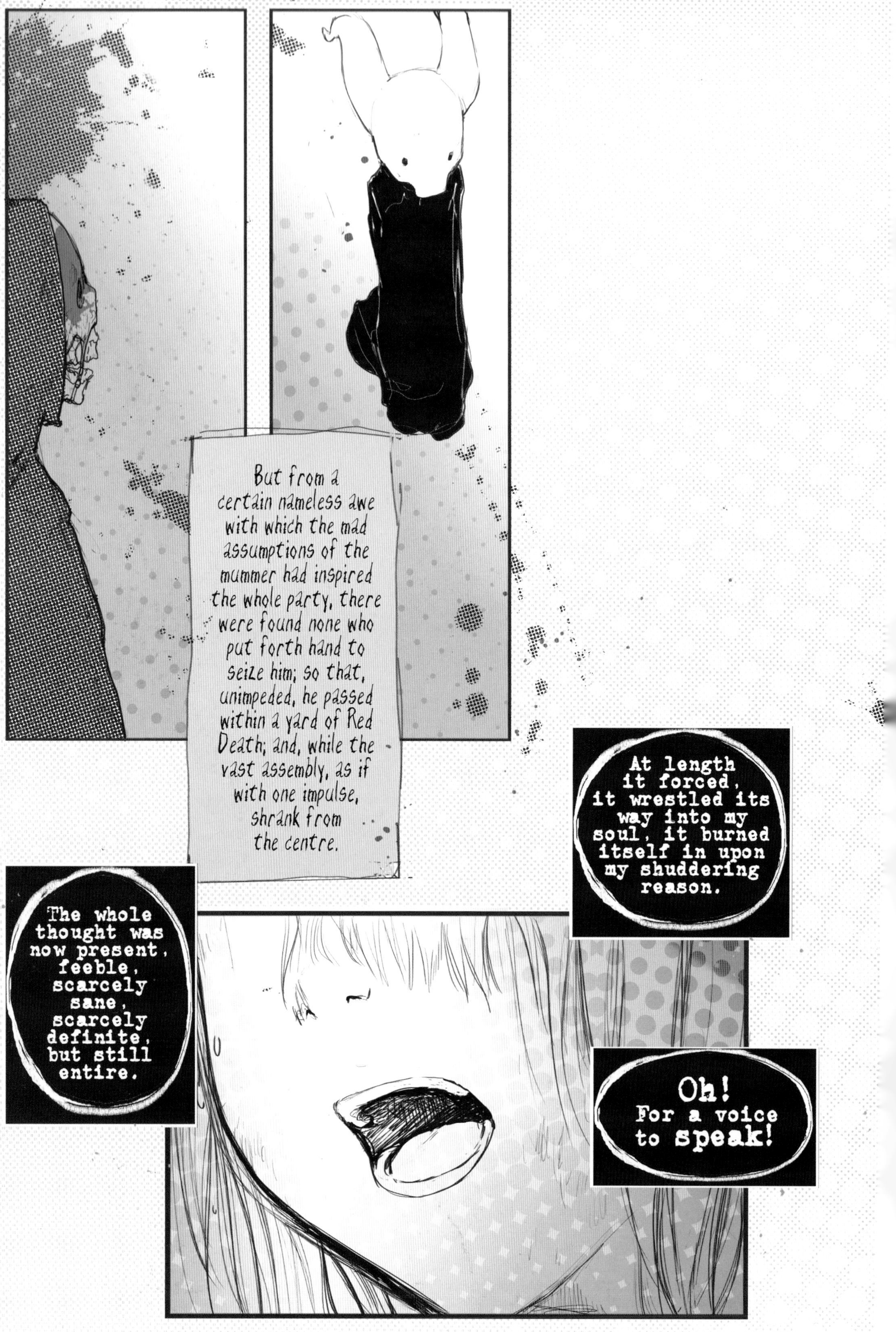
But from a certain nameless awe with which the mad assumptions of the mummer had inspired the whole party, there were found none who put forth hand to seize him; so that, unimpeded, he passed within a yard of Red Death; and, while the vast assembly, as if with one impulse, shrank from the centre.
The whole thought was now present, feeble, scarcely sane, scarcely definite, but still entire.
At length it forced, it wrestled its way into my soul, it burned itself in upon my shuddering reason.
Oh! For a voice to speak!

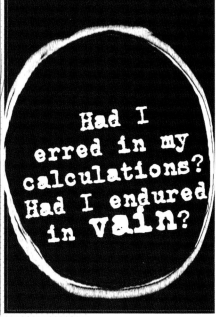

Had I erred in my calculations? Had I endured in **vain**?

He made his way uninterruptedly, with the same solemn and measured step which had distinguished him from the first, no movement had been made to arrest him.

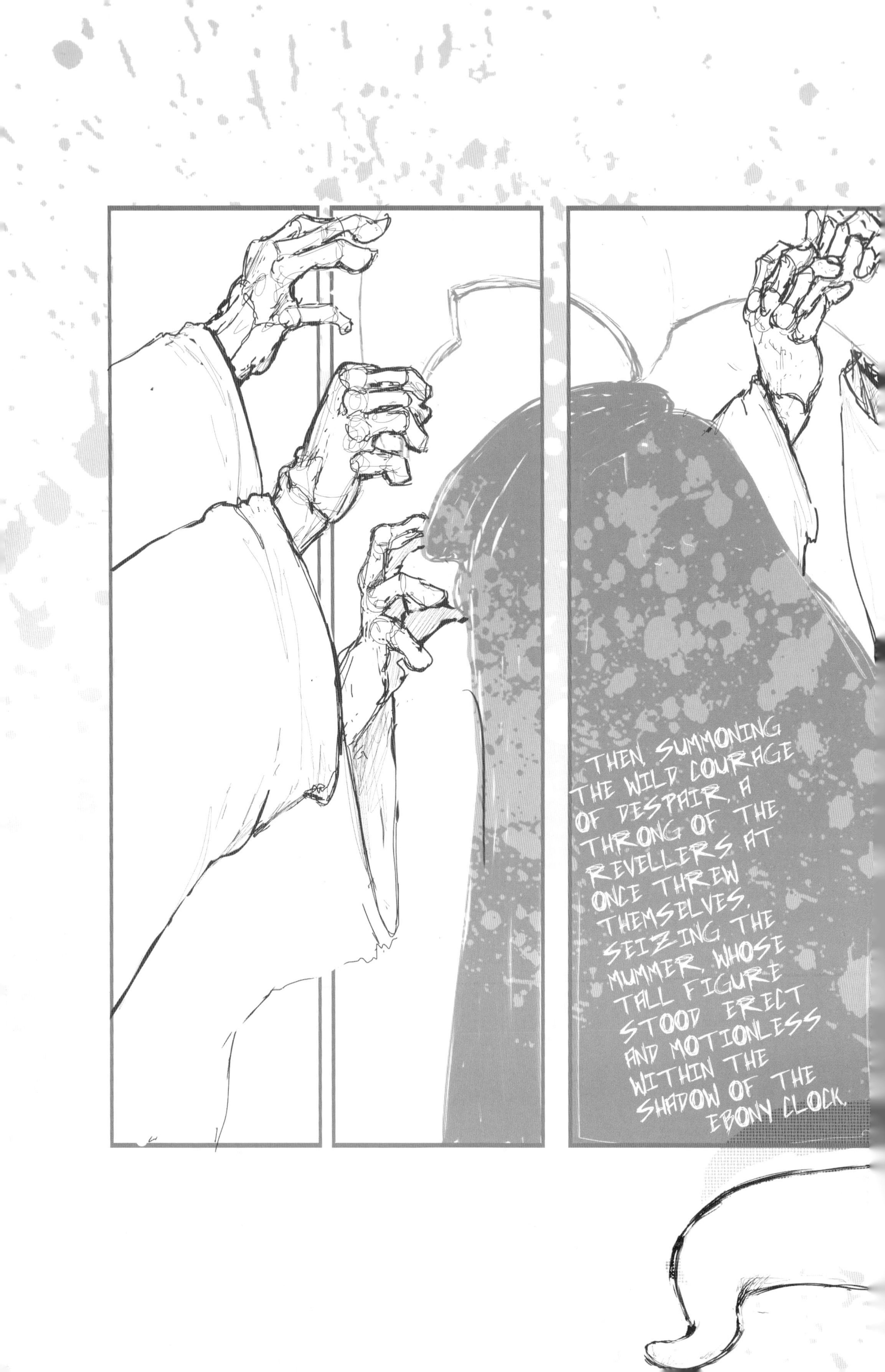
THEN SUMMONING THE WILD COURAGE OF DESPAIR, A THRONG OF THE REVELLERS AT ONCE THREW THEMSELVES, SEIZING THE MUMMER, WHOSE TALL FIGURE STOOD ERECT AND MOTIONLESS WITHIN THE SHADOW OF THE EBONY CLOCK.

I GASPED IN UNUTTERABLE HORROR AT FINDING THE MASK WHICH THEY HANDLED WITH SO VIOLENT A RUDENESS, UNTENANTED BY ANY TANGIBLE FORM.

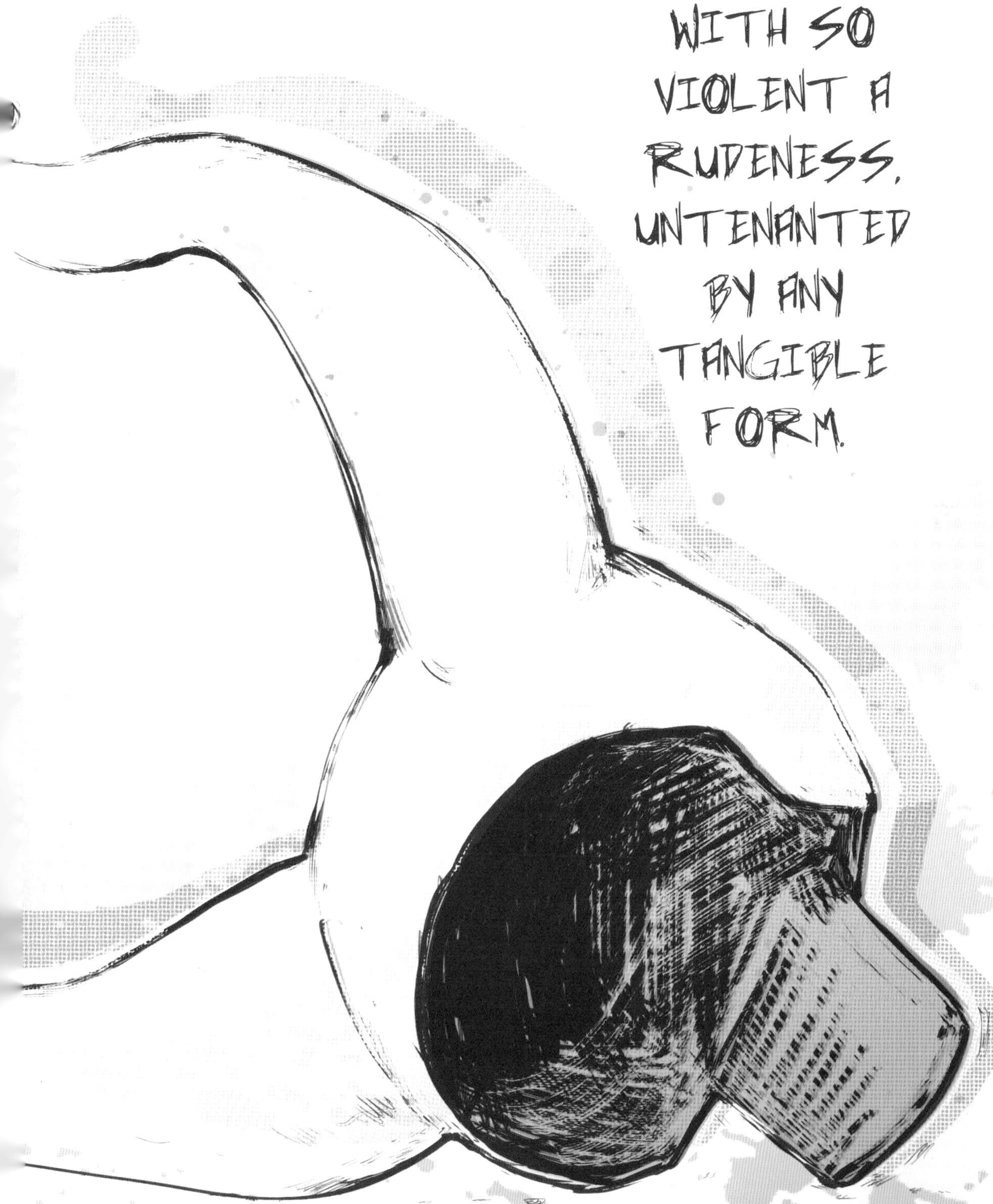

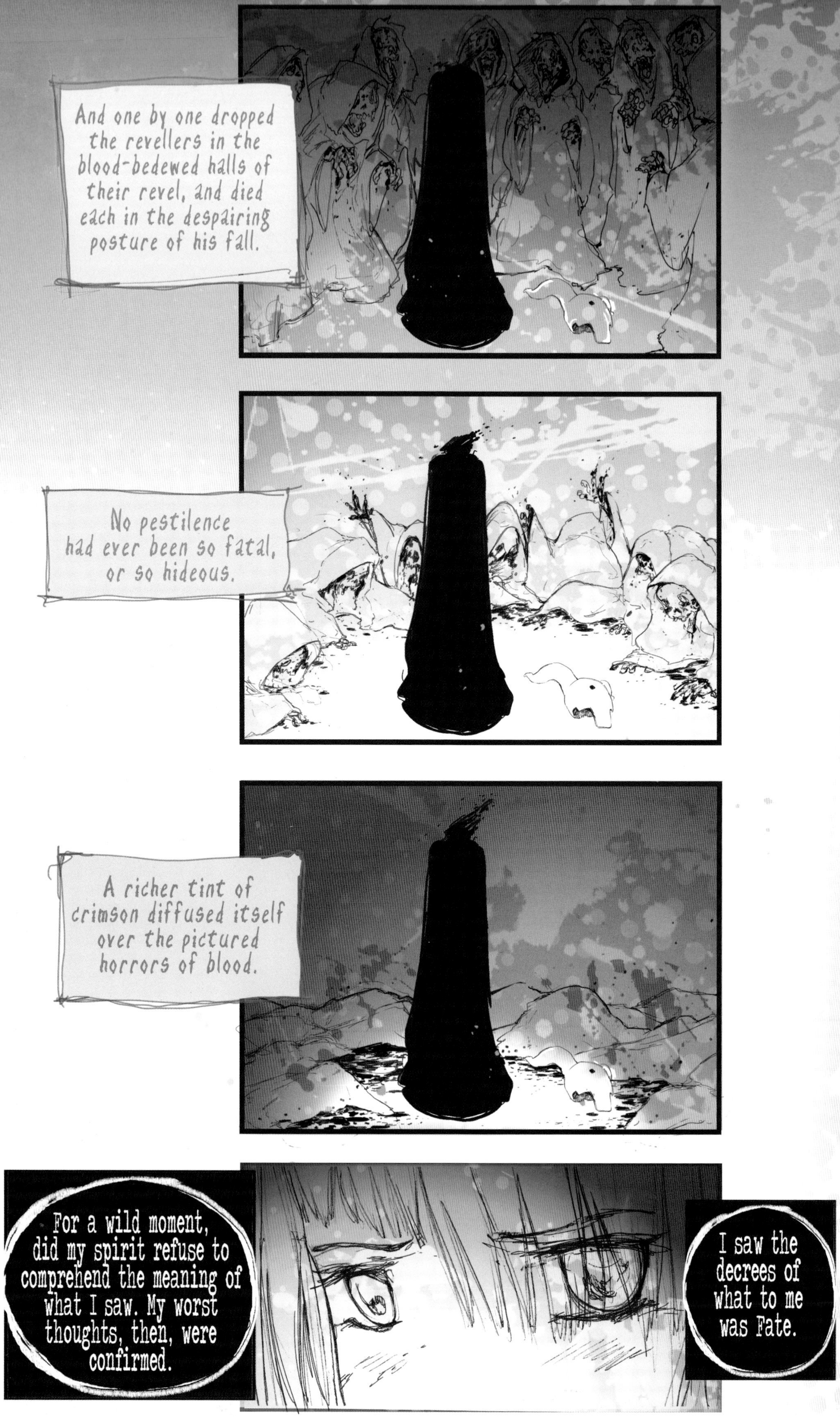

And one by one dropped the revellers in the blood-bedewed halls of their revel, and died each in the despairing posture of his fall.

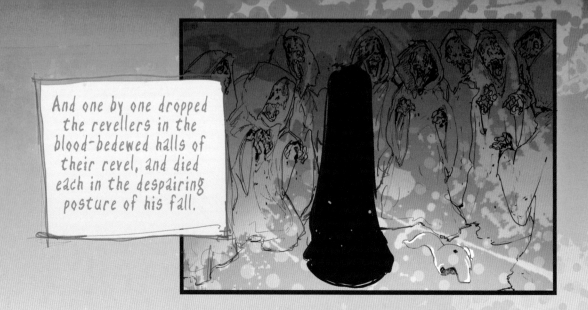

No pestilence had ever been so fatal, or so hideous.

A richer tint of crimson diffused itself over the pictured horrors of blood.

For a wild moment, did my spirit refuse to comprehend the meaning of what I saw. My worst thoughts, then, were confirmed.

I saw the decrees of what to me was Fate.

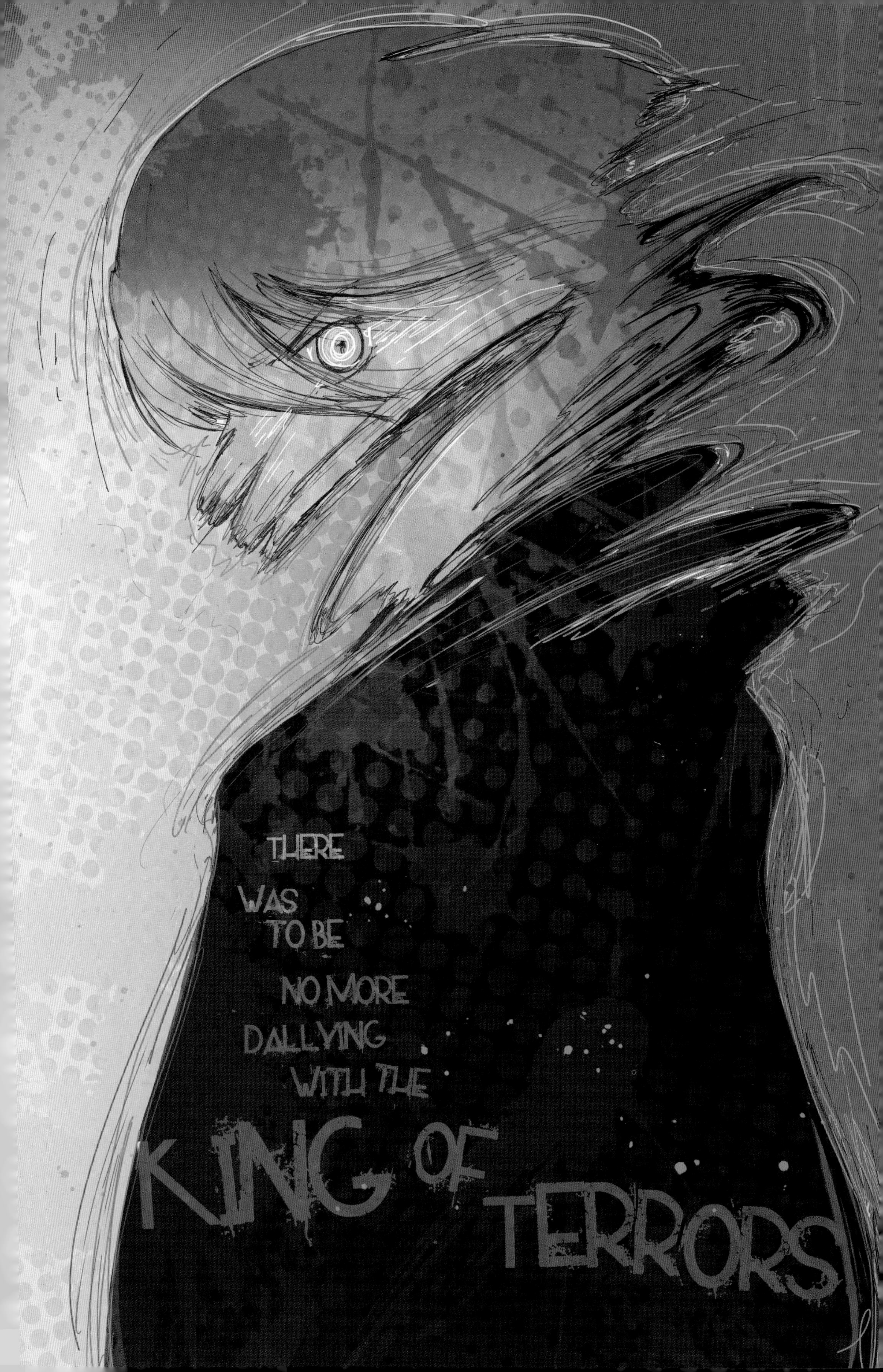
THERE
WAS
TO BE
NO MORE
DALLYING
WITH THE
KING OF
TERRORS

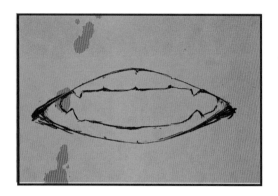

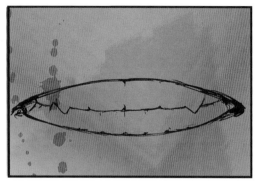

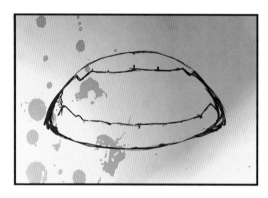

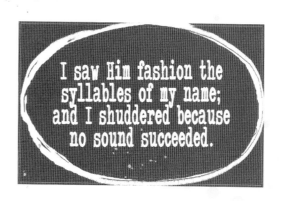

I saw Him fashion the syllables of my name; and I shuddered because no sound succeeded.

The truth at length flashed upon me. I had but escaped death in one form of agony, to be delivered unto worse than death in some other.

Once upon a midnight dreary,
while I pondered, weak and weary,

Deep into that darkness peering,
long I stood there wondering, fearing,
Doubting, dreaming dreams
no mortals ever dared to dream before;
But the silence was unbroken,
and the stillness gave no token,

While I nodded,
suddenly there came a tapping,
As of some one gently rapping,
rapping

All my soul within me burning,
Soon again I heard a tapping
somewhat louder than before.

with many a flirt and flutter,
In there stepped a stately raven
of the saintly days of yore
Then the bird said,
"**Nevermore**."

The raven, sitting lonely on the placid bust,
spoke only that one word,
as if his soul in that one word he did outpour.
Nothing further then he uttered-
not a feather then he fluttered-
He will leave me, as my hopes have flown before."

"Prophet!" said I, "thing of evil!- prophet still,
if bird or devil!-
- tell me- tell me, I implore!"

And the Raven, never flitting,
still is sitting, still is sitting
His eyes have all the seeming of a demon's
that is dreaming,
And the lamplight o'er him streaming
throws his shadow on the floor;

And my soul from out that shadow that
lies floating on the floor
Shall be lifted- **nevermore**!

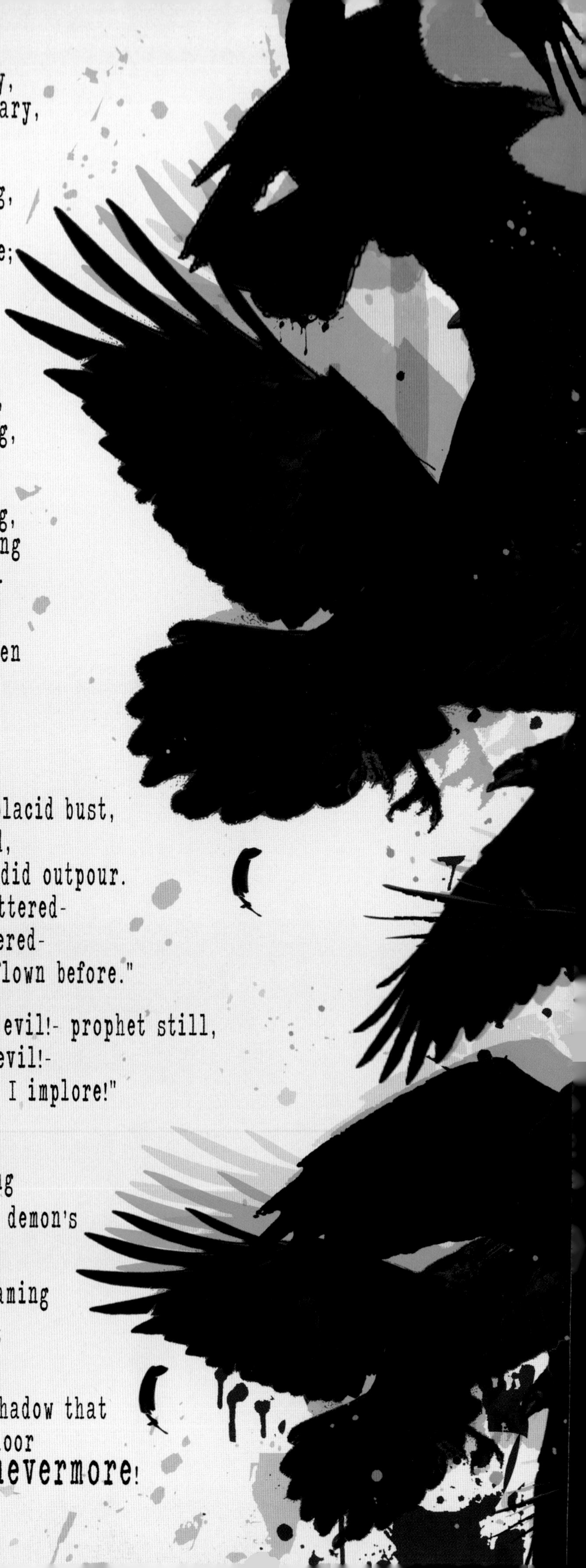

NEV

VERMORE!

NEVERMO

NEVERMORE!

RE!
VERMORE!

NEVERMORE!

MORE!

NEVERMORE!

NEV

MORE!

RMORE!

CHARACTERS

TANPOPO

Since she stepped onto the path of emotional discovery, Tanpopo — the superhumanly intelligent and strong-willed girl has grown to understand the impact and the depth of what was once out of her reach — feeling. While her origins remain an enigma, her purpose is clear: to seek out the meaning of human emotion.

KURO POODLE

The Devil in disguise, Kuro appears to Tanpopo in this disarming form, which she nicknames Poodle. He is mischievous, playful, adorable and seemingly innocent, but only Poodle knows what lies behind the mask.

KURO HUMAN

Always the kind looking gentleman, Kuro's purpose and promise towards Tanpopo takes on a more sinister form. When he reveals his deception, Tanpopo casts him away and he is no longer by her side as her companion and guide.

GHOST

He seemed a friend at first, but turns foe. As he whispers in Tanpopo's ear the Ghost plays the part of companion but, unbeknownst to her, Ghost is actually one of Kuro's minions. His counsel and guidance serve her in The City of Brass but when Tanpopo doesn't heed his warnings or take his advice, Ghost reveals his loyalty…and shows his true self.

CREATURE

A hideous being, banished and trapped in a chimney for eternity by the All-Might. Creature gives Tanpopo moral advice in choosing the path to follow and tries to forewarn her about Ghost's true nature.

RED DEATH

He appears from the pages of Edgar Allen Poe's "The Mask of Red Death," wearing the mask of a corpse, covered in blood; the symbol of his power. It is his masquerade that draws Tanpopo like a moth to the flame, and his dominion in which corpse-like revelers gather. He is terrible, brutal, and twisted; Red Death strikes fear into the heart and mind of Tanpopo.

MUMMER KURO

Silent and solemn, Mummer Kuro appears in the guise of an uninvited guest who interferes with Red Death's party. He arrives at Tanpopo's call, but is he her savior or her doom? The King of Terrors does not reveal his intentions, leaving her fate suspended, swinging like a pendulum between Mummer Kuro and Red Death.

As Tanpopo's journey continues, it reflects, in many ways, the journey we are all on — a journey to find ourselves, to connect with the world and with other beings; a journey to find understanding and a place where we belong while still maintaining independence. Tanpopo's journey of emotional discovery has not been an easy one, and in this second volume she is confronted with a horrible truth; betrayal from the one she believed was her friend and kept her safe. Naively trusting Kuro, we watch as truth is unveiled, and that same veil is torn from her eyes. And it hurts. It hurts to think we cannot trust those closest to us; it hurts to realize that perhaps we are truly alone in our goals because everyone has their own agenda — good, bad, just or unjustified. Where do we seek solace? Where do we find strength? What choices do we make when we cannot evaluate the consequences of the unknown? This, and more, is the challenge for Tanpopo in Volume 2. How we react to the circumstances that life presents to us is as much a personal, instinctual choice as the fight or flight response. Multiply that by a thousand— because Tanpopo is dealing with some of the strongest 'dark' emotions: anger, rage, fear and terror, for the first time! She is impetuous, dogged and prideful, storming off like a petulant child. While she may not show compassion or empathy, we hope the reader will. And we hope that the reader will find his or her own feet fitting Tanpopo's footsteps (since she wears no shoes) as we journey together through some of our favorite classics: William Shakespeare, Edgar Allan Poe and Arabian Nights. There's no end to the mystery we find in the words of the authors we draw inspiration from, both on and off the pages. The more we research, the more we bookmark, the more we discover about creative writing, storytelling and the journey of the human soul. Tanpopo's journey. And ours.

DEDICATION

We are grateful to have a willing and hungry audience for our work; you inspire us to dig deep into the meaning of emotion and reflect back what could be universal truths. We learn from you, from your insights and your interpretations. A big thank you to the staff at BOOM! Studios for your enthusiasm for our work and your dedication to creating valuable, beautiful literature.

— *Camilla and AdaPia d'Errico*

THANK YOUS

To the two Poe's in my life. You've inspired me, scared me and have always been there with a good story to share whenever I needed one.

— *Camilla d'Errico*

About Camilla:

Camilla is pop surrealist painter, illustrator, character creator and comic artist from Vancouver, Canada. Nominated for both Eisner and Joe Shuster awards, she has worked with Random House, Dark Horse, Image Comics and Tokyopop. Simon Pulse publishes her creator-owned graphic novel BURN, and SKY PIRATES OF NEO TERRA is published by Image Comics. TANPOPO, Camilla's passion project, has been embraced by fans and independent comics collectors for its highly original combination of classic literature blended with Camilla's unique West Meets East art style. She has collaborated with Neil Gaiman, Sanrio, Disney and Mattel.

See more of Camilla's work at www.camilladerrico.com

Visit the Tanpopo site at www.tanpopoandkuro.com

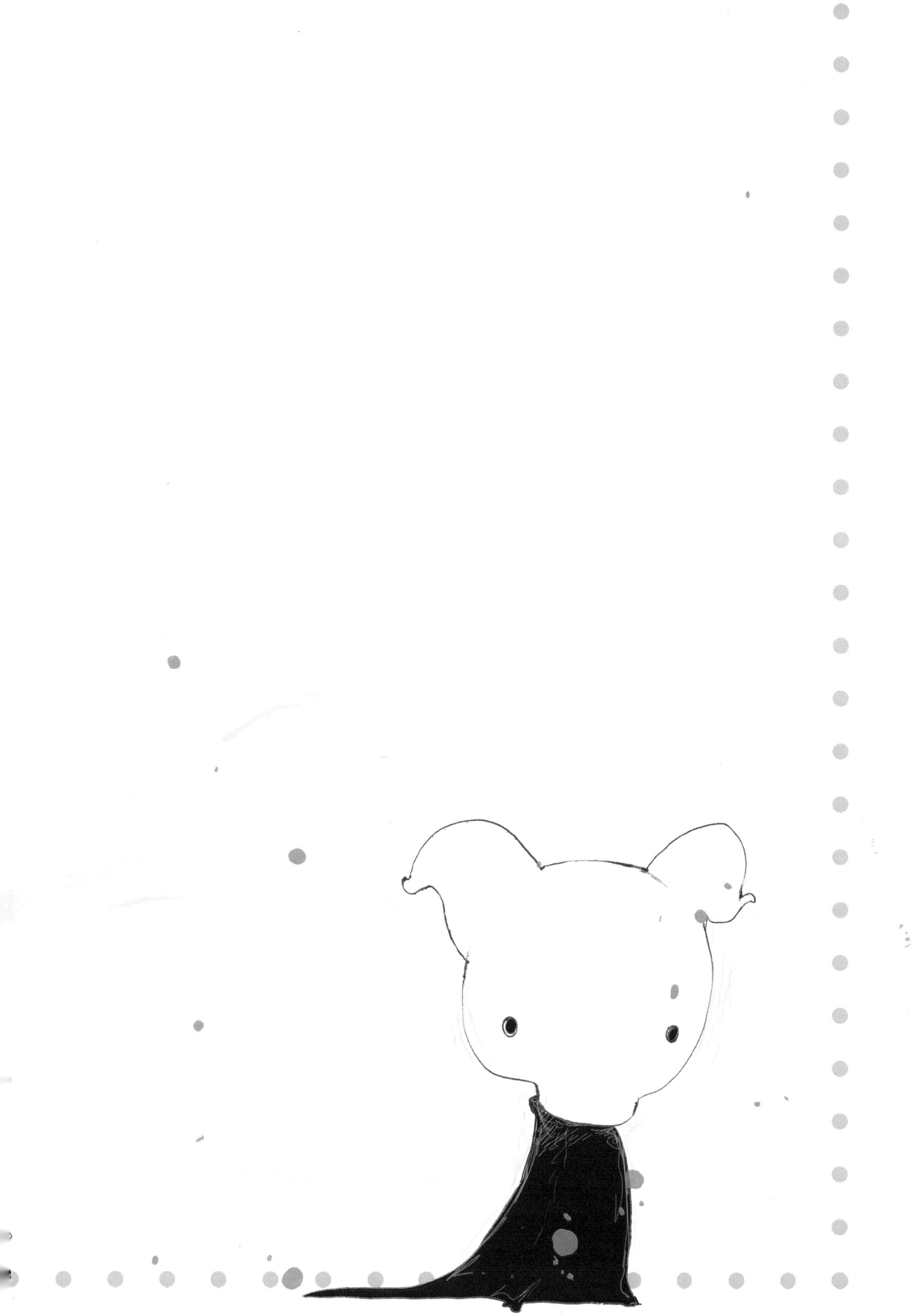